Cut, Print, and That's a Wrap!

For my many children and their extraordinary mother, Helen, who is my friend and my wife.

Cut, Print, and That's a Wrap!

A Hollywood Memoir

by
Paul A. Helmick

McFarland & Company, Inc., Publishers
Jefferson, North Carolina, and London

Library of Congress Cataloguing-in-Publication Data

Helmick, Paul A., 1919–
    Cut, print, and that's a wrap! : a Hollywood memoir /
by Paul A. Helmick.
      p.   cm.
    Includes index.
    ISBN 0-7864-0845-6 (softcover : 50# alkaline paper) ∞
    1. Helmick, Paul A., 1919– . 2. Motion picture producers
and directors—United States—Biography. I. Title.
PN1998.3.H455 A3   2001
791.43'0233'092—dc21   00-46460
[B]

British Library cataloguing data are available

©2001 Paul A. Helmick. All rights reserved

No part of this book may be reproduced or transmitted in any form or by any means, electronic or mechanical, including photocopying or recording, or by any information storage and retrieval system, without permission in writing from the publisher.

On the cover: The author stands by while shooting a scene.

Manufactured in the United States of America

McFarland & Company, Inc., Publishers
  Box 611, Jefferson, North Carolina 28640
    www.mcfarlandpub.com

Acknowledgments

    I most gratefully thank (in alphabetical order) friends and relatives who agreed to read the manuscript so that I might gain from their thinking and expertise: David Danon, Karen Givvin, David Hawks, Lisa Mitchell, Matt Moelter, Hugh Myers, Ken Pittman.
    The fact that some found it a remedy for their insomnia doesn't lessen the value of their contributions.

Contents

Introduction	1
It Just So Happened	3
The Sweet Sniff of Success	13
So You Wanted to Be in Pictures	19
Fixed Bayonets (1951)	26
Monkey Business (1952)	31
The Ransom of Red Chief (1952)	35
Gentlemen Prefer Blondes (1953)	38

River of No Return (1954)	43
How to Marry a Millionaire (1953)	59
Land of the Pharaohs (1955)	62
Nice Work, If You Can Get It	89
Breaking into Television	92
Marty (1955)	98
The Mad Hungarian	102
Defiant Ones (1958)	111
Teenage Thunder (1958)	114
Rio Bravo (1959)	118
Porgy and Bess (1959)	125
Thunder in Carolina (1960)	131
Hatari! (1962)	143
Man's Favorite Sport (1964)	164
The Great Race (1965)	168
Redline 7000 (1965)	171
A Guide for the Married Man (1967)	175
El Dorado (1967)	179
Funny Girl (1968)	184
Hello, Dolly! (1969)	194
The Cheyenne Social Club (1970)	202
Rio Lobo (1970)	206
The Migrants (1974)	240
Comes a Horseman (1978)	215
Chilly Scenes of Winter (1982)	220
And Now a Word	222
Annotated Filmography	225
Index	233

Introduction

On the shelf where this manuscript sat were several others written by people who found name, fame and fortune in the business of making movies. One of many ways in which this book differs from these is that the name, fame and fortune all seem to have escaped me.

My long sojourn in the business brought me in somewhat close contact with famous—and infamous—producers, directors and stars; the amusing stories and unforgettable experiences such privileged access gave rise to make up the contents of this book.

I hope I will be forgiven if I deviate from the absolute truth now and then. Because of my antiquity, I can't be expected to have a perfect memory for every detail or every word that was spoken. I have no intention of writing anything about anybody (with but a few exceptions) that might offend.

Introduction

Throughout this work you will come upon the words *movie* and *motion picture,* which I find myself using in place of the abused word *film.* Vehemently do I object to the use of the word *films* to describe what red-blooded Americans (and Peruvians, for all I know) used to call *movies* or *motion pictures* or just plain *pictures.* Even *shows* would be okay with me if somebody should ask, "Have you seen any good shows lately"? But *films?*

Or even worse, "An Oswald Offenbutcher Film." How about "A Film by Thelma Turnbuckle"?

Makes me wonder what the people who work at Eastman-Kodak, Fuji, Polaroid—the people who make the stuff we load in our Brownies and the stuff that runs through theatre projectors—put in the IRS form that asks their occupation.

I recently went to the Academy to look up some things I couldn't remember, and I was truly gratified to see emblazoned on the side of the beautiful building (once the City of Beverly Hills Water Works), a sign that read, "The Academy of Motion Picture Arts and Sciences."

And another thing: What are the Hollywood *filmmakers* going to call themselves when (and if) everything is shot and viewed on tape? Or some other yet-to-be-invented means of recording images?

My time, then, was the age when *films* were still *movies,* when movie stars seemed much brighter and closer than they do today, and when the studio system was still in full swing.

On beautiful summer days when I'm relaxing in the cockpit of a sailboat with some new acquaintances, after I've been asked what I did for a living and then what movie stars I've worked with, I'm frequently asked how I got into the business. That story, I suppose, is as good a way as any to begin.

It Just So Happened

Life didn't really start until I got into the motion picture business; or, more accurately, until my mother put me into it. No, she wasn't in it herself—she was just a darn smart lady who was determined to see the last of her four children (me) find a place in the entertainment world that she so dearly loved. In earlier days she had been an accomplished pianist and accordionist who had appeared in vaudeville when housewifery permitted, and she exposed me to that life whenever possible. But that doesn't explain how I happened to get into the business of making movies.

Mom was a gregarious person who liked gatherings, which was how she met a lady who was to become her lifelong friend and my entrée into the picture business. Mildred Lowe happened to be secretary to

Ed Ebele, general production manager of the newly formed production company 20th Century Films, whose headquarters were at the United Artists Studio (later to become the Samuel Goldwyn Studio, now owned by Warner Brothers, I think). That was in 1934 and I was in the eleventh grade at Fairfax High School. We lived only a couple of miles away from the studio, so it was fairly easy for Mildred to come to our house for a good lunch that my mother carefully prepared. And while they ate and talked, I washed Mildred's car, whether it needed it or not, rain or shine.

It was only a short time after I established my wash-and-rinse regimen that I received a phone call from Mildred, who asked me if I'd like to work after school and on Saturdays in the studio mimeograph department. I jumped at the chance, thinking not of a possible career in the picture business but of realizing every boy's dream of owning a car of his very own. My mother's dreams for me were much larger.

From school to the studio was only about a mile walk, so I worked after school and into the evening maybe two or three days a week. Somehow I found time to get enough of my homework done to merit get-by grades. If there were any child labor laws in those days, I was never affected by them. Most Saturdays found me "at the studio," as my mother liked to tell friends and neighbors. In those days, the studio's work weeks was six days long, and when pictures were in the shooting stage, you could be sure of working until midnight come Saturday. Darryl Zanuck, head of the fledgling company, worked hard to make a success of this new endeavor and, consequently, so did everybody connected with it. I would often be cranking away at a mimeograph machine, covered with stencil ink, when I'd get a call from somebody to run an errand or carry a box—anything.

One evening Mildred told me to find Mr. Ebele because Mr. Zanuck wanted to see him at once, adding that if I couldn't find him on the lot I was to search the three bars in the neighborhood. Being a studio production manager, at least in those days, may have been the most stressful job in the business. Ebele's idea of relaxing was to slip away for a drink or two, and that night, when this 15-year-old kid found him, he'd had many more than that. He roared his dismissal at me and told me to tell Mr. Zanuck what he could do with the job. Nevertheless he followed me, at a respectable distance, back to the studio and his session with Zanuck. In years to come, Mr. Ebele and I became pretty good friends, and I used to seek him out for advice.

Among my treasures is my father's teaching certificate, given to him by the State of Indiana when he was 16 years old. While he never attended college, he was a stickler for education, believing everyone entitled to—and responsible for—schooling enough to earn a living and not be dependent on anyone else. When it came to my working at the studio in my senior year, he put his foot down; I was to do nothing that could jeopardize my getting a high school diploma.

The investment business wasn't very kind to my dad in those days, and I sorely missed my studio pay check. I made a few dollars playing the accordion in a high school band, and a few more washing and waxing cars, but nothing like I had become used to by working at the studio. It was indeed a happy Thursday in June 1936 when I graduated from high school.

On Friday morning there came a call from Mildred. A job awaited me at the studio. I could start the following Monday. By this time 20th Century had merged with Fox Studio and was now 20th Century-Fox Film Corporation.

With great anticipation I drove my old roadster onto the employees' parking lot and reported to the much-expanded mimeograph-script departments. The merger was now seven or eight months old and judging from the hustle and bustle of both departments, Zanuck had lost no time in acquiring new writers and stories that were keeping everybody in the studio jumping. Departments were being expanded and many people were being added to the payroll.

It was a wonderful time for any young person to be alive and I knew it.

Besides operating mimeograph machines, which to my eternal gratitude were no longer hand-cranked but were run by electricity, I also had to distribute the assembled scripts to the various departments, executives, writers, and so forth. At first I would carry as many as I could around the lot, go back and get more, and resume the task, rain or shine, until they were all delivered. Many more scripts were typed, mimeographed, and distributed for movies that were never made than for those made and there probably always will be.

After much pleading, I obtained permission to bring my car onto the lot, load it up with scripts and quickly and almost painlessly get the job done. This was very important to me since a drive-on pass was a sign of prestige among my peers.

I don't remember how much I was paid in those days, but I do remember picking up her paychecks for my boss, Ruth Howard, on Thursdays and peeking at the amount—*$35 a week* ! I thought that if I could ever make that much money I could die happy. Little did I know.

My 1936 pass for 20th Century–Fox lot.

It wasn't long before I was given a job in the production office as a clerk-messenger boy. Two and sometimes three fellows did much the same type of work, and there was enough to keep us all busy. The production office always was, and may still be, the hub of activity of any studio. Consider that from 1936 through 1941, the studio was turning out no less than 48 movies a year and achieved the same production rate after World War II. That is a lot of production for just one studio. Warners, MGM, Paramount, Columbia, RKO, Republic, and Universal each probably turned out even more pictures annually. Hollywood was the promised land and almost anybody with any talent or just plain gumption could find a niche for himself—especially if he knew somebody or had a relative in the business and was willing to work.

Nowadays it seems the major studios make up for the lack of movie production with television production. This probably nets them more money than if they made theatrical features. It seems they merely release the biggest-grossing movies under their banners and have nothing to do with the making of the product. There doesn't seem to be any pride in a studio's making a product any more. Their only pride comes in their shrewd deal-making. What does it say about the great industry when Michael Ovitz, a very smart agent, was frequently proclaimed to be the most powerful man in Hollywood?

Jack Warner, Darryl Zanuck, Harry Cohn, L. B. Mayer and others derived a great deal of satisfaction from seeing who could make the best product—never for a moment neglecting the interests of their stockholders. But change was bound to happen.

But back to the production office and the learning process for this wide-eyed young giant-killer.

A studio committed to making so many pictures annually meant that frequently as many as six or seven were being shot at the same time. Virtually every part of the sound stages was being used for shooting, construction, or what were called "permanent sets." These sets included a theatre with audience seating, a full-sized stage and backstage. Another sound stage contained an ice rink (for the Sonja Henie movies, of course). And on another sound stage there might be a complete court room or maybe a hospital floor, complete with an operating room. Then, as in the case with 20th Century-Fox, there were the exterior sets: two streets for Westerns, two New York streets, a Chicago street, a Midwestern street, a small lake, a European street, a section of railroad track with a working locomotive and cars and, of course, a depot. Then there was another lot, the Western Avenue lot, located in mid-town L. A., filled with sound stages and the film laboratory. They soon acquired the "Ranch," several acres about an hour or so from the studio where many movies and the TV series *M*A*S*H* were made.

I suppose it is hard for this generation's movie makers to believe that many of these sets occupied land now known as Century City. Looking back over the many 20th Century-Fox pictures I worked on during my years there, it seems I've walked every square foot of land beneath the massive structures of Century City.

I want to explain the close and detailed coordination that was required by the production office and the various studio departments if all elements that made up movie-making were to operate smoothly. Involved was the construction of sets, electric rigging (scaffolding, wiring and lighting), dressing the sets with furniture, shooting scenes on the sets, holding the sets undisturbed until Zanuck and the producer and director were satisfied with the rough-cut movie, and then removing and storing the sets. These are just some of many functions of the production department. It is easy to see how by working there, I received an on-the-job education in movie making.

One of the reasons movie companies constructed their sets on stages and back lots was that this kept construction labor and material costs relatively low, and sets could be built and decorated to specification.

Then too, film required so much more light than it does now, and it often required careful manipulation of lighting and indoor shooting. On-location shooting has always been a part of Hollywood, but not to the extent that it is today.

After a year or so, Ed Ebele stepped down as studio production manager and a man by the name of William Koenig was brought in to take over the job. As the story went, he had been let go after a year at MGM. He must have pissed off somebody important at MGM, because we heard the only thing they had let him handle was collecting for the Red Cross. Prior to that he had worked at Warner Brothers. With him came Fred Meyer, Koenig's close friend and confidant. Before coming to Hollywood they had owned a couple of theatres in Milwaukee. Then there was Betty Russell, Koenig's secretary and my immediate boss. She wasn't easy to like and took some getting used to. I don't remember anybody getting used to Fred Meyer, though. He was called "Hatchet Man," and it became clear from the outset that his function was to ferret out which employees' services could be dispensed with. Several times a day he would slither in and out of Koenig's private office, and every week or so some person Meyer considered unnecessary would find himself seeking employment elsewhere.

It wasn't long before the head of the ladies' wardrobe department, a dapper fellow by the name of Bert Levy, was summoned to Koenig's office, where from behind the closed door we in the outer office could hear the two men shouting at each other. After a short while, the door burst open and out came the still-shouting warriors. And then the shoving began. The three large desks in the outer office were covered with quarter-inch glass, and my first impulse was to stand up and keep either of the combatants from falling and hitting his head on the sharp edges of the glass tops. I wasn't paying much attention to what they were arguing about. Levy claimed he had a contract and Koenig couldn't fire him. Levy stormed out of the building and Koenig sent for Meyer.

After a session in Koenig's office, Meyer emerged and announced that Mildred, Read Kilgore (the other clerk), Betty, and I were to write down on a piece of paper exactly what each person saw and heard during the fracas and he would collect our reports in 15 minutes. When he came to collect mine, I explained that I was too confused to hear anything said and that I was interested only in trying to keep the angry men from hurting themselves on the furniture during the shoving match. Back in Koenig's office he went with the other three reports and my blank piece of paper. When he came back he announced that I was fired for being disloyal. While I was getting my things together, Mildred, not about to see her poor, immature protégé banished from the movie industry after all her patient and kindly ground work had been laid, entered Koenig's office. When she emerged from the inner sanctum, she sadly explained to me that the best she could do was to get Koenig to agree that I was to be given a clerical job on the back lot. This I could have so long as he never laid eyes on me while he was driving to and from work across the lot.

It was with a heavy heart that I went home and told my mother the sad news. It was especially hard for her to take because my father had recently passed away, leaving her very little, and I was, in a fairly large way, responsible for keeping the family together. After digesting the tidings I bore, she said something like, "There's no way you are going to take that lying down!—I want you to go see him and on the way there, figure out something to tell him, whatever it takes to get your job back."

Saturday afternoon Koenig was in the habit of going to his home in Beverly Hills and taking a nap. His houseboy answered the door and I told him I was from Mr. Koenig's office and had to see him and couldn't wait until he awoke from his nap. It wasn't long before Koenig, in robe and pajamas, entered the living room, and when he saw how anxious and nervous I was, calmly seated himself on the sofa beside me. He patiently listened to what I had to say and when I was through, he admitted that perhaps he had acted a little hastily and was glad that I had come to talk things out with him. He even offered me a cold drink.

"I want you to report for work Monday morning like nothing ever happened. There will be a two dollar a week increase in your paycheck from now on." As he was showing me out the front door, he asked me what I wanted to be in the business, and when I said, "A director," he told me to work hard, make friends and stay out of trouble and he'd help me. While he still yelled at me once in a while and ranted and raved when I screwed up, I knew he was my friend. Other than my family, Bill Koenig was my most faithful correspondent when I served in the South Pacific during World War II. Had he lived, I do believe I might have had a chance to direct much sooner than I did.

One day while typing a letter on the executive stationery, with its magnificent letterhead, a horrendous thought occurred to me: What are they going to call my beloved company when the 21st century rolls around? I must confess that it still occurs to me when I hear the famous bugle blast that announces the picture. Although with most movie

Aboard Bill Koenig's yacht. *Top:* A picture I took of the "crew" (from left to right) Hazel Taylor, Mildred Lowe, Doris and Bill Koenig, my wife, Helen, Betty Russell and unknown. *Bottom:* Same crowd, but this time Koenig snapped the shot and I grinned for the camera.

companies changing ownership almost as often as Liz changes husbands, I don't have the same grave concern any more. Chalk it up as just another Y2K unsolved problem.

Betty Russell had a rather spacious private office adjacent to Koenig's where, about noon, she and Mildred would have their lunch. Early in the day, menus were brought from the Café de Paris, and the ladies phoned in their choices. Much to my chagrin, embarrassment, and humiliation, it almost always fell to this poor soul to walk the couple of blocks to the cafe's kitchen entrance, pick up the covered tray and deliver it to the waiting ladies. I no longer delivered scripts, so my drive-on privilege was revoked and I had to carry out this dreaded chore on foot unless it was raining, in which case I got to drive one of their cars. Here I am, this up-and-coming junior executive, making my way past the hordes of people on their way to lunch, and carrying a tray like a lowly busboy.

It seems impossible to move on without another Koenig story. Although the studios operated on a six-day week, if not much was happening, executives and department heads might take Saturday afternoon off. One such Saturday, when Koenig was courting a very attractive, well-educated lady from St. Louis (whom he eventually married), she and a lady friend, both swathed in furs, came to the studio for lunch. After eating, it was to be on to Santa Anita Race Track, where Koenig had a box from which to view the horse races. Apparently his houseboy had the day off, because Koenig was driving his spotless Buick limousine himself. After lunch, the ladies came to his office and I was summoned. He introduced me and told me that I was to show them around the lot while he finished up some business before heading for the race track. I was to drive them in his limo. Now, it had been raining the last few days, and they wanted to see the back lot, which had few paved roads. To get to the most interesting sets, one had to take the dirt roads, which after rains, were pretty slick and muddy.

Undaunted, I was driving on just such a road and giving the ladies my best spiel when suddenly the car began to slide into a ditch and came to rest partially on its side, smack up against an embankment. Right before my eyes and into the ditch went my whole future in the movie business. Seeing how calm the ladies were had a wonderful effect on me as I climbed out the driver's door and went to a nearby phone where I explained my predicament to the transportation department dispatcher. Within minutes a mechanic and his helper came with a tow truck, hooked onto the limo with a winch, and pulled us to safe ground. They told me to go straight to their department where the car washers were on duty, and within a few minutes I was back in Koenig's office with the ladies telling him what a wonderful time they had with me on the tour, making no mention of the harrowing experience.

Somebody almost always had to be in the production office after hours when a company (meaning a shooting unit) was working late, or when Koenig stayed on after Mildred or Betty had left for the day. That lot fell to one of the three clerks: Chuck Smith, Read Kilgore, or me. I dreaded my turn, especially when I had to break a date at the last minute. But occasionally, when Koenig was in a good mood and felt like talking to me, the extra hours passed pleasantly.

One day Mildred told me that I had gone about as far as I could without being able to take dictation. I could be privy to far more inside happenings if, when I was called to stay late, Koenig felt free to dictate a memo or a letter. Also, she and Betty could be relieved of their heavy loads if they could re-dictate some of their work to me. I immediately enrolled in night classes at the Beverly Hills Secretarial School and within six weeks was able to read back my own shorthand with only a minor mistake here and there. Koenig was anything but articulate, however, and I soon learned to listen for what he was trying to say, make notes, and then find the most direct and concise way to put it in writing. This was great training for anybody who might be called upon to tell a story without boring his audience to death.

There were quite a few stories about Koenig, but the one I liked best was this one: He determined, probably rightfully, that agents, when they got on the lot for an appointment with a director or a producer, would take advantage of being in the administration building by going from office to office peddling their wares, be they actors, directors, writers, trained dogs, or whatever they had for sale. Koenig felt the agents were causing studio employees to waste valuable time. He therefore issued an edict that he—and only he—could okay anybody to come on the lot, unless they had a regular studio pass. This undoubtedly saved the studio a considerable amount of "creative time" and was just fine until somebody called the city fire department to report a sound stage on fire. Adjacent sound stages were also being threatened by the fire. When the fire engines arrived at the studio gate, they were stopped by the studio police who dutifully sought Koenig's permission to pass the fire engines through! Alas, it took the production office considerable time to locate Koenig to give his okay. Most of the stage was consumed.

The Sweet Sniff of Success

One day I was told that I was being sent on location to Kanab, Utah, because they needed help on a big picture called *Drums Along the Mohawk*. The unit manager had specifically asked for me. Was this the big break I was waiting for? Was my latent talent finally being discovered?

When the train arrived in Cedar City, a car was waiting to take me and a couple of other people to a large Anderson camp that had been erected off the beaten path in the woods. Anderson-Dunham camps were famous for being able to feed and comfortably house large groups of workers where no suitable housing existed. They came into use in building the Boulder Dam (now Hoover Dam) in Nevada.

Studios discovered that by using these camps they would be able to shoot movies in places that were previously denied them because of a lack of proper housing. Everything, especially the food, was first class. They charged by the head for their services—and charged much more than a hotel or motel. Each unit had a wooden floor, wood sides about three-feet-tall, and the rest was covered in canvas. Each hut would have two or three comfortable cots, an efficient heater, and a few chairs. "Camp Drums," as director John Ford called it, had a community shower and toilet facilities, one unit for men and one for women, and a large mess tent. As I recall, Claudette Colbert had a hot-and-cold-water bathtub in her tent.

Ford insisted the camp be run strictly like a fighting ship. And he was the Captain. Nobody, including the stars, sat down at the white-table-cloth "dinner mess" until John Ford arrived and took his place at the head table.

After a long and scenic drive, I arrived at Camp Drums ready to assume my duties and make whatever valuable contribution to the movie I was called upon to make. It turned out to be typing call sheets and production reports, and other sundry duties, mostly clerical. Pico Boulevard in Nowhere, Utah.

A driver would bring me the daily call sheet from the set. While the driver waited, I would type it onto a stencil, run off the required number of copies on a mimeograph machine, and together we would go back to the set where I would hand a copy out to the cast and crew so they would know what was happening the following day and prepare accordingly. Then it was right back to camp for me. That was as close as I got to the action. Apparently they figured they could go on making the movie without any more help from me, until tomorrow's call sheet.

My office and sleeping quarters were in a tent I shared with the unit manager, a no-nonsense, no-sense-of-humor, no-fun and (as it later turned out) no-scruples sort. I got along with him just fine, but I still remember the night some of the movie Indians got drunk and started chasing him through the camp—into and out of our tent, where he ran around the stove with the yelling Indians after him. I never did find out what it was all about, but I suspect he tried to cut off their supply of booze.

Ford allowed no alcohol in camp (except for himself and a privileged few), and there was no way for the crew to get to the state-licensed liquor store in town. So, quite naturally, the boot-leggers had a field day, or rather a *field night*. Just try to deprive a movie outfit of its fair share of liquor, especially if there are a bunch of stunt men aboard! I was told there was also a bevy of beauties out on the road for those willing to pay for their services.

One late afternoon, after the company came in from shooting, Ford sent for me, my pad, and my pencil. He had decided that what was needed in the camp was a daily newspaper, and he expected me to take the dictation, type it onto a stencil, and run off copies on the mimeograph machine and place a copy at each table setting before supper for all to read—starting tonight. From his quarters I obediently followed him over to Miss Colbert's quarters, where we found Hank Fonda and two or three others waiting. They unanimously named the "newspaper" *The Camp Drums Bugle.*

In one upper corner box was the weather forecast. In the other corner, the quote for the day. Below was the gossip column, the names of the newly arrived and the dearly departed (mainly cast and bit players) and, of course, the editorial. There was much laughter and gaiety inspired by the cocktails and highballs as I struggled to set down on paper their brilliant quips and journalistic gems.

The third evening when all hands were gathered around the festive board, "Pappy," as a few of Ford's closest confidants were privileged to call him, stood up and summoned me to his table. When I got there, he announced, "Mr. Helmick will now explain to those whose knowledge of the English language is limited, what is meant by the word pasto*rial*, as used in the opening sentence of today's editorial. Quote: 'Here in this pasto*rial* setting where we find ourselves encamped.' Unquote. Mr. Helmick?"

I could only stand there thoroughly embarrassed and at a total loss for words until out came "Damned if I know, Mr. Ford. You said it." That brought on gales of laughter, including Ford's, who said directly to me, "I am quite certain that I said *pastoral,* and you may stand down. Thank you." Although I never worked an entire picture with him, we became quite good friends over the years.

One of my duties was to meet newcomers, show them to their quarters, and brief them on the way things were run in Camp Drums. One boring afternoon, an absolutely gorgeous young thing arrived, and it fell to this 19-year-old to do the honors.

After changing out of her traveling clothes, this beauty emerged from her quarters wearing white shorts, a white blouse, and a white ribbon in her dark hair. On our little walk around the camp, I learned that she was 16, had just become a contract player at the studio, and had been sent up here in the hope that Ford would find some little part for her, maybe as a soldier's wife or an officer's daughter, anything to gain experience.

Indeed, Ford did. After Darryl Zanuck saw the rushes, or dailies, in which she appeared, he ordered her sent right back to the studio. She would become a big star and he knew it. Her name was Linda Darnell.

Nepotism was apparent on any Ford movie. There would be his brother-in-law as the first assistant director–unit production manager (and a damn good one, too); his brother, Eddie O'Fearna, one of the second assistants; and, in the early days of Ford's career, his brother, Francis, often playing an important role. I've been told Francis was a much better director than John but didn't care much about directing, preferring to act. As for Eddie, I never saw him without an unpressed dark suit and tie, a chewed-on old pipe, and a crushed felt hat—be it winter or the hottest summer day. He didn't own a car, preferring to ride the streetcar, even to the beach where he'd go surf-fishing with some brew and a book or two. He was said to have read a book a day. When I asked him what kind of fish he caught, he said he never caught any because he never put a hook on the line. When I asked why, he explained that it would be too much work hauling the fish in.

When the Utah location shooting ended, it was back to the production office and the old routine. I was more convinced than ever that I had chosen the right career and that somehow I must get out of that office and on the set where it all really happens. But such good fortune was not to be—not yet, anyway.

My next brush with real movie-making came when someone in casting called and asked if one of the clerks could be spared to escort 14 Indians to Utah where they were needed for *Western Union*. (I think there were not that many real Indians in central casting, and about half the 14 were really Mexicans with long, straight, black hair.) I was given the train tickets, a few bucks petty cash, and instructions that it was my job to make damned sure that they arrived at the location *sans* any booze.

The train left at eight that night and I waited at the designated place until they all showed up. Judging by their gaiety and boisterous behavior, some must have interrupted alcoholic farewell parties to get to the train station. I managed to get them on the train before the conductor sent us on the way with his "All aboard!" I don't recall very much about the trip, except that the conductor and I had a hell of a time keeping some of my charges from going into the other Pullman cars and

October 1943 and I'm at Primary Flight Training at Garner Field, Uvalde, Texas.

annoying passengers. The train clickety-clacked its way through the night and the booze flowed freely until my Indians fell quiet. And fell is exactly what some of them did.

When we arrived at the Utah station, an elongated touring car, I think they called it a "flatiron," was waiting for us, and I loaded my charges and their luggage aboard for what I knew was to be a long, hot, and dusty ride through the mountains to the location. I was not in great shape myself, having had hardly any sleep.

After a few hours, it occurred to me that maybe the booze supply was not depleted after all, and I recalled my explicit instructions. Out came, "Hey, guys, I'm awful thirsty and would give anything for a little drink if anybody happens to have some." After some hesitation, one of the fellows with whom I had become somewhat friendly, reached into his duffel bag and produced a bottle of whiskey and handed it to me. I took a short swig and handed it back. Pretty soon, out came other bottles of assorted beverages. It was beginning to look like my ploy was going to work.

We even made a stop by a lovely shady stream, and as the afternoon wore on, their liquor supply wore down. By the time we came to our destination and I turned my charges over to the location manager, there must have been little, if any, liquor in their possession. Mission accomplished. I later found out there were plenty of Indians in Utah, but my Indians were being imported because of their special abilities, whatever they were.

Strangely, I don't remember how it came about that I made the break from working in the production office to becoming a second assistant director. I well remember, though, how welcome the change was. I was now on my way, with a fairly large increase in salary, a lovely wife, and a feeling that when my Mom talked about "my son in the picture business," I really was in the business of making pictures. Until the Japanese made the tragic mistake of bombing Pearl Harbor.

We were working on location at Avalon on Catalina Island that awful Sunday on a movie called *Rings on Her Fingers*. December 7th, 1941, marked the temporary end of my movie career and the beginning of a new career as a pilot and officer in the Army Air Corps. It was a wonderful experience, as it turned out, though most unwelcome at the time. But that's another story.

With the war over, it was back to 20th Century–Fox and picture after picture. Some I'm happy to remember, others I'm happy to forget. There were many locations such as Mexico, Australia, Europe, and the Western States. Lots of people and lots of living. I worked on a number of pictures during my happy post-war stint as second assistant director, including *The Pied Piper, Ten Gentlemen from West Point, Thunder Birds, Rings on Her Fingers, The Dark Corner, Road House, Nightmare Alley, Fury at Furnace Creek, Captain from Castile, The Fan, Come to the Stable, I Was a Male War Bride, Two Flags West, Broken Arrow, Ticket to Tomahawk, Love Nest, Kangaroo, Destination Gobi*.

So You Wanted to Be in Pictures!

Some of my favorite memories of those first pictures I worked on might be worth the telling.
Director Henry King (*Twelve O'Clock High, Jesse James, Alexander's Ragtime Band*) was one of my favorites, so I was pleased to be assigned to his *Captain from Castile* crew, even if it meant Mexico for three months. When King went location scouting, he did it in his own airplane and was a superb pilot with thousands of accident-free hours.
One noontime, he was having the catered lunch at the cast table (the exclusive eating place reserved for the director and the principal members of the cast) when I, sitting on the ground beneath a tree, heard

him arguing an aviation question with Tyrone Power, who was a decorated Marine combat pilot, and someone else, also a pilot, at the table.

Looking around, he spied me and, knowing of my military background, summoned me over to the table and posed the question to me. I anxiously looked over the several faces hanging on my answer. Fortunately, I was able to maintain my good standing with both King and Power; it was something the Air Corps neglected to teach me.

Though a great director, King was also quite a bore. Ask him the time, for instance, and he'd tell you how his watch was made. One early Sunday morning in the remote Mexican town of Uruapan, King, in search of one of the production people (and there were at least six of us because of the big money involved, probably less than two million), came to the hotel where many of the crew stayed. There had been a big storm the night before, and he wanted to see if the set, a campsite by a stream, had been washed out. I, the lowest in the chain, was the only one he could find, and I soon found my slightly hungover self in the back seat of his open convertible, the Mexican union driver in the front passenger seat. King was at the wheel as we made our way over the seemingly endless winding dirt road. Apparently he couldn't see me in the rear view mirror as I struggled to keep from heaving all over the side of his car, because he was praising me for all kinds of things I wasn't—including being a good boy on Saturday nights while the rest of his staff were out "filling the cup" and doing other things evil.

But my favorite recollection is being invited to a Sunday afternoon cocktail party given by three of King's favorite female crew members: Theresa Brachetto, script clerk; Carey O'Neil, wardrobe lady; and the hairdresser, whose name escapes me. Only a few people were invited, their quarters being small. Among those chosen was Tyrone Power, who asked if he could bring Lana Turner, who had come to Mexico to visit him. Here we are in this miserable, hot, dusty God-forsaken excuse for a town and he asks about the dress code. Carey told him, "Formal, of course."

The party was well under way when there's a knock on the door and, you guessed it, arriving is Power in white tie and tails with the lovely Lana in a full-length white evening gown. Without a trace of discomfort, they joined in, displaying not the least surprise at the less-than-informal way the other guests were dressed.

Fury at Furnace Creek was another memorable film. Kanab, Utah, was one of the favorite places to shoot movies. It offered everything: horses, wagons, cattle, lakes and streams, plains, a fort, two streets for Westerns, trucks, wranglers, and excellent housing. The Parry Lodge could handle the largest Hollywood unit. And the three Parry brothers either owned or managed everything that a movie company might need. They even catered the lunches, and the food served at the lodge was first class. I hope they became very rich because they certainly delivered.

Fury at Furnace Creek, a Western, was my introduction to Kanab. It starred Victor Mature and Coleen Gray, both contract players at Fox.

This was a period when Mature was very popular, and the studio moved him from one picture right into another, none of which was very demanding of an actor (which Mature was in name only). He was a likable fellow to be around, and for both the young and old waitresses at the lodge, positively lovable. I can only imagine the bickering that went on over who would get to take his breakfast to his cabin.

Mature had a good business going on the side. He sold television sets. That's right, television sets! In 1946, when television was in its infancy, any dealer who could get television sets from the manufacturers could sell them without even trying. It may be difficult for young people to believe this, but for only a few hours each day and only on two or three stations could you get programs of any kind, all bad, yet people loved it. Mature opened up a store on Pico Boulevard about a half block from the studio and hired an eager young man to run it. The store stayed open at night, and grips, electricians, prop men, directors—everybody, including me—could be found there after work putting their wages in Vic's pockets.

One day at about six in the morning at the studio on the Western street where we were to shoot, I'm checking to see that all is ready—doors all work, curtains on the windows, hitching posts upright, and so forth. I see this cream-colored convertible sedan parked in front of the livery stable, its radio blaring. In the car sat Mature with his electric shaver plugged into the lighter. He was using the rear-view mirror as he trimmed his beard.

"What in hell are you doing here so early, Vic?" I asked. "Your call isn't until eight-thirty."

"Glad you asked," he replied, pointing to his watch. "Put this on your production report. I'm here two hours and 20 minutes early, which is 14 minutes more than I was late day before yesterday. Want some coffee?"

It seems that besides his bosses' giving him hell for being late and holding up production, the front office contacted Mature's agent and lawyer and threatened to withhold what would have been a fairly large amount from his salary to offset what his being late cost the studio. I never heard how that turned out.

Maureen O'Hara and me in Australia.

As for the Spartan television set that Vic gave me a "good deal" on, it worked exceptionally well until we caught *inchitis* and just had to have a bigger picture.

Another of my favorite early experiences took me Down Under, where we made *Kangaroo*. Having been stationed in Australia a short time during the war, I developed a liking for all things Australian, so

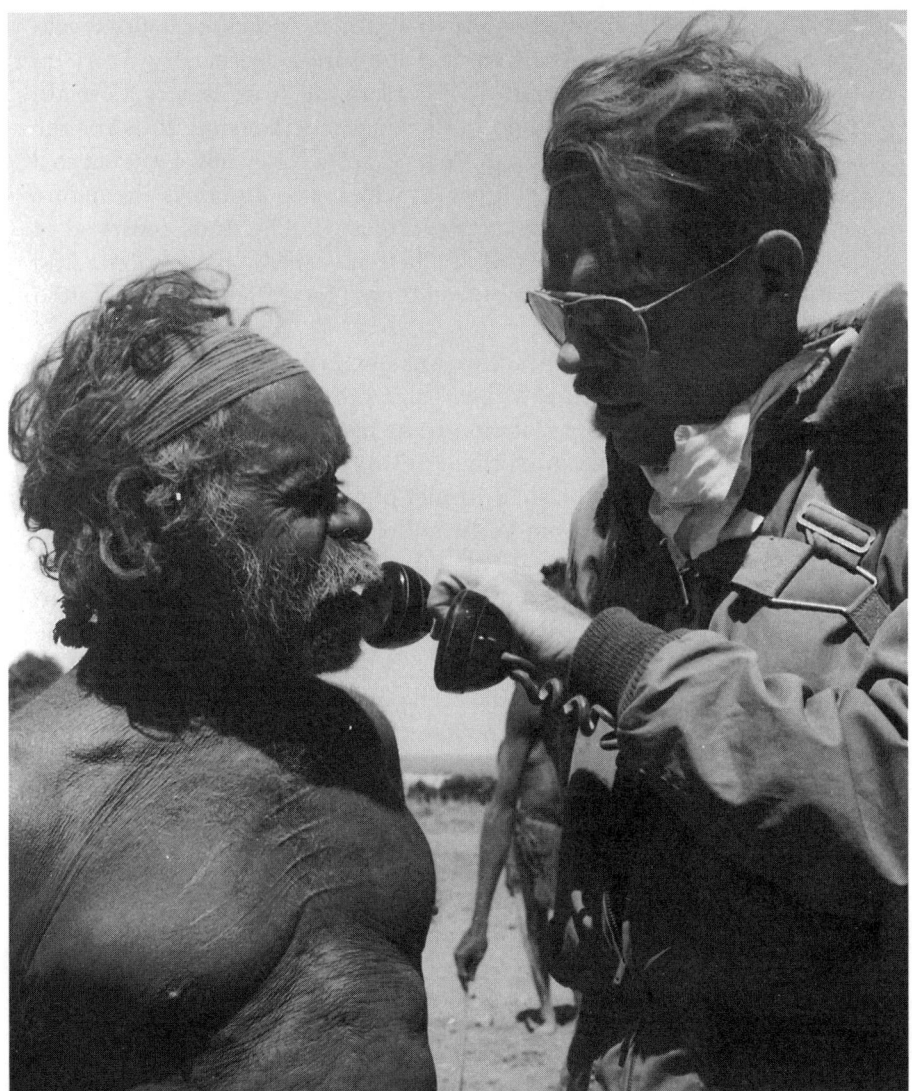

An Aborigine friend talking on my radio (which weighed at least 15 pounds).

I may have smiled a little when told that I was to be sent there on this movie. Their movie industry, while not exactly in its infancy, was not nearly as developed as it is today, and consequently our crew was made up of key people from Hollywood, augmented by Australians with little experience. Most of the equipment had to come from the studio, too. Looking at the product out of Australia now and for the past several years, those blokes sure were fast and superb learners!

The Australian government was planning to construct a certain project in South Australia and built temporary housing units for the workers near the remote town of Port Augusta. Our movie was set in a period that called for "early outback," which also describes the nature of the country in which our camp was placed. The units consisted of two-bedrooms, one bath, a tiny kitchen and small living-room. And the unit I lived in with the location auditor, a good friend named Harold Roth, became the office.

Some of the world's deadliest snakes thrive in Australia, and we needed one for our picture. When three brown snakes were delivered to our associate producer, Bob Snody, he had the nut who caught them put the gunny sack containing the writhing devils in a galvanized wash tub and store them in the shade under our porch.

When I came in from work and Harold told me what Snody had done, it only made me dislike him more than I already did, and afraid of snakes as I was, I carried the wash tub over to Snody's front door, knocked on it and said some rather nasty things when he opened it.

When we tried to shoot the scene of one of the snakes crossing a dirt road, it was very hot and the handler couldn't get any of the three to move. I think he finally tied a thread to its neck and pulled it across the road.

Fifteen-hundred head of cattle were gathered for the big stampede scene, and for some reason, the head cameraman, Charley Clarke, thought I should drive the camera car. Now, this vehicle was a specially built truck that carried five cameramen, about six cameras, batteries, film, the company nurse, the script clerk and the director, Louis Milestone *(All Quiet on the Western Front, Les Miserables)* and his wife, sitting in director's chairs on the top platform. It was grossly overloaded.

When the signal was given for the drovers and effects people to startle the cattle into panic, we began to move fairly smoothly as I edged the car alongside the herd, with Charley telling me on the headset to speed up or slow down. Just when we got going good, the wind changed and I was blinded by a great cloud of dust the cattle made. I began to gradually slow down. That's when I could feel the cattle bump the car. By the time we were completely stopped, several more hit the car, and I wondered about the operator of the lowest camera (Scotty McEwen), who was about two feet from the ground. When the dust settled, nobody was hurt but Charley actually picked hair out of the matte box of the low camera. I think I asked the wardrobe man for a change of underwear and trousers.

Fixed Bayonets (1951)

After "doing" five months in Australia as a pitifully underpaid and overworked second assistant director doing the work of three good men, I was just getting reacquainted with my family when I was summoned to the production office to pick up a script for my next assignment. Without opening the cover, I asked if, by any conceivable quirk of fate, it might possibly be a bedroom-parlor-and-bath (meaning that it would be shot mostly on a sound stage) and I would be spared having to take off for God-only-knows-where for God-only-knows-how-long.

"One of the Western states," I was told.

Back at the cubby-hole of an office where, along with a couple of other in-betweeners, I was hanging out, I pondered the best way of telling my wife, Helen, that I would soon be off on another location, leaving her to cope with two kids and a house that needed a lot of work. About to pick up the phone to call her, and all the time feeling sorry for myself, an idea flashed into my head. Dialing the office impulsively, I asked my dear friend and benefactress, Mildred Lowe, if she could get me in to see Ray Klune, the studio general production manager and my big boss.

"Be here in ten minutes," she replied. Now I was committed.

Entering the plush inner sanctum of a very busy and important executive can be a trying experience for a nervous creature like me, especially if he's there to ask for what might be considered an outlandish favor. Realizing that I had passed the point of no return, out came: "Mr. Klune, you are looking at a very tired man who has just spent five months chasing cattle, kangaroos, and aborigines around Australia in the hot sun."

"Well, if you're that tired, why don't you sit down and tell me what you want me to do about it," he replied, gesturing to a chair in front of his massive desk.

"I've been told I'm off on another location, and judging from the thickness of the script I was given, it might just be forever," I whined, "and I need a rest before taking on another location as a second assistant."

"Well, Paul, if all you want is some time off, we ought to be able to arrange that," he said.

Before he could push buttons, replacing me on the picture and setting me free—without pay, no doubt—I found myself saying, "But Mr. Klune, I don't have any vacation time coming, and I can't afford to take time off on my own. Could you please give me just one picture as a first assistant so I can rest up? And then I'll be ready for anything, anywhere."

He just looked at me and then: "You are sitting there telling me that you want me to promote you to a much more responsible job that pays a lot more so you don't have to work so hard and can get a rest. Have I got that right, Paul?"

In light of the cold hard facts as he presented them, I could only shrug my shoulders and reply, "I guess so, sir!"

He just sort of smiled and said simply, "Well, I'll be damned!" And without another word, he dismissed me with a wave of his hand and resumed doing whatever he was doing when I interrupted him.

Back in the cubbyhole a couple of hours later, I was pondering whether I had done irreparable damage to my movie career when the phone rang and I was summoned to the office immediately. With a wry smile, Mildred handed me a new script and told me to report to Sam Fuller, telling him I was his first assistant director.

Some men smoke a cigar as if it were their just reward for some heroic deed they had performed, or as though they were relishing every moment spent with a dear friend. Sam Fuller was one such sort. A small man, he was seated behind a large desk covered with hand-written notes. He greeted me warmly as I introduced myself and found myself a seat.

He said we were going to make a Korean War movie he had scripted and was scheduled to begin shooting in about a month, and it was called *Fixed Bayonets*. What he didn't say was that he had already made a Korean War movie he had scripted, which was called *Steel Helmet*. Both featured the same star, Gene Evans. The main difference, I was to learn, was that one story takes place in the summer, the other in the winter.

I liked this man and began to like him even more when his great-looking secretary advanced into the office bearing a tray of fixings for the evening highballs. There were three glasses, a bottle of Jack Daniels, and a bowl of ice. She thrust a glass in my hands and began pouring without as much as a "say when." After she did the same for the boss and herself, Fuller toasted me with a hearty "Welcome aboard!" and exhorted himself to make a great movie. I should add that this ritual was faithfully observed every evening during the preparation and shooting of the picture.

Sam was well qualified to write and direct movies like this one and *Steel Helmet* and *The Big Red One*, since he had been an infantry combat reporter for the military service newspaper "Stars and Stripes." Listening to some of his war stories left no doubt about his being right in the thick of it during World War II.

It was fitting also that his office at Fox was in Park Row, so named because it originally housed the New York writers William Fox had under contract. Several had been hired away from newspaper reporting much as Sam had been.

Lucien Ballard was a cameraman who was married to the lovely movie star Merle Oberon. He had gained a certain fame in the industry from a recent movie he shot in which there was a fairly long scene with five or six people seated around a table. The characters were playing poker and planning a robbery. The scene had been rehearsed the previous day. The next morning when the scene was to be shot and the director arrived, nothing seemed to be happening on the set regarding lighting. Lucien, relaxing in his chair, told the assistant director he was ready to shoot, and when all the actors were in their places, Lucien reached over the table and pulled the chain to turn on the bulb in the single, green-shaded lamp that hung over the table. The scene, shot with only that light, became a classic.

Anyway, Lucien was fast, had a good sense of humor, didn't take anything too seriously, including himself, and he and I hit it off famously. Knowing this assignment was my big break, he went out of his way to make my job on a tough picture an easier and more pleasant experience.

If you didn't see *Fixed Bayonets*, it was about a platoon of American infantrymen fighting the war in the mountains in the dead of winter. Several guys who played the GIs went on to become notable stars. Later I heard that Jimmy Dean was one of the GIs but I can't remember him being in the cast.

The entire picture, except for a few stock shots (scenes taken out of a film library or shot by an outside cameraman specifically to order), was photographed on Stage 8 at 20th Century–Fox. No explosion was big enough for Sammy, and while he was very safety-conscious, both Lucien and I made sure risks were kept within bounds and at a minimum. Nevertheless, Sam kept asking the special effects crew for larger bursts when the mortar shells exploded. He got them, too, as evidenced by a large crack in the stucco over the entrance to Stage 8.

Upon arriving on the set every morning, Sam was furnished two six-shooter pistols loaded with blank ammunition. These were carried by Sam in two large holsters that were belted onto him. Sam fired these pistols when he wanted to cue an actor to react to something off-scene, to fall, or almost any other occasion he had to give a cue. On a certain afternoon, the press was invited to visit the set to watch us at work and interview Sam and the actors in between shots. A small bleacher had been set up on the sidelines during the lunch period where the press, including Hedda Hopper and other famous columnists, was to sit and watch. Scheduled was a certain death scene in which one soldier says goodbye to his dying buddy, who lying in the cold and wet snow, bleeds copious amounts of blood, utters his last words, closes his eyes, rolls his head to one side, and dies.

Now this sort of scene calls for exquisite timing, and Sammy, leaving nothing to chance, decided to cue the actor to close his eyes, roll his head, and die. With his cue gun, of course. We rehearse it. Lucien and his crew light the shot, and when they're ready to shoot, Lucien disappears, presumably to the men's room. Except instead, he heads for the ladder, where a waiting prop man hands him several phony stuffed ducks. The dying soldier utters his last sound, closes his eyes, and—BLAM!—Sammy fires the cue to die and down flutter five dead ducks that land right in front of the press, who react with great laughter. Sammy, guessing that I had a hand in the caper, barely spoke to Lucien or me the rest of the day.

The picture came in on schedule and on budget, which of course was a feather in my cap, and while Sam and I were having a final evening drink together in his office, he pulled out his checkbook, wrote out a check for $100, handed it to me, and simply said, "Thanks." He then poured us another drink and took a puff on the ever-present cigar. I had grown to really like and admire the man, and I was so damned grateful and proud I almost cried.

Checking in at the production bungalow before heading home, I ran into Max Golden, the assistant general production manager, a very nice guy. I wasn't the least bit reluctant to show him the check, which he promptly took in to show Mr. Klune. As far as Golden was concerned, there'd be no more second assistant directing for this lad.

The time came for Mr. Zanuck to run a rough cut of the picture with Sam Fuller, Zanuck's aides, Lefty Hough (Ray Klune's assistant), the film editor, and whoever else Zanuck chose to have. These runnings were never scheduled much in advance and invariably took place any time between nine at night and three in the morning in Zanuck's projection room. Lefty told the story like this: When the showing was over and the lights came up, everybody waited for the great man to speak. After several silent moments, Zanuck, having heard about Fuller's method of cueing, pulled out a pistol and began firing—live ammunition! The bullets ricocheted off the concrete walls and the astonished members of the audience either tried to hide behind their seats or run out of the room. The dangerous prank was a huge success, at least for Zanuck. *Fixed Bayonets* was only mildly successful, but I still remember it fondly.

Monkey Business (1952)

Much to my pleasant surprise, Howard Hawks came back on the lot. In Europe, he had been making *I Was a Male War Bride,* or at least parts of that movie. Cary Grant had come down with a bad case of yellow jaundice and was unable to work for months, which of course brought production to a halt. When he was well enough to resume work, Hawks and the studio decided to finish the picture back at the studio and at local locations around Los Angeles.

While in Europe, Hawks had foreign assistant directors as well as a foreign crew (which he spoke of in a disparaging manner). Disgustedly, he told about the English crew going on strike because, on one afternoon tea-break, the teacart didn't have raspberry tarts! So when he was ready to finish the picture here, the office assigned

Arthur Jacobson as first assistant, an excellent choice, with me as the second assistant director, an absolutely splendid choice. For me it was the beginning of a long and wonderful association with Hawks.

Three years later Hawks returned to the studio for another comedy with Cary Grant, *Monkey Business*. Remembering me, Hawks tells the production office that I will be his first assistant. The only pictures he made from this time on that I didn't work on were those made while I had other commitments. At least I like to think that!

This time, Ginger Rogers was the leading lady, and a real lady, if I ever met one. That wonderful gentleman Charles Coburn played a prominent role, as did Marilyn Monroe, who at this point in her all-too-short career, couldn't quite "find" herself among the big-time, heavy-hitting company into which she was thrust. I remember Grant and Rogers seemed to be aware of this and tried quite visibly to make Marilyn comfortable.

I'd like to forget a certain feature player in the picture, an ornery and very miserable chimpanzee whose name would not be mentioned here even if I could remember it.

We had sent a script to the chimp's trainer, and the primate must have read it, too, because when we interviewed them at the studio, the chimp was A-1 perfect, doing all his tricks and obeying commands, certainly living up to his reputation as the best-trained chimpanzee in the business.

But when we began shooting and it came time to do his stuff in front of the camera, it became another story. If he didn't run away on the stage, he'd simply refuse to obey his trainer. In all fairness, there were some days when he'd arrive at work in a good mood and turn in a respectable performance. Such days, however, were few and cherished. Needless to say, Hawks, who was as fine a writer as any in the business, revised the script and eliminated several of the little stinker's scenes that—who knows?—might have made him a superstar. Like Kermit, or more recently, Babe.

That Hawks didn't brook insubordination was well known.

In his earlier days, Hawks wrote and directed two-reelers, comedies, Westerns, whatever. Monte Banks was a popular comedian, maybe a leading man, too. Hawks was making a silent movie with him at the time Banks was at his peak of popularity. One day, Banks started to tell Hawks how a scene should be done. Hawks listened, giving Banks a steely stare (which I've seen many times, occasionally aimed at me). Telling Banks they were losing the sunlight, he then directed the actor to get on a train that was waiting a few hundred yards up the track.

Monkey Business *(1952)*

When the train stopped near the camera, he was to get off and run across to a nearby two-story house, go in the front door, and slam it shut. When Banks wanted to know why and what came next, Hawks explained that they must hurry before they lost the light and that he'd explain later. The shot in the can, Hawks then made a shot through a window of Banks entering the house and running across the room and crawling into the fireplace.

That shot completed, Hawks shakes Banks' hand and tells him he's finished in the picture. When Banks protests, Hawks merely tells him that he doesn't want to work with him anymore, that he's too difficult. He goes on to tell him that another actor in blackface and Banks' wardrobe will be seen emerging from the chimney and assuming Banks' part for the remainder of the picture. Needless to add, Banks never questioned Hawks again! Or so he told me.

Another time, Hawks was making a picture (*To Have and Have Not*) with Humphrey Bogart and Lauren Bacall at about the time the two fell madly in love, and they'd get attacks of the "cutesies" (Hawks' expression). They'd come up with all sorts of ideas of things they might say or do, all lousy, according to Hawks.

After taking just so much of them, he had the cameraman tie off the camera and put white tape on the floor to indicate the camera side lines. He then told the actors to do their scene any way they pleased, doing and saying whatever they wished but to do it all within the boundaries of the white tape side lines. He then announced that he was going out to the Santa Anita Racetrack to watch a horse he owned run. Not only did they behave from then on but he told me they sent him a case of good liquor.

So no one on the set of *Monkey Business* was surprised when Hawks wrote the ornery chimp out of several scenes. We still had shots that required the monkey's cooperation, however, and we all earned our money trying to keep him in line. There was a scene, for instance, of a board of directors' meeting room in which the chimp was required to sit attentively in his chair along with Grant, Rogers, Coburn and several other people. The beast was just fine in what little rehearsal Hawks did, but no matter how clever we were about not letting him know when the camera was running and we were making a *take*, he'd scamper off and disappear up the chains holding the scaffolding and thence go on up to the ceiling grids of the big Stage 5.

Off went the lights and everybody relaxed while the trainer, chagrined, embarrassed, and mad as hell, went looking for the little bastard. Sometimes it took thirty or more minutes to coax him within grasping distance, whereupon the trainer would get a firm hold on him and proceed to beat the hell out of him. The resulting screeching and crying was enough to tear your heart out. This happened a couple of times until Mr. Grant quite emotionally told me that if the trainer beat the chimp just one more time, he, Grant, was going home! The trainer seemed somewhat relieved when I told him, but also said that was the only way the animal could be worked. I said something about him and his little chum being among the unemployed if he hit him one more time.

We tried the scene again, and once more the chimp took off, disappearing up into the grids, about sixty or seventy feet from the stage floor. Up the stage wall ladder went the trainer, but to no avail; all his coaxing and pleading fell on the chimp's deaf ears. Down he came sans chimp and shrugging his shoulders, told Hawks that he'd get another chimp, maybe two, and we could try again tomorrow.

I could see almost an entire afternoon's work going down the drain. The loss certainly wouldn't enhance my standing with the production office. I heard myself saying, "Maybe he'll come to me, I think he likes me," and I headed for the ladder. That ladder seemed never to end as I climbed upward. I tried not to think about my fear of heights. Not daring to look down, I found myself on the catwalk with the evil little bugger, who seemed rather glad to see me. Without too much pleading, he came to me and put his arms around my neck. I talked to him and petted him soothingly, wishing that somebody was doing the same to me. As I contemplated carrying the recalcitrant ape down the ladder, it occurred to me he might be getting ready to bite me just for the hell of it.

When the cameraman saw us on our way down the ladder, he had the lights turned on and the actors took their places. The trainer and I put the chimp in his chair where—miracle of miracles—he stayed long enough to get the master shot. We easily enclosed the chimp within the set for the remaining close shots.

Cary Grant, noble man that he was, inadvertently sent me up that ladder and to the catwalk, where I scored several Brownie points with Howard Hawks, who knew I had come to work with a powerful hangover that day.

The Ransom of Red Chief (1952)

It was while *Monkey Business* was being edited that Darryl Zanuck approached Hawks with the idea of getting him to direct *The Ransom of Red Chief*. It was the only comedy among five O. Henry stories Zanuck wanted to make into a single "A"-quality feature picture. Zanuck asked four of the top 20th Century–Fox directors to contribute their services, since the shooting schedules, like the stories, were short. All four had agreed. Hawks was not a contract director but had earned a lot of money when he did make a picture there. When Zanuck asked Hawks, he refused, and offered to do it for $50,000. At least that's what Hawks told me.

My guess is that the two of them had a big fight in Palm Springs the previous weekend over a croquet game, which wasn't unusual, and Hawks wasn't giving Zanuck anything for free. Talk about a love-hate relationship!

And this wasn't the first time the two friends had butted heads.

Some years later, while Hawks and I were on a plane going to London, he told me of the time when he'd just finished a picture and decided to go to Paris for a little fun. He'd hardly settled into his hotel room when he got a phone call from Zanuck, who was in Europe on business. Zanuck asked Hawks if he was up to a night on the town.

"Sounds good to me, Darryl, as long as you don't bring your stooges along," replied Hawks.

When Hawks walked into the designated nightclub, Zanuck was sitting with two henchmen and a gorgeous French actress who was giving Zanuck her rapt attention. Instead of walking out, Hawks joined them and within minutes was on the dance floor with the actress.

She asked, "Is that really *the* Darryl Zanuck, the vice-president of 20th Century–Fox Studio?"

Hawks confirmed that he certainly was exactly that, and after a moment, she asked, "But how do you know?"

"Because I'm the president," Hawks replied.

Next morning, Hawks was awakened by a phone call from Zanuck: "Howard, did you by any chance get that French girl's phone number?" he asked. "She disappeared before I had a chance to get to know her."

"No, Darryl, but she's right here with me if you'd care to talk to her," replied Hawks. "Want me to wake her?"

Anyway, that's the story he told me.

Ransom of Red Chief starred Fred Allen and Oscar Levant and a kid by the name of Lee Acker. Both Allen and Levant were very funny people on radio and then television. Levant was also a gifted pianist— the concert hall variety.

The very idea of two sour and cynical men like Allen and Levant going up against an obstinate, clever, devilish, smart-ass little boy like Acker promises good comedy, and the good script in the hands of Hawks meant a lot of laughs on the set. While Allen and Levant didn't become bosom buddies, the two men were constantly working out business and coming up with gags, many of which Hawks accepted, but it seemed to me they were trying to top each other instead of thinking of what worked for the movie.

The shoot required a real bear, and we certainly picked a winner. I think his name was Bruno. If anybody tells you they know of a tame

The Ransom of Red Chief (1952)

adult bear—I mean one that can be depended upon to be sweet and gentle around strange people and that will be obedient to its trainer—don't you believe it.

The stage the hideout camp was built on was rather small, and the set was a wooded place where three people might hide out while waiting for the ransom money. The entire set was surrounded by a day-or-night sky backing. We kept the part of the backing we weren't photographing raised for ventilation. Between the bear pee, the campfire smoke, and the rotting greenery, it got to smelling rather ripe on the stage after a few days.

It's my contention that most movie animal trainers necessarily have to be a little funny in the head to choose such a way of earning their daily bread. Bruno's man was no exception. No matter how the trainers attempt to buddy up to the brute, it was no go; there was a definite conflict of personalities. There were times when the bear would behave quite well and please us. At other times, with Bruno's will prevailing against the trainer's, lots of patience and film were spent to finally get the shot.

For those of you who might have occasion to get a bear to walk down a path in the woods and not stray off to one side or the other so as to take a half hour to find and coax back to the starting place, here's how it's done: After all else has failed sprinkle Sloan's Liniment on both sides of the path and the bear won't cross it but will try to get away from the smell. So will your camera crew!

One scene called for the bear to come out of the woods and into the clearing where Levant and Allen were stretched out sound asleep by the glowing campfire. Ignoring the sleeping figures, the bear was supposed to eat their food that was loosely wrapped in a cloth. Dummies dressed in the actors' double clothes were used while they lit the shot, and then the trainer wanted to do a couple of rehearsals. On the very first one, Bruno entered the clearing, stopped, looked around, and made straight for the dummies, grabbing the Levant dummy's head in his mouth and violently shaking it. Getting Levant to come out of his dressing room after some wag told him what happened wasn't easy.

Gentlemen Prefer Blondes (1953)

My promotion to first assistant director wasn't permanent. After *Ransom of Red Chief*, I found myself as second assistant on a hot Nevada location doing a picture called *Destination Gobi*. The only redeeming and rewarding thing about the assignment was my association with the director, Robert Wise, with whom I'd worked on *Two Flags West* in 1950. Robert Wise was truly a gentleman, and I wish I had been invited to work with him on his later movies.

Business conditions became lean, and fewer movies were being made at Fox. I suppose I was lucky to have any sort of job when I was assigned as first assistant on *Gentlemen Prefer Blondes* with Howard

Gentlemen Prefer Blondes *(1952)*

Hawks as director. The sky turned blue again, and I went about breaking down the script and working out a production board for scheduling the picture. The production office wanted Hawks to agree on a schedule. He saw no reason to come to the studio, so it fell to me to take the production board (we called it a "cross-plot board") up to his house in Brentwood. It was known as Hog Canyon Farm, a beautiful estate that until recently had also been part-time home to his race horses. The house was a large, two-story Colonial, comfortably and tastefully furnished, I guess by his second wife, Slim Hawks, from whom he was divorced.

With only a cursory glance at my schedule, mostly out of courtesy to me, he declared it just fine and then proceeded to ask me questions about the war and what routes and South Pacific islands I flew between as a pilot in the Air Transport Command. Rummaging through some drawers, he found a set of military maps printed on fine silk. They had been intended for use by downed pilots and were marvelous souvenirs for any air crew member who served in the area. (With all the overwater flying I did, I don't know why I was never issued a set.) Hawks told me to take whichever ones I wanted.

There were several things about the picture I wanted to discuss with him, but he would have none of it. Instead he took me out to his row of workshops where he was building a sleek sports car with a fiberglass body. (In those days, most people had never even heard of fiberglass.) Then he showed me a large swimming pool that had been built during the war years out of materials he scrounged from various sources with the help of people in high places.

Having worked with him before, I knew it was premature to try to pin him down about a schedule or anything that didn't pertain to either casting or story, both out of my domain. My bosses, however, were oblivious of this fact, so I had to go through the motions of scheduling. I am sure, judging by his patience with me, that Hawks knew I had to come up with something.

It wasn't long before things began to happen—Jane Russell and Marilyn Monroe were set for the leads and were to begin extensive rehearsals with Jack Cole and his assistant, Gwen Verdon. Hawks came to the studio for a few hours almost every day to work with Joe Wright (the art director), Billy Travilla (the costume designer), the casting directors, and me.

By the end of a couple of weeks into rehearsal, Marilyn was constantly late in arriving at the studio, sometimes by an hour or more. I had to show this on a daily production report, and Sid Rogell never failed to notice this fact. He was the new general production manager who had just taken over the job. He was not the most lovable fellow I'd yet met. Summoning me to his office, he told me to phone him the next time Marilyn arrived late.

True to form, she showed her up-all-night face about an hour late. As ordered, I called Rogell to report it, but not before I called Hawks to come and listen in, which he did. Both of us hid in a little rehearsal hall office without a ceiling that allowed us to hear the whole conversation. Knowing her all too well, we had to learn for ourselves what sort of dialogue she'd think up to lay on Rogell. He politely introduced himself and proceeded to firmly tell her that her frequent tardiness would no longer be tolerated, that hereafter she must show up on time. In the syrupy "Lorelei" voice she used in the movie, she explained, "But Mr. Rogell, I'm not at all late. I started rehearsing at seven o'clock this morning, planning out in my mind all the things I wanted to do in the number we're working on. I can't wait to show Mr. Cole my ideas. I'll bet you weren't even awake that early." Whereupon Mr. Rogell, defeated, left, quite speechless.

While I've worked on several big musicals, I cannot be considered an authority on dancing. But as you view *Gentlemen Prefer Blondes*, it's quite plain to see that the style, particularly the movement of the arms and hands by Monroe and Russell, is being copied by many of today's dancers. This style was taught to Monroe and Russell by Jack Cole and Gwen Verdon, two very pleasant and talented teachers. Gwen was not only a great dancer but also was a good actress. Unbeknownst to her, I urged Billy Gordon, the 20th Century–Fox casting director, to go to the rehearsal hall, meet her and watch her work. Unfortunately for the studio, he never did. Another nudge I gave him, again to no avail, was to get the studio to provide Marilyn with a decent automobile. Here's a girl making a picture that inevitably was going to propel her to stardom yet not receiving a salary large enough to drive a dependable car. Under term contract to Fox, she was steadily getting more important and larger parts, but her salary didn't seem to rise. The studio had a deal with Ford Motor Company to provide dollar-a-year cars and trucks in exchange for movie exposure. Several of the executives and department heads drove the free cars, and I figured the Studio could loan Marilyn one, at least for this important picture. I've no idea where or how she got the junk car she drove, but one had to believe her when she'd plead car trouble for being late for work. I never said anything to her, but she sure had a lax agent, whoever he was, at that time.

A good portion of the movie takes place on an ocean liner bound for Paris, and several sections of the ship were built on sound stages. One set even included a fairly large swimming pool where a big production number took place. One day we were shooting in the ship's cocktail lounge with several dancing extras and a studio orchestra. The scene was between Marilyn and the inimitable Charles Coburn, the character actor with the monocle, who, in reality, had the hots for Marilyn. In the scene, they were dancing and talking. I don't know how such a scene is done today but the best way to do it then was with a "dancing dolly." The camera is mounted on a tripod on a small, three-wheel dolly that is easily moved about by one grip. The sound boom man also moves with the dancers. What with the lighting there are several things to coordinate which means more rehearsal than usual for Hawks. By the time he got the scene worked out, we broke for lunch, after which Hawks laid down for a little rest. After lunch and after the cameraman finished lighting the set, I continued to rehearse the scene. We arrived at the moment when it was time for Hawks to appear and take over, but when the second assistant told him we were ready, he just nodded. By now I knew better than to persist in anything with him. You only told him something once. When he didn't show up on the set, everybody relaxed, except Mr. Coburn and Marilyn, who, getting the orchestra to keep playing, danced like two lost-in-the-crowd lovers. A Latin piece, as I remember. The crew and the extras loved it.

Then the orchestra, as if on cue, played the introduction to the lovely "September Song," and we were treated to Coburn singing it to Marilyn. He was about 70 at the time, and after seeing him with this gorgeous young girl, the song and the moment took on a special meaning. We were all rather sorry when Hawks showed up and we went back to work.

A few days later we were shooting a scene in the main dining salon of the ship with all the actors and an expensive crowd of dress extras, an orchestra, uniformed waiters, and fine food.

I had worked on two previous movies with George Winslow, the "kid with the foghorn voice," as he was billed, and I thought I was aware of all his tricks. Believe me, he had plenty. It was 4:30 p.m., and just about all the above mentioned people were to go into quarter-checks (one-fourth more to their daily minimum pay) at 5:00 p.m., so I alert Hawks and the cameraman, even though I knew we could easily finish before five. With everybody ready, I send for the dreaded Winslow, only to learn that he has retired to the men's room—with a couple of comic books. I keep everybody in place and at the ready for when the kid, refreshed and relieved, makes his appearance. Ten minutes go by. I ask his mother to check on him, and she reports back to me that he'll be through shortly.

The closer it gets to five, the angrier I get. I collect the mother and together we go after him. At about thirty seconds before 5:00, out of the stall he appears, comic books in hand. By the time the camera is rolling, it's very expensively after 5:00.

It has been my good fortune never to have to work with him again. Come to think of it, he isn't a kid any more. Hell, he's probably collecting Social Security!

Even after working on six pictures with Marilyn (starting with *Ticket to Tomahawk*), it never occurred to me how little sex appeal she had for the various staffs and crews she worked with. That is, until Hawks brought up the subject over lunch one day, and I couldn't agree with him more. I remarked that the male stars she worked with didn't appear to get excited about working with her, not even Robert Mitchum, who had more than an ordinary interest in the female species. Nor do I think it bothered my wife one whit when Marilyn phoned me late at night to ask what scenes we were shooting the next day or if I could possibly make her set call later in the morning. Contrast this with the effect a mere *photograph* of her produced. I don't know, but I'd be willing to bet her photograph sold many more times the number of calendars than Betty Grable's, Lana Turner's, or any other girl's photograph did. I recently read that had Marilyn lived, she would now be 67 years old. What would she be like and what tales would she have to tell, had she lived?

River of No Return (1954)

Perhaps the production office felt I needed a breath of fresh air after *Gentlemen Prefer Blondes,* because off I went to Guatemala on a second unit operation called *Treasure of the Golden Condor.* It was headed by Delmer Daves, a well-known and popular director (*Broken Arrow*) and starred Cornel Wilde, Anne Bancroft, and Fay Wray. We were there for only a few days' work, making background shots, process plates, and a few scenes putting the principals in the locale of the story—Lake Atitlan, Antigua, and the Mayan ruins of Tikal. Altogether it was interesting and I remember Guatemala fondly, regardless of its citizens' propensity for perpetual revolution.

A few years earlier, I was the second assistant on *Broken Arrow* and worked with Delmer Daves, the picture's director. He was a rather large man whose hobbies were calligraphy and collecting and analyzing rocks. Wouldn't you know I would be dragooned into the wrong hobby. On the survey trip to Sedona, Arizona, it fell to me to walk behind Mr. Daves, who hurried and took giant steps. I was carrying a huge canvas bag in which I placed the rocks he picked up as we traversed the state of Arizona (or so it seemed). By the time we got back to the Anderson camp at the end of the day, I was one lame and aching rock caddy.

One sunny day before we started shooting, Ray Klune, my big boss, and Ray Moore, the head of the location department, flew to Sedona in the company plane. Stanley Goldsmith, the unit manager and my immediate boss on this picture (and a man who just happened to hate anybody who had been an officer during World War II), sent me to the airport to meet them. When we arrived at the camp, it was time for lunch, and I found myself seated next to Klune. I was trying to answer his questions as best I could when a driver who had been to Flagstaff approached and whispered in my shell-like ear just loud enough for Klune to hear, "I put the pint of bourbon and the change under your pillow." Ray Klune just looked at me. I think I sort of squirmed and smiled like Stan Laurel.

Ray Klune must have become tired of being the studio production manager, because word got around that Zanuck made him a producer. I felt very flattered when he had me assigned to his first picture. I told him as much when I reported to him. He was highly respected in the industry. His greatest accomplishment was being Selznick's production manager on *Gone with the Wind*. He worked on several other Selznick movies also.

Klune was rather small of stature and you'd never peg him to be the outdoor sportsman he was. Any weekend or holiday that he could get away would find him freezing in a duck-blind, or at some mountain stream or lake with a fishing rod in his hand. So I wasn't the least bit surprised when he told me in the jargon of movie-making that we were going to make a low-budget, no-name, small-crew, fast-director movie to be called *River of No Return*.

I was to be the combination unit manager/assistant director, and we were going to camp out in tents with a cook and one helper to feed us.

Klune explained that the first order of business was to find great scenic locations that audiences hadn't seen before. So Addison Hehr, an amiable, bright, young art director and I were dispatched to Idaho, where the actual River of No Return flows. We were to photograph any possible locations and not return until we had explored all possibilities, however remote they might be. After viewing our still photos, Klune would then go with us to see the places for himself.

River of No Return *(1954)* 45

It took only a few weeks to find what we considered spectacular locations, and back to the studio we went, pleased with our efforts and hoping Klune would be, too.

When our film was developed and our slides organized, a projector and screen was set up in Klune's darkened office. As the show began, Addison and I provided narration as I operated the projector. There were a few other people in the office, as I recall.

The "show" was moving along quite well, and Klune appeared to be pleased with what he was seeing. That is, until onto the screen flashed a picture of me posing beside a river, proudly displaying two enormous trout, one in each hand. With only the slightest hesitation and without comment, I pushed the button and moved on to the next slide.

"Put that slide back on!" roared Klune.

"But, sir, that slide wasn't supposed to be—" I pleaded.

"Put the slide on, *now!*" he ordered, and so I did.

"Tell me, Paul, just when did you find the time to catch those fish?" he inquired with a challenging note in his voice. It was obvious that he had never seen such huge trout before. It was also obvious that he was vitally interested.

"Well, sir, it was at the end of a very long day—and we felt that a little recreation would be in order," I lied.

He replied, "You'll be lucky if you don't find yourself recreating in the unemployment line. Move on. Oh, and see that I get a copy of that picture."

The truth was, we were driving along the South Fork of the Salmon River late one afternoon when, right beside the river's edge, we came upon a shack where an old man was unloading his fishing gear from a beat-up old car. When we stopped to ask him some questions about the area, he told us that he'd been upriver, fishing a new spot that proved very good. Opening the trunk of the car, he showed us several giant-sized trout. Seeing my admiration, Addison asked him if he could take my picture holding one of those big devils in each hand.

It wasn't long before there was a shooting script. And I can only guess at this, but I bet when Darryl Zanuck saw the possibilities of a big, major picture, the whole project took on a decidedly different complexion. A new writer was assigned and Klune was no longer the producer. He was replaced by Stanley Rubin, a decent sort, as I remember.

Oh, and Otto Preminger became the director!

When I was a second assistant, I had the dubious pleasure of working with Otto Preminger on *The Fan* and found him a less-than-

Me beside the Snake River with two beauties that I had nothing to do with catching.

River of No Return *(1954)*

endearing fellow with absolutely no redeeming qualities. When I heard that he was to be my immediate boss, I figured that my days—nay, hours—were numbered. Having witnessed how he treated people, including me, I knew there would be a tremendous conflict of personalities. Still, I didn't ask to be taken off the picture. Feeling as I did, it's hard to believe that I finished the picture with him—and a few years later worked with him again on *Porgy and Bess*, although I was exceptionally well-paid for that exercise.

Late one winter afternoon, Otto sent for me. When I entered his office, there sat Marilyn Monroe, who, he announced, would be working with us on the picture. Instead of saying, "But, my dear Otto, you've got to be making a joke!" I merely shook hands with her and said something like, "How nice!" As much as I admired Darryl Zanuck and his exquisite business judgment, I figured that between engaging Preminger to direct an All-American Western and compounding the error by pitting Monroe against Preminger, Zanuck had simply lost his mind.

The size of the production crew grew daily, and it soon became apparent there would be no camping-out or roughing-it type of locations for this movie. It was to be first-class all the way. This meant the Idaho locations so remote from motels, hotels, airports, and even train depots, would be spared our contamination.

New locations were the next order of business and the location department determined that a good possibility would be Alberta, Canada, with its spectacular scenery and the Bow River. Another factor was to choose the best place, weather-wise. Dr. Irving Krick, the inimitable weather prophet from Cal-Tech, gave his blessing on the area. So off Preminger and I went in the studio airplane with the cameraman, Joe LaShelle, and a few other key people. It was early in May and the motel where we stayed was just re-opening after a long harsh winter. The Bow River, the other star of our movie, lacked any road along its course, so to look at the locations along the river we had to travel on horseback. We hired riding horses and a couple of wranglers to go along, and we dressed ourselves in borrowed ponchos and hats, the better to cope with the miserable, drizzly cold day. When we were assigned our mounts, Otto asked for and got a nice gentle horse, which he immediately named "Horsie."

Probably since the very first motion picture, certain protocol has been practiced. One rule that sticks in my mind is the director always goes first. This holds not just when the crew scouts locations, but at the end of the shooting day, as well. Especially if the road back to town is

Rare evidence of happy times in the company of Preminger. We're at a Sunset Strip nightclub, celebrating the end of our work on *The Fan*. From left to right, Tom Dudley, Lefty Hough, Edna Bowen, me, my wife Helen, and Sid Bowen.

unpaved and dusty, an auto or truck should never leave the location before the director's car.

Otto somehow and erroneously perceived that I was at ease whilst astride a horse, whereas he probably would far prefer walking in the mud to being on a horse's back. He summoned me to ride alongside him on the pretext that he had some profundities for me to retain and act upon. Be it acknowledged that I was anything but an equestrian, and that I had not the slightest interest in becoming one. Notwithstanding, I gave my steed a little urging and pulled up alongside an unmercifully bouncing Otto. He evidently forgot what I was supposed to learn and remember, because all he said was, "Paul, just stay right here with me."

After a couple of minutes of bonding with my director, my inner voice admonished, "Don't miss this opportunity, Paul, because it will never come again." With that, I gently urged my mount to move the slightest bit faster, knowing his mount would instinctively do the same. Distracting Otto with small talk, I waited a moment or two before repeating the process of accelerating our animals a little more. After three or four such urgings, we found ourselves in a most uncomfortable gait. Seeing Otto's frantic expression as he tried desperately to keep from falling out of the saddle, I reached over and grasped his horse's bridle and slowed both our horses down. It was hard to keep from at least smiling as he thanked me gratefully. Of course, the guys behind us knew exactly what I was up to but said nothing, at least not at the time.

The road north to Jasper opened for the spring season, and we all piled into a Volkswagen bus which had a sliding sun-roof. Once in Jasper we switched to two sedans for the location scouting. It was early afternoon when we approached the Jasper Lodge. Though it wasn't officially open for the tourist season, it was already engaged in housing, feeding, and training the large staff of young people they would employ during the spring and summer.

We approached the lodge from the rear, where we saw two bears sniffing around the enclosed lean-to in which were kept the hotel garbage cans. Our driver told us that when the bears come out of hibernation they are desperate for food. Otto, seated between me and the driver, thought the bears fascinating and cute and told me to roll down the window so he could call them closer. One came, all right, lumbering straight for the car and my open window, which I proceeded to roll up with alacrity.

"What are you afraid of, Paul? The bear just wants to say, Hello," the nature-loving Otto explained.

"I don't think so, Mr. Preminger," spoke the driver. "The bears are awfully hungry come spring, and you never know—" And suddenly the bear was pawing at the window, the huge face looking at us with what I deemed a vicious leer—and not two feet distant from my face. At the time, nearly all cars had outside door handles that turned downward to open. Apparently the bear's paw found the handle and the door opened slightly. I frantically grabbed the inside door handle and held the door shut while the driver pulled the car away and began a lecture on just how dangerous the hungry bears could be.

The survey trip successfully completed, we returned to the studio to find that Robert Mitchum had been set for the male lead opposite Marilyn Monroe. While I don't recall anybody asking me, nevertheless I thought it was superb casting—two animals loose in the wilds!

In looking at the swift current and turbulence of the Bow River, I could foresee a difficult problem, and though it wasn't exactly in my domain, I was concerned about it. The problem would be how to get steady, moving background shots. In those days such background scenes were called process plates. I never did know why or how they came to be called that. Every studio had a separate department known as the process department whose function was to make and handle process plates. These scenes were projected on a screen to show movement or background behind the actors as they acted on a set in the foreground. For example, in this movie the actors would make their escape traveling down river on a raft. For long shots, stunt doubles would ride and steer the raft down the treacherous river. But close-up scenes would have to show the actors on the raft with the background moving in sequence with the progress of the raft down river. The river was so turbulent that background scenery shot from a boat going down river would be jerky, rough, and uncontrollably unsteady. In those days we had no access to helicopters or any of the fine technology movie makers have available today. It might be said that while we were short on technology, we were long on entertaining scripts that didn't have to rely on explosions, vivid sexual encounters, ridiculous car chases and vicious displays of man's inhumanity to man to keep audiences awake.

When we were looking for locations in Idaho, I ran across one of those airboats that operate in very shallow water, such as they use in Florida swamps. I even met the fellow in Lewiston who built it, Clem Somethingorother. It occurred to me one day that an airboat might provide a steady camera-platform for continuous background shots of the scenery along the riverbank as the airboat made controlled drifts downriver with the current. I called Joe LaShelle, the cameraman, to see what he thought of the idea, and, of course, he was in favor of any tool that might make for better photography.

After getting permission to look into the possibility of using his airboat as a camera platform, I phoned Clem in Lewiston and broached the idea. The boat was to carry the cameraman, a certain weight of equipment, and himself to pilot the thing. Clem was most enthusiastic, certain the airboat would work just fine, and promised me it would be easy to strike a fair deal. We decided that when I notified him, he was to drive up to Canada, towing the airboat behind his station wagon.

When our whole company was assembled just prior to the start of shooting, Clem and his machine arrived. He was wide-eyed and unabashedly awed when he viewed the mighty Bow River for the first time. With a handful of interested onlookers watching, this man of courage—but not too many smarts—unloaded and launched his machine and fired up its airplane engine. Not liking the way it sounded, he decided to put off the trial run until the next day.

At the appointed time the next afternoon, Clem again ran up the engine. Its sound meeting his approval, he gave the order for us to cast off the lines that bound him to the shore. I should explain that in this instance, the airboat was to be operated just the reverse of how it normally would be operated if it were on a swamp or slow moving body of water, where the engine's propeller would be pushing the boat forward. On this fast-moving river, the engine would be used to work against the current to hold the boat back and control the speed as the boat drifted down the river. Once free of the bank and out in the river, Clem gave it the throttle and got control, as planned.

Things were looking just fine until the engine was heard to emit a couple of coughs and sputter to a choking death. Clem frantically tried to restart the engine as the boat moved out of control and perilously close to some large rocks near the shore. Realizing the danger he was in, Clem gave up, albeit reluctantly, and abandoned ship. He swam, splashed, and scrambled to the bank where he watched his beloved craft smash itself to pieces on the rocks and slowly drift out of sight. We were grateful Clem wasn't hurt, and we helped him gather up the pieces until darkness overtook us.

At supper that night, Clem didn't seem much bothered about the accident and the loss of his machine. Actually, he was more concerned about whether there would be any customers awaiting his services when he arrived back in Lewiston. There was a well-traveled, narrow, and very crooked highway running alongside the winding river near Lewiston, and speeding motorists frequently went off the highway and wound up at the bottom of the river. A local mortuary had a deal with Clem to give him a goodly share of the funeral costs if he dove down and recovered bodies and hauled them in his station wagon to the funeral home.

Finding myself in need of some additional work clothes, I took the opportunity to go shopping in Calgary before shooting was to begin. A car was being sent to the Calgary airport to pick up the arriving stunt doubles, so I hopped a ride. The double for Marilyn was Helen Thurston, and for Mitchum it was Roy Jensen. Both were expert water stunt people. For the kid actor, Tommy Retig, we had a midget named

Harry Monty. I had worked with all three on other pictures and liked them all. Besides working in pictures, Harry owned a thriving television and appliance store.

As we rode along in the car, I noticed that Harry wasn't his usual cheerful self.

"Anything wrong, Harry? Didja get airsick on the plane?" I asked.

Up spoke Helen, "Can I tell him, Harry?"

"I don't really care," replied Harry.

"He'd doubled Tommy Retig before, so the casting office called Harry for this job," explained Helen, "but apparently they forgot to mention that this was mostly a whitewater job."

"So?" I asked.

"He can't swim a stroke and is deathly afraid of the water," Helen replied.

"We've both promised that we're not going to let anything happen to him, no matter what," offered Jensen.

The sun was just setting when we came to a decent-looking restaurant and we pulled off the highway for supper. After a round of cocktails, the waitress came to take our orders. When she came to Harry, he was decisive: "I'll have the filet mignon, medium rare," he said. At that moment, the Devil took possession of me and I couldn't help myself.

"Don't do it, Harry," I warned.

"Don't do what, Paul. What are you talking about?" he asked.

"It's very simple, Harry. If you're really worried about not being able to swim, you should start right now to do something about it," I replied.

"Like what? What's swimming possibly got to do with my eating a filet mignon? I have either a steak or prime ribs just about every night, and sometimes for lunch, and I don't see what—"

"I'm going to tell you something for your own good, Harry. I just don't want to see anything happen to you," I interrupted. Looking him squarely in the eye, "Don't eat another piece of meat until you finish this job, and that's all I'm going to say," I told him.

He looked at me stunned. "What am I supposed to eat if I don't eat meat?" he asked, as if I were writing his dialogue.

"Fish, Harry. Fish for breakfast, lunch, and dinner. No meat, no chicken. Just fish. Any kind of fish, Harry," I replied

Harry looked at me like I had just stabbed him. "But I hate fish. I've always hated fish. Just the thought of—"

"*Fish*, Harry. You'll be swimming like a pro in nothing flat. Right, Roy?" I said and turned to Roy for support.

River of No Return *(1954)*

Roy rose to the occasion, as I knew he would: "He's right, Harry. Did you ever see a fish that couldn't swim?"

With the addition of two big stars, a big-time director, cameraman, and a complete second unit, the company had grown to well over a hundred people. The Banff Springs Hotel could easily handle our entire troupe as well as another fairly large company from Universal Studios that was making a Royal Canadian Mountie picture with Alan Ladd starring and Raoul Walsh directing.

When we moved to Jasper, it was a different story: we were scattered all over in different motels and lodges. The elite, the elegant, the above-the-line folks were, of course, in the best place, which was a picturesque lodge with comfortable cabins and an excellent dining room. The only reason a peon such as I was quartered there was because the assistant director should be near the director to handle notes, change in calls, meetings, whatever. Kind of a tradition, I suppose.

It was early evening of the first Sunday we were there that Preminger, along with his wife, came storming out of the dining room just as I happened to be crossing a small clearing toward my cabin. When I heard him calling my name, I could tell from the tone of his voice that all was definitely unwell. Those in the business who have worked with him know exactly what I mean. There was no escape for me; I prepared for the worst.

Red-faced, fiery-eyed, and sputtering, he instructed me, "I vant you to get a reservation right now and send Sid Bowen [the unit manager] back to the studio. I don't vant him on the picture!"

Shocked, I dared to ask, "What happened? What did he do, Otto?"

I won't even try to remember his exact words, but the gist of the story is that when they went in for supper, the dining room was crowded with townspeople as well as our people, and Otto was told there would be a few minutes wait for a table. I ventured to ask, "Did you call ahead to make a reservation? A lot of local people—" But that was as far as I got before he exploded:

"He should have made sure there vas a table for me whenever I decide to eat. I don't vant him around. Now get us a car so we can have supper in town."

Entering the dining room, I spotted a driver having supper. "You're on the clock as of this minute at double time. Get a car and take Preminger wherever he wants to go. He's waiting outside."

Walking back outside to the waiting Preminger, I found myself getting madder than hell and I couldn't help it. "A driver went to get his car," I said simply and started to walk away.

"Make that reservation like I told you," he instructed.

"Otto, I'm going to make two reservations, because I'm going too," I found myself saying.

"Vat do you mean, Paul. I'm not blaming you," he said.

"When a man like you can fire somebody who has spent 30 years in this business and is tops in his job, when you can fire him because he didn't reserve a table for you, then I'm in the wrong business," I said and then hurried away before I became any more enraged.

Back in my cabin, I began wondering about a lot of things:—How about that family you're responsible for? What about the disappointment of those people who helped you get this far? Maybe Otto was just showing his great power in front of his new wife and really didn't mean it? How about Ray Klune, who trusted me to get along with Preminger? How am I going to break the news to my good friend Sid Bowen, with whom I'd worked on several pictures?

A couple of hours later, my phone rang.

"Paul, vill you come over to my place for a drink? I vant to talk to you about what we're shooting tomorrow," he said.

I don't think Otto could ever say to anybody "I'm sorry," and sincerely mean it. I could tell just from the tone of voice that this was the best "I'm sorry" the man was capable of. Once again, all was well in Jasper, until the next time something pissed him off, anyway.

Over a brandy in Otto's quarters, absolutely nothing was mentioned about the incident, but you can be reasonably certain that Otto had a reserved table for the duration of our stay. And Sid Bowen never knew what happened. How I ever became the assistant director on *Porgy and Bess,* which Otto Preminger directed a full five years later, remains a mystery to me.

Since the last Marilyn picture I worked on, she had met up with a rather unlikable lady named Natasha Litez, who became her drama coach. If there's anything a director doesn't need, it is having someone other than himself tell an actor or actress how a scene should be played. My guess is Marilyn finally figured out—or maybe somebody told her—that she was a tremendous asset to 20th Century–Fox and that she could have things pretty much as she pleased, including Otto's head on a platter!

There was something catlike and furtive about Natasha. I have a mental picture of her slinking around the set, standing in the shadows as she watched a scene being rehearsed or shot. Here was her modus operandi: When the director would approach a new scene, Natasha would lurk somewhere in the background, watching as the scene was being worked out and staged. The director usually discussed with the actors, collectively or individually, what he wanted to see on the silver screen. After the camera crew set marks for the stand-ins, Marilyn and Natasha would retreat to her dressing room where Marilyn was told Natasha's version of how she should play the scene. To what extent Marilyn listened to her will never be known.

When it came time for the scene to be shot, Natasha would assume her place where she could watch unobtrusively, but still where Marilyn could glance at her after the take for her approval or disapproval. If the director said "print" but Natasha disapproved, Marilyn would ask for another take on one pretense or another.

It didn't take Preminger long to realize what was going on and to react accordingly. This might be compared to the atom bomb exploding over Nagasaki! While Natasha had permission to be with Marilyn on the set, as best I recall, there was nothing said about her sort of co-directing along with Otto.

When Otto vented his anger at Marilyn, she must have realized the high esteem in which Zanuck and the stockholders held her, because while there might have been a few tears, she gave it right back to Otto.

Me and Otto Preminger—in between fights.

Makeup Artist Allan "Whitey" Snyder and me helping Marilyn Monroe over the rough spots. Note her sprained ankle in cast.

Listening, one got the distinct impression that perhaps they didn't hold each other in very high regard.

For the next few days, the tension on the set between the two of them made things unpleasant. Natasha, as I recall, stayed mostly in the dressing room, leaving Marilyn to get through her scenes as best she could. And Marilyn wasn't getting much help from Preminger, either, because there was a minimum of words between them.

When Otto complained to Darryl Zanuck that he was having great difficulty working with Marilyn and asked him to straighten her out, back came a telegram from Zanuck to immediately start getting along with her and do the job he was hired to do or he would find himself replaced by another director.

Even so, director and star continued to share a minimum of words with each other. Most of Otto's instructions, coaching, or comments, were conveyed through Mitchum or me. With time, their relationship improved considerably, but for quite a while, it was Mitchum who made things work.

There was a period in his career that I considered Robert Mitchum among the top leading men. Put him in a picture with a good script, a director who knows his craft, a strong leading lady, some believable action that belongs, and you've got a winner. Of course, he has to belong in the part, not miscast as he was in the mini-series *Winds of War*.

There's one more incident involving Otto Preminger that I must relate because it spelled the demise of my career at 20th Century–Fox and thrust me out into the real world.

Back at the studio we were shooting a big night scene on the back lot. There were lots of extras, horses, and wagons, with tents and big areas to light, which meant there were extra electricians and grips. It was Saturday night and approaching midnight when it became obvious we couldn't finish until much later. We had permission to work Tommy Retig, a minor, only until midnight. While I thought I knew the rules of the unions and guilds, it turned out I didn't, because I called everybody and everything back for Monday night. This cost the studio big bucks because everyone working on the set got paid for Sunday even though they didn't actually work on Sunday. Suffice it to say, I really fell from grace with my bosses.

One more Marilyn story:

One beautiful Canadian morning, Marilyn showed up for work in a particularly pleasant mood. While she was never cross or abrupt with crew or staff members, she seemed to be more enthusiastic than she usually was first thing in the morning.

She waited until after lunch before taking me aside and asking me if I could please rearrange the schedule so she could have a whole day off. Joe DiMaggio was coming to see her, and they needed some time alone. Everybody knew they were in love and that it was more than a fleeting romance. I, for one, really wanted to see this thing succeed.

I must say that when I explained to Preminger how it would be possible to oblige her, he was most cooperative and readily agreed to my revised schedule.

After a day off, Marilyn returned to work happy as she could be. A few hours later, DiMaggio showed up in a rental car and even stayed for lunch with us. If it had been the president himself, the crew couldn't have been more thrilled. I think DiMaggio may have been a little embarrassed by all the attention.

Sometimes when I think about her, I wonder how different her life might have been if things had worked out for Marilyn and DiMaggio. Lord knows he really loved her.

So what did Harry Monty order for supper? Try as I may, I can't remember.

How to Marry a Millionaire (1953)

It was when they called me into the production office and told me I was assigned to *How to Marry a Millionaire* as a second assistant that I realized to what extent I had fallen from grace for my goof on *River of No Return*. But when I learned that Johnny Johnston, the unit manager, and one of the best they had, had been demoted to first assistant on *Millionaire,* I didn't feel quite so deflated.

There is an expression to describe a movie that is easy to work on. After reading the script for *How to Marry a Millionaire* I realized that for once I was handed a bedroom-parlor-and-bath picture that could be "phoned in." I was almost happy to step down and coast for awhile. Besides, I was seriously thinking about going into the fast-growing television field and, if not, of going into the independent field, where the best money and greatest opportunities were.

At that time, the assistant general production manager, the respected Lefty Hough, was a man whose opinion was highly valued. When I spoke with him on the subject of television, he felt strongly that while it certainly had a place in the future, mainly in sports, it would never be a threat to the big studios. He compared the novelty of television to the novelty of radio, saying that it would soon wear off just like radio did. He predicted that television fare would consist of broadcast sports competitions. The teams would be owned by big corporations, such as Ford Motor Company and General Electric. Sports programs would be augmented by news and special events. When I see the slop that's being served up with each new television season, I almost wish he'd been right.

While I awaited the call from TV or independent movie-making—which was to come sooner than I'd expected—I had fun working on *Millionaire,* despite my disappointment at being demoted. The actors were most professional and the atmosphere could only be described as elegant, with the fabulous Travilla costumes adorning Lauren Bacall, Betty Grable, and Marilyn Monroe. The handful of leading men performed from a compelling script by Nunally Johnson. The settings by Lyle Wheeler exhibited upper-crust New York's life style. I got the feeling that everybody in the cast and crew, and the director really liked each other, which was something of a rarity in my recent experience.

The studio chose wisely when they picked Jean Negulesco to direct. Not only was he a recognized painter but a suave Continental gentleman whom ladies took to on first meeting. Joe McDonald was among the top cameramen in the industry and completely up to the challenge of the new medium, Cinemascope.

Before I could approach the possibility of getting into the coveted independent field, it approached me. Warner Bros. phoned me to say that Howard Hawks wanted me to work for him on a picture he was preparing to make in Egypt and Europe. How soon could I join him? they inquired. I asked the usual questions: How long, how much? "Four or five months, and a little above scale, but with a per diem allowance," they answered. I said I'd let them know after I talked to my family.

It should be explained here that although it was Warner Bros. who signed the check, I really wasn't working for a major studio but for Howard Hawks, who invariably owned the stories and scripts and also a large percentage of the picture. His attitude was that he was merely

How to Marry a Millionaire *(1953)* 61

using Warner Bros.' money, their facilities, and their releasing organization.

When I told my wife about the offer, it was a hard decision for both of us because it meant, once again, being away from my family. We had just bought a big house with all the attendant expenses and many more to come, and the money would be heaven-sent. No doubt I was in an excellent bargaining position. I was engaged on a job, lowly though it seemed at the time, but one that nonetheless was paying the bills.

When I called Warners back, I agreed to take the assignment if they'd up the salary considerably. When they agreed to my asking price, I told them the date I could leave and the deal was on.

My memory is a little fuzzy on whether I left *Millionaire* early or stayed to the end, but I certainly remember Warner Bros. coming up with almost twice the money that I ever made at 20th Century–Fox. There was more than a little soul searching about whether I was doing the right thing by leaving my alma mater after more than 16 educational years. I knew everybody and every nook and cranny of the 20th Century–Fox lot and the Western Avenue lot, which was always very active and loaded with sets. The only other time I had left the studio was when I joined the Army Air Corps during World War II.

Coincidentally, the other demoted fellow, Johnny Johnston, got the call to go independent about the same time. He had become a favorite of Joe Mankiewicz *(Letter to Three Wives),* who wanted Johnny to join his newly formed production company in Italy as soon as he could, and at a lot more money.

Even now, so many years later, I get excited at the thought of heading off for Europe and the real unknown. There's many a young member of the director's Guild of America who knows what I'm talking about.

Land of the Pharaohs (1955)

It wasn't until the studio car came to pick me up that the full impact of this commitment hit me. I was close to tears at having to leave my home and lovely family, and yet I was terribly excited at going off to Europe and Egypt to meet and deal with brand new challenges, and to work with and learn from a man I considered a brilliant picture-maker, Howard Hawks.

En route to the airport, I offered silent thanks to 20th Century–Fox for providing me with the education and experience that enabled me to make this move.

In January of 1954, there were no direct commercial flights from Los Angeles to England. The Warner Bros. travel department had me staying overnight in New York at the Astoria, and then I was off for

LAND OF THE PHARAOHS

HOWARD HAWKS'

ASSOCIATE PRODUCER
ARTHUR SITEMAN

ASSISTANT DIRECTOR   SECOND UNIT DIRECTOR
PAUL HELMICK   NOEL HOWARD

COSTUMES DESIGNED BY
MAYO

Pacific Title Company created the main title credits for *Land of the Pharaohs* on blocks of wood.

London on the Pan American Clipper the following late afternoon. It was the most enjoyable airplane trip I've ever taken.

My instructions were to join Howard Hawks in San Moritz, Switzerland. I boarded a train in Zurich and happily shared a drafty compartment with a most genial Swiss couple who never ceased talking. After getting settled into a comfortable hotel room, I checked in with Hawks on the phone, and he invited me to meet him for supper in the hotel dining room. When I walked in, there was Hawks and his new bride, Dee, a beautiful and very smart young lady, hosting a distinguished group over cocktails: Harry Kurnitz, Bob Capa, Jack Bloom, and William Faulkner.

Kurnitz was one of the fine screen writers of the time. Bob Capa was the head of Magnum Photographers. During the Spanish Revolution, Capa was the photographer who asked Hemingway to run across the street in front of a tank for a second time because Capa missed his shot the first time. A photo by any of the Magnum photographers was almost assured of publication in *Life* magazine. Jack Bloom was a writer I think Hawks met in Paris. I rather suspect the original story for *Land of the Pharaohs* was his idea, although I never asked. Finally, there was William Faulkner, who had worked with Hawks on one or two previous pictures. Once, on a hunting trip with Clark Gable and Hawks, Gable asked Faulkner who he thought were the best living American writers. Without hesitation, Faulkner replied, "And then Hemingway and Steinbeck." Or so Hawks told it.

After introducing me and ordering a drink, Hawks made the mistake of asking me if my hotel room was satisfactory.

"Thanks, I just couldn't be any more comfortable. These Swiss think of everything. There's even a footbath in my bathroom," I elaborated.

Hawks, after a quick glance at Dee and the others asked, "A footbath?"

"Well, I guess so. What else could it be?" I asked.

Faulkner burst into laughter and the rest picked it up. Not knowing how to react, I just smiled and sipped my drink.

I honestly think only Hawks knew that I wasn't trying to be funny, that I had never even heard of a bidet, much less ever seen one.

The next morning, I had breakfast with Hawks, and he explained my reason for being there: I was to sit in on the story conferences, which were held for a few hours almost daily. He made it quite clear that I was to listen and say nothing. He wanted me to get a feel for what the

Land of the Pharaohs *(1955)* 65

movie was to be about. It was going to be a tremendous undertaking, and I should be thinking about how to accomplish what he and the writers were dreaming up.

The writers usually worked in the morning in Hawks' suite, and after lunch he and sometimes Dee would go skiing. That is, until he either broke or sprained his leg (I can't remember which). After that he spent the afternoons getting therapy treatments in the baths.

Dee was getting bored, I think, and wanted to get on down to Rome. Hawks must have decided that I had absorbed enough and suggested that I go to Rome with her and set up some casting sessions in advance of his arrival. The story conferences would continue in Rome when Hawks was able to travel comfortably.

One of the first persons I met in Rome was Tenny Wright, the general production manager of Warner Bros. and one of the finer men in the business. We both stayed at the Excelsior Hotel and had dinner together almost every night. Robert Wise was making *Helen of Troy* in Rome, and Tenny was overseeing it while also getting our company set up financially.

After the war, all the major American studios had plenty of frozen funds all over the world and would use that currency to make pictures abroad where feasible. Tenny had a lot to do with whatever that involved.

Tenny was usually an early-to-bed sort, but one night after supper, I conned him into going to Bricktop's, a popular cellar club just off the Via Venito. We listened to some music and chatted with a few movie folk who happened to be there. When we got back to the hotel, we went to the bar for a nightcap. When Lauren Bacall and Humphrey Bogart, who were in Rome making John Huston's *Beat the Devil*, saw Tenny, an old friend, they insisted we join them. Bacall was on Bogart's case about something or other, and it was kind of amusing to see her browbeat the toughest guy Jack Warner ever made.

It wasn't long before Hawks arrived in Rome from Switzerland, where he was regaining the use of his leg under the care of the ski-injury experts. As I recall, Kurnitz and Faulkner showed up a few days later, the latter having gone to Paris to be with a young lady he'd taken a fancy to and to go on a binge which, allegedly, he was wont to do in Europe. I was told by Hawks that Faulkner, when drinking, could become troublesome. But because he was honored by France with one of their highest awards, the Legion of Honor, and always wore the little rosette in his lapel, the gendarmes, on seeing this little flower of power, considered his offenses less offensive, and even offered him safe haven when necessary.

Mr. and Mrs. Hawks and her toy poodle had a suite in a much older and more elegant hotel across the Via Veneto from the Excelsior, and there the story conferences resumed, usually in the morning, as I recall. On the days when we didn't have casting sessions or screenings to attend (to see actors and actresses at work), there really wasn't much for me to do after lunch. When Faulker told me he knew of a great place for lunch, I jumped at the chance to join him.

It was a place called Georges, only a couple of blocks from the hotel and maybe the best restaurant for an American in all of Rome. I haven't the slightest idea what we talked about during those long lunches. The thing I do remember is Faulkner's Southern graciousness. With the assistance of the martinis and the well-chosen wines, he made me feel completely at ease. One memory I have is telling him that, compared to mine, the local spaghetti was unpalatable. He remarked he'd like to come to my house and try it the next time he came to Los Angeles. I sorrowfully report he never made it.

Another memory I have is Hawks suggesting I find another luncheon companion or dine alone. I learned long ago that when he "suggested" something, that was an order not to be questioned.

We soon left the warmth and glamour of Rome for cold and slushy London. A car met us at the airport and whisked us to the Hotel Claridge, where Hawks had a suite and I lived in luxury in a spacious room. Between meeting actors and actresses and going to screenings, we were kept busy.

At this point, I think I should mention a little known idiosyncrasy that was part of the Hawks method of making movies: He played solitaire! It took me quite a while to figure it out, but I eventually concluded that during those games he did much of his creative thinking and decision-making, and anyone foolish enough to interrupt him during the process was at considerable risk. Once a game was over and before the next began, you could talk—but only if it was very important, short, and simply couldn't wait.

Once, long after *Land of the Pharaohs*, he really teed me off about something and the devil in me took over, compelling me to take a card out of his solitaire deck. Do this to a highly competitive man who went limp at the very thought of losing, and you may just destroy him—or yourself, if you're caught! Three or four days later, I was in his office reading while he was playing away at his damned game and, lo, he played out his last card and smiling hugely, pronounced himself a winner! Imagine, winning at solitaire without all the cards!

One dreary, wet London afternoon, Hawks called me to join him in the lobby. He told me only that we were going someplace. Bundled up against the cold, we hailed a cab. Before long I found myself with Hawks in the Rolls Royce showroom, greeted by a dapper representative—you'd never make the mistake of calling this guy a salesman—who led us to an absolutely smashing Bentley "motor car." It was a coupe, and I climbed into the spacious rear seat while Hawks moved into the driver's seat.

Silently, we oozed out into the afternoon traffic and soon found ourselves in the suburbs, all the while the representative answered Hawks' questions, never selling. He didn't have to. With its gorgeous silver body and its soft, genuine gray leather upholstery, this was the automobile for Howard Hawks!

Over supper, all we talked about was that car and its price, a mere $26,000, as best I remember. This was 1954, don't forget. In all the time I knew him, I never saw him get excited about anything, but it was plain to see that he was passionate for this automobile.

The next day, I asked him if he'd decided anything about the Bentley. He said he was thinking about it, but no decision yet. It was then that I started giving him a pitch that Cal Worthington would have envied. At the time, he owned a 1947 Cadillac convertible that had served him well, as I pointed out, and he deserved to treat himself to this beautiful new machine. I could see my words dispelling his doubts, like sun burning the morning mist. I kept at it. He'd always cherished his cars, hadn't he? No one took more care in maintaining—nay, pampering—his autos, right? Well, then, who better to give this delicate beaut a good home? Could he answer me that?

Hawks had made an appointment for later that day with one of the big chiefs of the Bentley company, obviously to talk a deal. This pleased me no end because once a decision was made, we could get on with the business of making a movie, instead of talking cars most of the day and night.

Arriving at the dealership, we were ushered into a plush office where I heard the damnedest story ever. Get this: For a substantial discount, Hawks will feature this car in a big picture he is preparing to make which would be seen by the whole world, with the leading man—and I think he named John Wayne—driving it in several scenes! And of course, he'd need a backup car just like this one "in case of an accident, don't you know."

I sometimes wonder what story Hawks would have told had the chief asked what the movie the Bentley would appear in was all about. As it was, the meeting was adjourned most cordially with the chief promising to take up the matter with his superiors.

Never once did I presume to ask Hawks if the movie he was about to make that starred John Wayne and the Bentley had anything to do with pharaohs, pyramids, and maybe a sphinx, although I was sorely tempted to during the next few days. Instead, I was the soul of discretion, and I believe he really appreciated my silence on the subject. Having been around the man for four previous pictures, I was beginning to understand him, if only a little bit.

While Hawks was a most generous man and rather loose with money, he had a thing about besting car dealers. I'll bet he never in his life bought a car on which he didn't get a "good deal." But more about that later.

One evening we went to supper at the White Tower restaurant in Soho. When the maitre d' and owner approached us, he bowed and said, "Good evening. Your usual table, Mr. Hawks?" "That'll be fine," Hawks replied, and we were led to a table adorned with a single rose. During supper, Hawks told me that he hadn't been in this restaurant in five years, since making *I Was a Male War Bride* (which gives you some idea just how unforgettable Howard Hawks was). It was a unique restaurant. The owner's mother sent enough beautiful Sicilian roses each February day to grace every table.

The day before we were to leave London, Hawks told me that he was going to a party with an English friend of his and I wasn't invited. I would just have to find something to do by myself. I was a little miffed at not being invited as I'd met his English friend who was full of life and wit and a party with him would have been fun. But in reading the newspaper, I saw that *The Big Sleep* was playing at a theatre club, and not having seen this Hawks success, I had the concierge arrange a ticket for me.

The next day on the flight to Rome, Hawks asked me what I had done the night before.

"There was a theatre club playing some of your movies and I went to see *the Big Sleep*," I answered.

Several moments lapsed before he asked: "What was it about?"

He's asking me what it was about? A loaded question, maybe?

"Mr. Hawks, I haven't the slightest idea," I replied, looking him straight in the eyes.

Land of the Pharaohs (1955)

"You are the first and only person I've asked that question who gave me an honest answer. *I still don't know what it was about!*" and he smiled, putting me at ease. And that was the end of that.

Back in Rome, the first discordant note on this project struck, loud and clear. On a dismal, rainy, winter-time late afternoon, I'm soaking myself in the bathtub and looking forward to an evening of fun and frolic with my cousin and best friend, Colonel Irving Eells. He was in a rather high position representing the U.S. Air Force in Italy. I never asked why he and his family were living it up in Rome at my, a taxpayer's, expense. He had a handful of officers under him who were almost as party-loving as Irv was.

Anyway, the spell was broken by a guy brazenly entering my bathroom and letting me know that he was the production manager and my boss. His name was Art Siteman and he had flown up from Egypt for meetings with Hawks. The word "gentleman" was invented for Howard Hawks, and I was astounded that he would have hired such a brash, arrogant, crass type as this Siteman was.

"I'll tell you what, Art Siteman. If you'll get the hell out of my bathroom, I'll meet you in the bar in thirty minutes. Now, if you'll excuse me!" and I think he got the idea that it was just possible that maybe I didn't much like him and that I might be a little hard to push around.

When we met in the bar I tried to be upbeat, smiling, and pleasant. I asked him about his background and got him to talk about his favorite subject, himself! He had no impressive credits, and I began to understand why Warner Bros. was sending over unit manager Chuck Hansen as a watchdog. Later, when the going got tough, I was most grateful for Hansen. When I most needed a good Hollywood second assistant, Chuck jumped right in.

After listening to Hawks and the writers discuss certain scenes to be shot in Egypt, I began to get concerned about getting a couple of good American second assistant directors to help me. When I voiced my concern to Art Siteman, he put my mind at ease by saying that he'd already hired the best in Europe and Egypt. My immediate and main assistant was the top first assistant in France, and Siteman said we were lucky to get him. He'd be in Cairo when I got there. Well, when I saw him, he appeared to be about my age and one look convinced me that this fellow was a highly capable, easy-to-get-along-with assistant and would be an efficient worker. When he greeted me in French and I greeted him in English, however, we were both non-plussed. What

Siteman was thinking of I'll never know. Obviously, there wasn't enough time for him to learn English or me to learn French. I was determined that I wasn't going to be responsible for sending this man back to France where he would suffer embarrassment, if not disgrace, because of the stupidity of Sitemen, and he stayed for a few weeks before returning to Paris and another job.

Hawks revived what might appear to be a practical and interesting idea of building interior sets on a giant revolving platform located outdoors. The platform would be divided into two, three, or four sections, depending on the size of the sets built on it. The reason it had to revolve was to take advantage of the movement of the sun throughout the day, thus minimizing the number of lamps to light a scene. To a certain extent, this was successfully done in the silent movie days though I don't think anyone used a revolving stage. As for dependable sunlight in Egypt, I'd hazard a guess that nobody under the age of 80 can remember having seen a cloudy day in Cairo. Anyway, the idea never came to fruition, and I think it was the production designer, Alex Trauner, who persuaded Hawks to shoot our interior sets in Rome.

Hawks had another interesting idea. Intending to use two cameramen on the movie, he hired both Lee Garmes, whom he considered the best interior cameraman, and Russ Harlan, whom he considered the best exterior cameraman. Both men had been nominated for Academy Awards. They each brought along their own assistant cameraman, key grips, and electric gaffers. In Egypt we either had two camera crews or Garmes would shoot what little second unit work there was. When we got to the interiors in Rome, one camera crew would rig, pre-light and shoot a set while we were utilizing the other crew to shoot the one they had previously pre-lit. This was a good idea in theory but a lousy one in practice.

One afternoon, Hawks asked me to go out to the Rome airport to meet Russ Harlan, who was going on to Egypt with us the following day. Having never met Russ, I inquired, "How will I know him?"

"Gary Cooper. Just look for a tall slim guy who looks like Gary Cooper," instructed Hawks.

In his Western-style suit and felt hat, Russ not only looked like a leading man, he moved and talked like one—in the rough, that is. Introducing myself, I sensed almost immediately something amiable in him, and somehow knew we'd be friends, and I think Russ may have felt the same. It was a sad day for me and many others who knew him when Russ died the very year he was nominated for both the black-and-white

Land of the Pharaohs *(1955)* 71

and color (*To Kill a Mockingbird* and *Hatari!)* Academy Award for photography, a high and rare honor. Joe Camel did his job well.

So it was on to Egypt where within a day or two we'd meet Alexander Trauner, the French production designer who would be responsible for the "look" of the picture; a French construction foreman; a French scenic artist; and a French costume designer; and sundry other crew members. Then there was Don Stewart, the American special effects man; an English property master, and the unit manager, Chuck Hansen. Noel Howard, an American who called Paris his home, was hired as second unit director, but the way it turned out, there really wasn't much second unit work. Noel proved a great help to Trauner, his good friend, and to Hawks and me.

The survey party moved around in a group, looking at villages and towns that might form a base for sets that Trauner could adapt and augment as needed. Then there were the obvious sites: the pyramids, the Nile and its islands, the verdant farms and the stone quarries. When we'd drive into a village and get out of the vehicles, the stench was almost overwhelming, and I wondered how the crew—to say nothing of the actors—would handle such conditions. And what about the construction crew? And, lest I forget—as if ever I could—the begging children who would appear out of nowhere and surround us. They seemed oblivious to the swarms of flies crawling over their eyes and runny noses. It was heartwrenching. Then there were their prize possessions, the cattle, the pigs, chickens, goats, dogs, and cats roaming in and out of the mud houses.

Trauner had each of the three selected villages cleaned up and sprayed with insecticides, so when we went to shoot there was hardly a trace of odor or flies.

Almost all the crew, certainly the key people and the actors, lived at the Mena House, which was a very old and serene hotel across the highway from the Cheops pyramid and the Sphinx. It was quite old, quite English and at least in those days, had possibly the worst food anywhere on earth—and maybe any other planet. But there was great service and a splendid bar, however small. The rooms were quite large, featured big bathrooms, and were nicely furnished with comfortable beds equipped with mosquito netting. There was no air-conditioning, but the temperature wasn't too bad at night, at least in my corner room.

The dining room is best described as very sedate, with white linen setting off the dark wood beams and paneling. The tuxedoed maitre d' wore a stiff collar and commanded robed waiters who didn't speak

English but smiled hugely. A string trio playing chamber music did their best to divert attention from the atrocious food. It seemed all carefully designed to bring on a severe case of homesickness to the weary traveler or dislocated moviemaker. I'll bet anything there's a McDonald's or Burger King within a block of the hotel now.

It wasn't long before the shooting crew of Americans, French, English, and Italians began to arrive. The Egyptian movie industry provided a few technicians, all of whom spoke and understood enough English to get by. I was really impressed with how we all melded together after only a day or two of shooting. All of my eight assistants, Greek, English, and Egyptian spoke both English and Arabic, and depending on who would translate in the fewest words, I would choose which one would be my interpreter for the day. I even learned a few words and phases in Arabic, like *action* and *very good* and *once again, please.*

Unless it's happened to you, you've no idea how it feels to be the last one chosen for a team game. I know because one hotter-than-usual Sunday was the day of the big golf tournament, and I had volunteered my questionable ability, only to be chosen as a last resort. The course was small, only nine holes, completely walled-in, and a lot browner and sandier than it was green. The wall was high enough so that an adult camel could barely peer over it, which is what happened from time to time. My caddy, an Egyptian kid of about 12 or 13 who spoke and understood English quite well, coached me and provided me with the proper clubs, and as a result I came in with a creditable score. I had taken a liking to him even before the final tally and had decided to make him my assistant on my personal payroll at, I think, 20 dollars a week.

On Monday morning he was waiting for me outside the hotel, and off we went to work. When we arrived at the location, I gathered whichever of the second assistants showed up for work and introduced them to my new assistant. I noticed the guys sort of snickering when I introduced him as "Ali Baba," the name he had given me before the golf game. He was one proud and happy kid when I told him to call me Paul. He was a smart kid, dependable, quick to learn; I found myself worried that Hawks might have him doing my job on his next picture.

What was immediately noticeable was the great respect and admiration Hawks commanded of one and all. The crew wasn't used to working with a director who was soft-spoken, likable and easy-going yet firm, and who therefore got what he wanted with ease.

Hawks was never one to shoot a lot of takes of a scene. He usually printed the first, second, or third take, much to the disappointment

Land of the Pharaohs *(1955)*

Ali Baba, my 12-year-old golf caddy and personal assistant at the end-of-Egypt party.

of many actors. Like John Ford, there wasn't much coverage of a scene because they knew how to stage their actors and where to put the camera. With all due respect, their movies required assembling more than editing by the film editors.

I would say that of all the big-time directors with whom I worked, Hawks made the fewest takes and still rehearsed his actors less than any other director. Probably part of the reason was that the actors frequently helped re-write the scene just before it was to be shot. Many of the still-living actors who worked with us will attest to this.

On almost every set, including exteriors, there was a quiet place with a big table and several chairs where Hawks would gather the actors and a secretary or script clerk and go over the notes he had scribbled during the night or early that morning. He explained the gist of the scene and what he hoped to get from it. It might well go something like this: "Duke, what would you say if Walter [Brennan], who has been peeking out the jail window, limped over to you and told you a pretty girl in a bright red dress just got off the stagecoach." And Wayne, knowing very well the Hawks way of making good scenes, would put a twist on the scene that wasn't thought of by the writers or Hawks.

And so it would go until Hawks was satisfied with the scene, at which time it would be re-typed and a copy would be given to the actors while they were getting made up and into costume. This routine was not practiced on every scene, or every picture, for that matter. Many times Hawks had the script pretty much as he wanted it before shooting. But if he rehearsed a scene and found it didn't work, he'd tell everybody to relax or take a walk while he and his actors headed for the table. If the writer was available, he'd send for him or her. Leigh Brackett was probably his favorite writer during the years I worked with Hawks.

Hawks had an old-fashioned, brown-leather briefcase that accompanied him on every movie. It was really beat-up. In it were a couple of legal-size yellow tablets, several pens and the amended script and notes from each writer, plus his own notes, and always a deck of playing cards. He'd remove old material only when starting on the next movie. Toward the end, I witnessed him turning it upside-down, and out came various foreign coins he'd gathered over the years, golf tees, a few loose keys that probably fit doors of various offices he'd had over the years, and maybe a hotel key. On some movies, the briefcase would bulge out so far he couldn't buckle the straps. Now that I think of it, we should have had that briefcase heavily insured because if anything were to happen to it while we were shooting, the picture would have ground to a halt.

Land of the Pharaohs *(1955)*

With each passing day of shooting, the weather got a little hotter, making it increasingly difficult for me and my assistants to work with the hundreds and often thousands of recalcitrant extras. Initially, the plan was to use soldiers from the Egyptian army as extras with one or two of their English-speaking officers echoing my instructions in Arabic on the public address system. Nice try, but it soon became apparent that the men held nothing but contempt for their officers, and only when the officers screamed and yelled threats did anything happen. We soon got tired of listening to them and I asked them to let my team try, explaining that the process was taking altogether too much time and getting too few results. Things got a little better, but not much. While we were in Switzerland, Hawks had told me that the Egyptian government had promised him, via Art Sitemen, the use of the Egyptian army personnel as extras at no cost. Such was not the case; I soon learned that we were paying the army officers for every man. I don't know if the men actually ever saw any money or not.

Hawks and me at work.

76 Cut, Print, and That's a Wrap!

An Egyptian army officer relaying our instructions to his soldiers as Hawks and I look on helplessly.

To supplement the soldier-extras, we finally used labor contractors, who not only furnished laborers but transported them to and from the locations and paid them. This arrangement worked out quite well for a while, and there seemed to develop a feeling of competition between the military and the civilian groups, with the army officers commanding their people and the contractors overseeing their own charges.

Then along came Ramadan, which, according to my dictionary, means "to be hot, the hot month. The great annual fast of the Mohammedans." All of which means that besides being thoroughly drained by the searing, inescapable heat, the Egyptian extras were starved and dehydrated from abstaining from food or drink all day and standing beside a great phony rock waiting for that loud-mouth American son-of-a-bitch to scream *haraka* ("action") at which time they were to grab hold of a rope and pull a giant rock across the desert.

One excruciatingly hot day, we arrived at the pulling-the-stone-blocks-across-the-desert location, and while Russ and the crew were getting ready, we noticed that the sky was getting darker and that the

Land of the Pharaohs *(1955)* 77

breeze had become a wind. Not a cloud in the sky. Russ kept looking at the hazy sun through his glass and shaking his head. One of the officers told us that we were experiencing a type of high sandstorm that occurs every year about this time and that it might last anywhere from a few days to a week or two. I hadn't liked this guy from the moment I met him, but now I really despised him. Kill the messenger!

It was a dust storm all right, but with very little wind where we were. The visibility lessened to a point we not only couldn't match scenes previously shot, but objects were mostly in silhouette.

In spite of all my prayers, and those of other fed-up but under-fed Americans, the next day was equally bad. Along about the fourth day of waiting for the air to clear, I casually said to Hawks, "You know, I wonder if we really need these few scenes that are left to shoot." Along came that cold, steel-blue look that made me wish I were a sacred scarab hidden in the hot sand.

"It's not too hard to understand, Paul. Maybe someday, when you get nice and comfortable in the cutting room, and you find yourself

Me, far left, and one of my assistants, far right, didn't have enough sense to get in the shade.

Top: Hawks and I confer amid the scores of extras, the crew, and the unrelenting heat. *Bottom:* In the shade this time, Hanks explains something to an English-speaking bit player as I look on.

looking for the scenes you never shot, you'll remember," declared Mr. Howard Hawks, maker of movies.

With the sand storm came even greater heat, and when it finally cleared up enough to allow us to shoot, it was a tremendous effort to get a scene organized for the cameras. In a *Life* magazine photo-story done at the time, they showed pictures of dead camels being dragged away by jeeps as well as a sheltered area out of the sun where heat-stricken extras and crew members were treated. What sap called movie-making an art form?

A local sheik sent an invitation to our entire group to join him and his family for a gala banquet at his palatial home on a certain Saturday night, and having heard that this man was a lavish host, we looked forward to a feast.

His house was built around an open oval-shaped area, somewhat like the Mexican style of building around a central patio. Instead of a garden, the sheik had chosen to have a sandy arena because he was an expert horseman and had a stable of beautiful Arabian horses. We, his guests, were seated at tables on a raised platform surrounding the arena where we were served highballs and cocktails of choice prior to and during supper.

A small orchestra played Egyptian music, and a couple of rather plump belly dancers performed throughout the meal. Russ Harlan and I were seated at the same table, along with some other people. The food was wonderfully tasty and plentiful. We ate like it was Thanksgiving.

It was during coffee that the sheik disappeared. Shortly thereafter, mounted on one of his favorite horses, he charged out of a sort of tunnel into the arena. He circled the arena and then proceeded to put the beautiful horse through its paces, making it do his bidding. At the end of the routine, he proudly acknowledged our applause by having the horse make several low bows to the audience seated around the arena.

It was when he bowed in front of us that Russ jumped over the rail and into the arena where he strode up to the sheik and spoke to him while stroking the horse appreciatively. Somewhat reluctantly, the sheik dismounted and turned the animal over to Russ.

I can see the picture now as I write this: Russ, his coattails flying, going all out around the ring and then doing the same tricks that the sheik had performed, including the bows. Russ then dismounted and led the magnificent animal back to its owner. Just showing off! Had I been the sheik, I think I would have kicked Russ right in the ass instead of graciously shaking hands with him. I later learned that Russ owned a small horse ranch in Vista, California. When Russ wasn't shooting pictures, he trained horses.

Early on, when we were looking for locations, we were taken to a stone quarry where, allegedly, some of the great blocks of granite used in building the pyramids were cut. Surveying the giant chasm, Hawks turned to me and asked, "How many people will you need to make this busy, everybody doing something, everybody working!"

When you are young and impressed with yourself and filled with an abundance of self-confidence and a short supply of good sense, you might find yourself casually answering, "I'd say with five thousand, it'll look pretty busy."

Turning to Russ, Hawks said, "What if we put a big boulder between both sides of the quarry and do a motorized pan of the camera past the boulder and then Paul moves his five thousand people to the other side of the boulder—we'll have ten thousand."

"Sounds okay to me, Howard. I can tell you, though, that the light is going to be pretty flat in the afternoon. I don't see any place we can put the camera other than right here," replied Russ and gave me a look.

"What time do you want to shoot, Russ?" I asked, taking the bait.

"Between eleven and eleven-thirty," he answered.

"We'll be ready at eleven," I stated quite simply and maybe with a slight touch of drama.

On the scheduled day, Hawks stepped out of his car and after the usual "good mornings," I called for a rehearsal to show him what we had staged.

"Let's just shoot it," he said. And that is what is in the movie!

All departments got behind me and put forth their very best to make certain that my boast of being ready at the promised time was made good. The assistant directors and I held night meetings, using blown-up still pictures I had a photographer shoot of the quarry. Each assistant was responsible for the action in his assigned area and used a bulky walkie-talkie radio for communication with me. As the trucks and busses arrived at dawn, the extras were herded into changing areas where they undressed and put on our costumes and wigs. From there, they went into enclosures where their bodies were sprayed brown (the average Egyptian man's body is white). Those who carried props—such as mallets and chisels, water bags, ropes, and whips—were given them, and then the assistant directors took over. It was really quite an organizational effort, for which Chuck Hansen, the Warner Bros. unit manager, was primarily responsible. Even now, after all the years, when I see a

Land of the Pharaohs *(1955)* 81

One of the stone quarries from which the Egyptians cut the giant blocks used to build the pyramids.

movie that uses large numbers of extras doing things besides standing or walking, I ache just thinking about the poor assistant directors and their tired feet.

Only by being very careful of the food I ate—no vegetables or fruits with skins on, no milk, no lots-of-other-things—had I avoided getting sick, as several of our people did. Now, it happened my wife had gone to college with a girl who married a man on the staff of the American embassy in Cairo. Because in my letters home I was always complaining about the food, my spouse prevailed upon this nice couple to invite me to an "old-fashioned, midwestern, Sunday supper." They lived in a large apartment in a fashionable district on an island on the outskirts of Cairo. Any Nileophile knows where it is. When I arrived, my hostess told me the menu was roast beef, mashed potatoes and gravy, and chocolate cake for dessert, all ingredients imported from Europe. To shorten the story, the day after that good old all–American supper, I was about as sick as I've ever been before or after.

Across the street from the Mena House was a walled area that we used as our compound where our vehicles were kept and where the shops were located that built our props. The props (weapons, vases, utensils, and so forth) were made or adapted by local craftsmen. Then there were the musical instruments (drums, horns, cymbals, and stringed instruments) which were copied and made from models found in the pitiful Egyptian museums. I say *pitiful* because of the meager support the museums received from the government. It is undoubtedly true that the British and other foreign archaeologists, whose excavations were generously supported by their own governments, were able to claim the best and most important artifacts for the museums in their own countries.

There is a sequence in the movie that depicts the pharaoh's triumphant parade. Prominent in the parade is a band of extras marching and playing the instruments as our technical advisors envisioned they did in ancient times. When my team and I got the whole thing organized and I saw a rehearsal, it made me think how interesting it might be to score the picture with various sounds that audiences hadn't heard before, or at least to augment the usual orchestral instruments.

We had several scenes throughout the picture in which we used atmosphere orchestras and small musical groups. *Source music* it is called. There was nothing to prohibit adding new sounds that the composer might wish to use on those occasions as well.

When I mentioned the idea to Hawks that evening, he seemed to be as excited about it as I was. That is, he might have twitched an eyebrow. Tell that man that three of his horses came in win, place, and show in the Kentucky Derby and he wouldn't get excited!

Toward the end of shooting in Rome, I had our replicas of the various instruments carefully packed and shipped to Dimitri Tiomkin, Hawks' composer of choice during that period of his movie-making. I also wrote Tiomkin a very diplomatic note, not hesitating to say that Hawks thought the idea was at least worth his exploring. I'd never met the man but had heard that he could be very temperamental. (We would eventually butt heads while working on *Rio Bravo*.)

The Bible and Cecil B. DeMille tell us about Moses working a miracle and parting the Red Sea so a bunch of anxious-but-happy refugees could beat a hasty retreat from a mob of unfriendly Egyptians. So it was with our little band of moviemakers when word came down from the heavens that Hawks couldn't conjure up any more work for us in the land of the Pharaohs; we were to journey northward to the heart of the Roman Empire—Roma!

It was with light hearts and heavy appetites that we packed our belongings and headed for the Cairo airport. Like most of the cast and crew, rather than stay in a hotel, I chose to take a small apartment in Pereoli, a rather nice district on the outskirts of Rome. My cousin (the Colonel) and his wife kept my kitchen stocked with food from the American Military PX.

I had decided some months earlier that I hadn't been endowed with sufficient courage to drive a car or, for that matter, a Sherman Tank in Rome. So a car and driver picked up and returned three or four of us each day. If I needed a car in the evening or on Sunday, I'd just hang onto it. This was a nice arrangement, since the driver spoke fair English and knew my favorite haunts, including the location of my cousin's apartment. Between the Colonel's huge Ford station wagon, his sports car, the studio car, and an occasional taxi, I never wanted for transport.

We had sets on sound stages at two different studios, and Trauner kept the Italian studio shops and their fine craftsmen busy building our magnificent sets. All the sets were under Trauner's direction, and the construction was carefully supervised by the French art specialists. Trauner was the master of forced-perspective sets, and I feel safe in saying that English and American art directors learned from his work. He could create an illusion of a huge palace interior on a stage whose dimensions might actually be one third the size of the perceived volume. He later worked on several pictures in Hollywood, mainly for Billy Wilder, I believe.

As the summer wore on, the heat in Rome became intense. The sound stages we worked in were not air-conditioned and the ventilation systems were inadequate. It became difficult for the actors to get through even a short scene without perspiration dripping off of them. The problem was given to Art Siteman, and I will say that he rose to the occasion with alacrity. There were no air conditioning units of adequate capacity to be found in Italy, but Siteman managed to find some large units in Switzerland or Germany. When they arrived, Trauner adapted them so that the cold air was blown into the sets.

We weren't always confined to a sound stage, though. History has it—or, at least, Howard Hawks and his writers have it—that it was mandatory for a pharaoh to perform an act of great bravery once each year in front of some of his subjects, including his queen and members of his court.

For our pharaoh, it meant taking the charge of an angry bull full in the chest after the bull was goaded by a few nutty guys with a death-wish who teased and tortured him. The location chosen for this sequence was on the seacoast, a few miles north of Napoli. It featured a large villa that was easily revamped to our ancient period, and it already had a sort of rodeo ring with bleachers. Anyway, it was a welcome relief to get out of Rome and the studio sound stages for a couple of days.

We imported five bullfighters along with two fighting bulls from Portugal. Jack Hawkins, the fine British star who played the lead, our pharaoh, showed a certain reluctance to perform the stunt himself, so one of the gentlemen from Portugal who most resembled Jack was chosen to do it for him.

All went off just as planned. So why am I telling this story? Well, on the day the bullfighters arrived in Rome, an Italian interpreter whom we sent to meet them at the airport told them that there would be a day or two until they were needed to work. After wardrobe fittings, they would be free to sight-see, shop, or whatever they liked, and if they would please tell him what they'd most like to do he'd try to arrange it.

"Have an audience with the Pope and go to a whorehouse," came the reply.

I don't remember how I came to be invited but one evening I found myself dining in Hawks' favorite Italian restaurant. My dinner companions included Dee (Hawks' wife), Enid (Dee's sister) and her new husband—Groucho Marx. Oh, and Dee's French poodle. For some reason I can't recall, Groucho took a dislike to the service or the waiter, and loudly got on his case, very much to Hawks' embarrassment. Hawks said nothing, but I could tell there was no love lost between the two, and I left their company as soon as I could. That was the only time I saw a dog in a European restaurant, but I learned it was quite common and accepted.

If Hawks became interested in something or someone, it was practically impossible for me to get his attention back to making movies. He was always polite, but the more he thought he was being pushed, the more engrossed he'd become. I learned early on to mention something once, and only once.

The Italian crews took a bit of getting used to, at least the crews we had. Like all Italians I ever knew, they were very social and fun-loving and seemed to thoroughly enjoy working with us as well as with

Land of the Pharaohs (1955)

each other. One morning when Hawks arrived on the set he noticed one of the Italian electricians reading an automobile magazine that had pictures of the latest foreign cars, together with all the details, their horsepower, speed, price, and so forth. Hawks started a conversation with the guy and lost himself, thumbing through the pages and discussing, each man in his own language, the merits of each car. No matter how much I yearned to re-capture his interest in making the movie, it was not to be until the last page had been turned. In time, we got him back to business, but after he rehearsed the scene and while the crew was lighting it, Hawks sought out his new buddy and resumed their car talk. This went on all day, and I noticed another Italian got into the act with his magazine. At the end of the day and after Hawks had gone home, I called the crew together and announced that the next son of a bitch who showed up on the set with a car magazine of any kind was fired. "Is that clear? Fired!"

Next morning, I felt my warning hadn't fallen on deaf ears, because I saw no evidence of car magazines. It wasn't long until the director drove up, and when he walked onto the stage, every single Italian and most of the other crew, as if they'd rehearsed it, produced a car magazine for him to check out! Even Russ Harlan had a copy of *Road and Track*!

I have a deep appreciation for color, most likely the result of having spent four years living with olive-drab, tan uniforms and shades of jungle green while in the Army Air Corps. *Land of the Pharaohs* features a gala party scene in which the pharaoh, his significant other, as well as his queen, members of his court and would-be courtiers, all lie around feasting and generally debauching. Part of this scene is a six- or seven-member orchestra whose musicians are scantily dressed and playing their weird-looking instruments. When we were putting the scene together, I felt that color was conspicuously lacking and suggested to Hawks and Harlan that we make up each of the musician's bodies in a different color. Neither one took keenly to the idea, but Hawks said go ahead and try it. He no doubt hoped that after I saw the multi-colored band I'd see what a lousy idea it was—which is exactly what happened. Back the musicians went for normal makeup.

Hawks' deal with Warner Bros. precluded their seeing any film until he was ready to show a rough cut or until he chose to let them see something. The English film editor the studio wanted us to use turned out to be lost in Wonderland. He was continually at a loss when Hawks asked to see a rough assembly of certain sequences. We finally gave up and sent him back to London. At Howard's request, the studio then sent over one of their top filmeditors, Rudi Fehr, a most competent man who in very short order got things under control. After assembling two spectacular sequences that filled the Cinemascope screen with thousands of people doing interesting things, Hawks shipped them off to the studio for Jack Warner to lick his chops over.

Hawks and I usually had lunch together in the studio restaurant, and it was during one of these lunches that he told me about a cablegram he got from Jack Warner, who after seeing some footage, offered Hawks a million dollars cash for his interest in the picture. That was a fairly large amount of money in 1953. While he didn't ask me outright, I suggested he take it, my reasoning being that this was turning out to be a most expensive picture, and by the time it showed a profit and he received his share, he might be very glad to have the up-front profit. I don't think he took too kindly to my line of reasoning. But then, he didn't know I was a firm believer in Omar Khayyam's admonition: "Ah, take the cash and let the credit go. Nor heed the rumble of a distant drum."

There came the morning we were to shoot the big confrontation scene between the pharaoh (Jack Hawkins), his aspiring lover (Joan Collins) and her secret lover, the pharaoh's captain of the guards (Sidney Chaplin). We began to rehearse the beginning of the scene between Collins and Chaplin, and they couldn't say or do anything right, which was unusual for either of them. In spite of the great makeup artistry of Emile Lavigne, Collins looked like hell, and Chaplin looked little better. It soon became apparent they were in no shape to perform for the camera, even if they had been able to remember their lines. Hawks had seen enough.

"When was the last time either of you so-called actors had any sleep?" he asked. Not waiting for an answer, he charged, "Here you both are, getting the biggest chance of your lives, making more money than you've ever seen, and you don't feel any responsibility to me, the other actors, or this crew. Instead of taking care of yourselves, getting to bed at night and thinking about what you are doing, you're out raising hell all night!"

They both looked like they were going to cry. I glanced over at Noel Howard for his reaction to his buddies' getting raked over the coals. He just shrugged sympathetically.

Relentlessly, Hawks continued: "Just look around you. You don't see anybody else coming to work all hung over and unable to do the job they're being paid to do!"

Land of the Pharaohs *(1955)*

In between shots, getting a breather outside the Rome sound stage. From left to right: Sidney Chaplin, me, Joan Collins and Jack Hawkins, the pharoah.

He looked around at the crew and his steely gray eyes settled on me.

"You don't see my assistant here carousing all night and unable to do his job. Unlike you people, he feels a certain—Oh, Hell! Paul, I'll be at my apartment when these people feel like they're ready to work."

Looking back over the years, I wonder if Hawks ever learned that the four of us—Noel, Sidney, Joan and my sinful self—attended a party together and ended the evening or early morning pitting driver Sidney and co-driver Joan in Sidney's Aston Martin against driver Noel and co-driver Paul in Sidney's Ferrari (he collected them). Sidney and Noel both lived in Paris, so they found speeding through the zany Rome traffic not at all daunting.

I remember one pit-stop we made in a piazza where from a first floor balcony, Sidney regaled the citizenry by singing arias, making up Italian-sounding words as he poured his heart out in song. Very funny. He even had the police laughing!

In later years, whenever *Land of the Pharaohs* was mentioned in front of Howard Hawks, he took great delight in telling how, when the Egyptian government discovered that our character "Vashtar," the architect of the great pyramids (played by James Robertson Justice), was Jewish, they banned the movie throughout Egypt. I wonder if that ban was ever lifted.

I've been quite surprised by how many people have said this is one of their favorite movies.

Nice Work, If You Can Get It

Flush with money and delighted to be able to spend some time with my growing family and recover from what seemed at the time an eternity of hard work, I was not eagerly seeking another assignment. Nor were any potential employers seeking me! After a couple of months, I began to wonder if the phone would ever ring. Also, after about eighteen years of almost steady employment at 20th Century–Fox, I woke up to the realization that (a) by choice I had cast my lot in the independent field, and I wasn't really known away from Fox; (b) the way to get jobs was to hustle for them, at least until you became known in the independent field; (c) when you do get a movie, you'd better deliver a 110 percent piece of work; (d) and oh, you'd better have more lucky streaks than unlucky ones!

Of course, having a few friends who are disposed to helping you can be invaluable.

Another source of employment was and maybe still is the directors Guild of America. When a member finishes a job or is near finishing one, he must call in and have his name put on the availability list. Then when a producer is seeking to hire a member, he phones the guild and is read the list of names and phone numbers. If the member is new or unknown to the studio, an interview might be scheduled. I've obtained my share of jobs through this method, and at least an equal share of humiliating and humbling rejections as well.

Then there was the *Hollywood Reporter* and *Variety*. In the Friday issues were published lists of pictures in production, as well as pictures and TV productions in preparation. Also listed were names of producers and directors and production managers, how to contact them, and their tentative start dates.

Yet another job source that probably doesn't exist anymore is the Formosa, a watering-hole and restaurant directly across the street from United Artists/Samuel Goldwyn/Warner Bros.—whatever name the studio has now. Whether you are trying to hire a movie or TV crew or you just want to let it be known around town that you are "available," drop in late in the afternoon, find a seat at the bar, say hello to Lindy, the bartender, and Jimmy Bernstein, the owner, and whomever you know at the bar. It was my experience that you could find some of the top people in almost all areas of production either preparing or wrapping a job and, if there didn't happen to be a key grip sipping a highball at the time that you needed one, ask Lindy.

An interesting and little-known aside: Every year at Christmas, Jimmy would put on a Christmas dinner and party for orphans beneath a giant tent with labor, entertainment and presents provided by many of his patrons, who were insulted if they weren't asked to do something.

They are both gone now, but I wonder if either Jimmy or Lindy knew what a great hiring hall they ran.

Just down the street from the Formosa was a new producing company called Eagle-Lion Productions. It was run by partners Aubrey Schenck and Howard Koch. Their specialty was low-budget theatrical movies. I knew Koch from 20th Century–Fox, where he used to carry film from cutting rooms to projection rooms. Genuinely liked by one and all, he left little doubt that with his inherent smarts and discerning manner he would go a long way in the business. This is precisely what he did, and his career included running Paramount for several years. It was through him that I was hired as the first assistant director on *Desert Sands* and worked under director Les Selander. Immediately upon meeting me, Selander told me that the man he wanted wasn't available, so he went with whomever they hired on what he said was to be a very tough location picture (Yuma, Arizona) with a short schedule. If he meant to insult me, he sure succeeded.

As a result, I really busted my behind to make everything go along more smoothly and efficiently than he'd ever experienced. After the first couple of days of shooting, he and I were buddies and holding our evening meetings with shoes off our aching feet, highballs, and room-service dinners. There was nothing and nobody notable about this 1950 release. It was just another notch in my belt. But like every picture, it was a totally new experience. And it was work, after all.

Breaking into Television

I never quite adjusted to the phone going for long periods of time without *ting-a-ling-ing* for me. There's no feeling like not being needed or wanted when you're in show business, especially when you think you can do the job some other guy has much better than he does it. This sums up my state of mind when I got a call from an actor I'd worked with on two Hawks movies, Bill Self. He had become the producer of a very successful TV series, the *Schlitz Playhouse of Stars*. That was in the days when a half-hour series had one producer, no executive producers, no associate producers, no line producers, no co-producers — just a plain producer, who along with a story editor (Sid Bidell) and a secretary or two, managed to turn out a good program each week. It's no great wonder so much of television is so lacking in quality these days. By the time all the superfluous workers are paid, there is probably no money left for good writers.

Bill asked me if I'd like to come aboard as the first assistant and try it for awhile.

"I'd be enchanted," I replied. And indeed I was for about a year and a half until the series came to a temporary halt.

With a superb staff and crew, we'd make each half-hour episode in three working days of nine or ten hours each. The ingenuity of Serge Krizman, the art director, coupled with production manager Ralph Nelson's common sense, resulted in our rarely having to leave the sound stage. Bill drew from about five directors, infrequently hiring an "outsider," and he chose directors with the same fastidiousness he chose the stories, which were wonderful.

The director would have a one-day rehearsal, which was really a "read-through," with the cast. This was an anthology series, so each episode was different. Bill would engage a *star* or at least a *name* or *face* people might recognize, usually good actors, and support him/her with other competent hims/hers.

Many of the stories came from magazines like *The Saturday Evening Post, Collier's,* and *Liberty,* and Bill hired good writers to do the teleplays. Those magazines published some good fiction. And of course, writers came up with original material written just for our show. Sid Biddell, the story editor, really had his hands full, but he kept calm and did his job well.

One evening a few days before Christmas, Bill, Sid, Mary Jane (Bill's secretary), and I were having a drink in Bill's office, and Sid was complaining how tough it was to come up with good stories. More to needle him than anything, I scoffed at him, declaring to one and all that by the second of January, I would place on Sid's desk a complete teleplay, written in my spare time. It would be good enough that Schlitz Brewing Company, the ad agency, and Bill would buy it. I even offered to bet money on it.

"No more drinks for Paul," declared Bill, without further comment.

Even though the story I had in mind was simply a matter of remembering some of the people and situations from my experiences in the South Pacific during World War II, I worked long, late, and hard in order to place the manuscript on Sid's desk by January 2.

The following Friday I was summoned to Bill's office, congratulated, and handed a check for my teleplay. Shortly after, he offered me the job of directing it. I gratefully accepted.

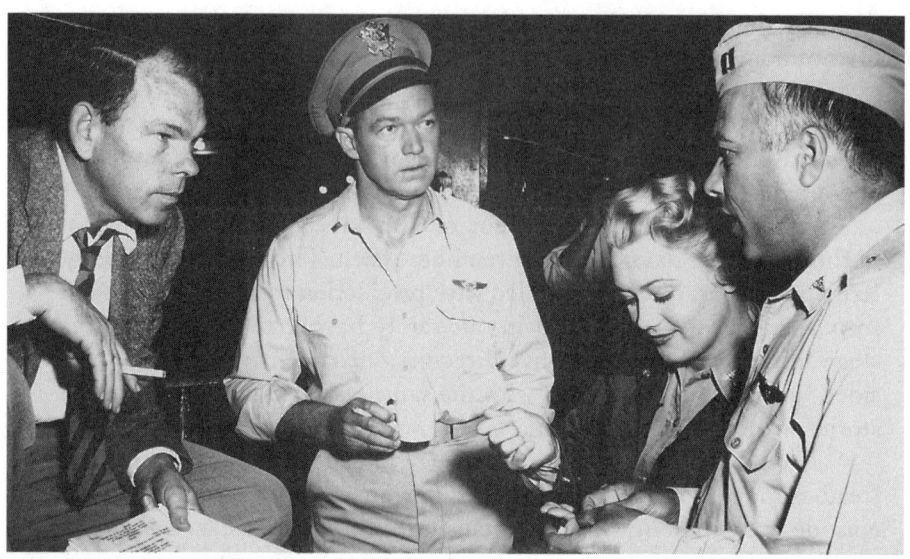

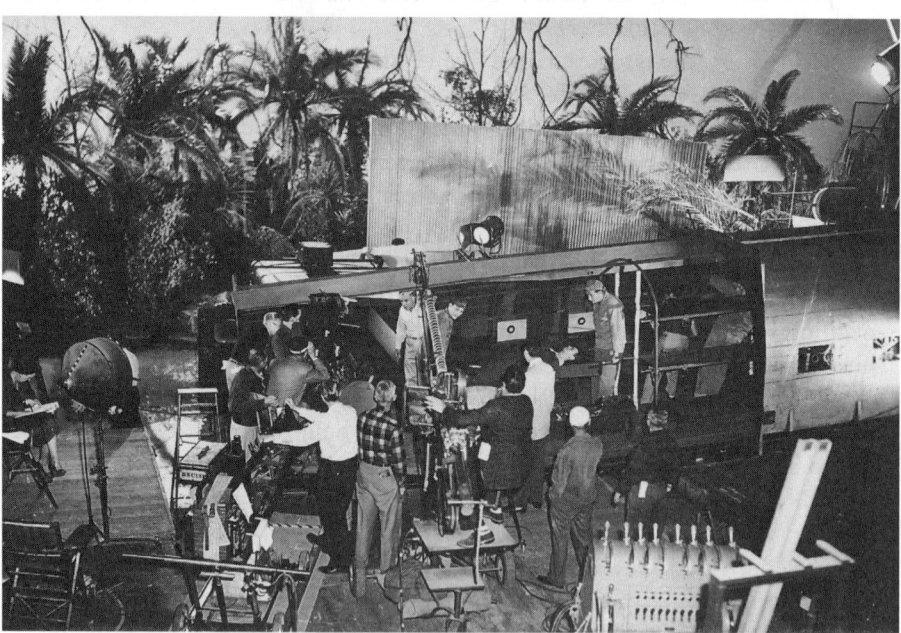

Top: Me directing Bill Williams, Marcia Henderson and Edward Platt in the *Schlitz Playhouse* episode I wrote. I also appeared in the Schlitz commercial. *Bottom:* the C-47 mock-up that enabled us to shoot scenes inside the plane. Note the tropical backing for parked scenes.

On the Friday evening it was shown on network television, Bill called and offered me another episode to direct. I'd read the script and thought it was lousy and needed re-writing to make it even passable. I said as much to him and offered suggestions on how I would re-write it, but he declined, saying that the "committee" had already okayed it. Rather than direct something I would be ashamed of, I told him I would pass. This attitude has led me time and again to substantial financial mistakes, but I'm not a bit sorry. If you want to put yourself on the market as a director, you must be ready and willing to direct whatever material you are being paid to direct, not just the scripts or teleplays you approve of. At least until you get to be a Sidney Pollack or a James Burrows. Still, I couldn't bring myself to think that way.

It was my good fortune to stumble into directing television commercials, and for the most part, I really enjoyed the work. A good friend, Tom Conners, became associated with Marty Ransahoff, a New York TV commercial producer who came to Hollywood with just enough money to rent a two-room office at General Service Studio and hire a secretary. Marty was a great salesman, and even before he could get stationery printed, he started getting commercials to produce. All he needed was people and facilities. This is where Tom, with his connections and his savvy, fit in. I happened on the scene shortly thereafter, and after working as assistant director on only a couple of jobs, Marty and Tom sold me as a director. It was a great and lucrative way to spend my days when I wasn't working on a long-term feature picture.

Those were the golden days of making commercials here on the West Coast when the ad agency people were largely situated in New York. Thus, it was quite a treat for them to come out here on business and live much higher off the hog than they did back home. Maybe it still is the golden age, for all I know. With fat expense accounts, many of them ensconced themselves at either the Bel Air or the Beverly Hills Hotel, and that's where Marty could be found, wining, dining, and wooing the agency account executives and sometimes their clients. If he wasn't at the office, that is.

I met many bright and interesting agency people from New York. One, Bob Carlson, was a producer on the Ford Motor Car account with the J. Walter Thompson Agency. Now retired, he lives the life of a country gentleman in Nipomo, California. Bob was and still is a class act. My wife still chuckles, remembering the hot summer days when Bob would spend much of a weekend frolicking in our swimming pool with our kids and eating hot dogs and hamburgers—when he could

Here I am in Oakland directing Henry J. Kaiser, builder of Liberty ships and Jeeps. He's on the far left; I'm third from the left.

have been living the good life offered at the Bel Air Hotel. We laugh when we think of the important and unusual work we did together, and now, in our antiquity, we're reduced (or maybe elevated) to exchanging recipes!

We both agree that if called on to make TV commercials today, we'd be hopelessly lost. In modern automobile commercials, the idea seems to be to show as little of the product and as much of the happy buyers as possible. And when you do show the car, have it in situations and under conditions that only well-paid stunt drivers could handle.

Neither Bob nor I can quite figure out the "wandering camera" technique that prevails in commercials these days. I'm only guessing that some Madison Avenue brain reasoned that with every third person on earth brandishing a video camera and frantically searching for the subject, the TV audience would feel better if they saw on the screen that paid pros were having the same difficulty. Then, it is hoped, the audience will feel good enough about themselves to go out and buy the toothpaste or whatever.

I have yet to theorize why some misguided directors allow or cause the same *wandering camera syndrome* in their theatrical features.

Television, in one category or another, provided a welcome source of livelihood for a couple of decades. My experiences working on pilot shows, weekly shows, movies of the week, and commercials are too numerous to mention. I was on more jobs that were canceled or unsuccessful than on jobs that were completed and successful. However the job turned out, I was happy to pick up the paycheck.

Marty (1955)

It was late afternoon when I found myself sitting in the office of Ray Klune, my ex-boss at 20th Century–Fox. Now he was a big man with Hecht-Hill-Lancaster Productions, a newly formed company. Klune was not exactly new in the independent field. Before he came to 20th Century–Fox he was production manager for David O. Selznick on *Gone with the Wind* and other big Selznick pictures. After a brief exchange of pleasantries, he sent me to another office to meet Delbert Mann, fresh from New York and now in Los Angeles to direct his first Hollywood movie. This was to be a theatrical version of *Marty*, which was originally produced in New York on the TV program series *Playhouse Ninety*. That was in the days before tape, and *Playhouse Ninety* shows went on the air live. Several fine directors and actors came from that difficult school.

Marty (1855)

What is a successful young TV director supposed to look like? I don't know what I expected, but I found myself shaking hands with a tall, smiling, rosy-cheeked fellow about my age who radiated sincerity and affability. Before a minute had passed I guessed that this was to be a very pleasant experience.

Mann then took me to an adjoining office where I met the inimitable Paddy Cheyevsky, the author of *Marty*. He had been brought out to Hollywood to work on the screenplay. There never were two more dissimilar people than Del and Paddy, but they certainly complemented each other in the net result. Paddy was in on everything, not just the numerous re-writes demanded for adapting an already great script to the silver screen. He seemed to dedicate himself to making sure that the integrity of his creation was protected in every detail: the sets, the furnishings, the props, the wardrobe.

I recall the afternoon some of us Hollywooders thought Paddy went a little too far. We were preparing to shoot on the set showing the exterior of a corner bar, including a bit of the street, the curb, and the sidewalk. Marty and a couple of buddies exit the bar and stop to play a

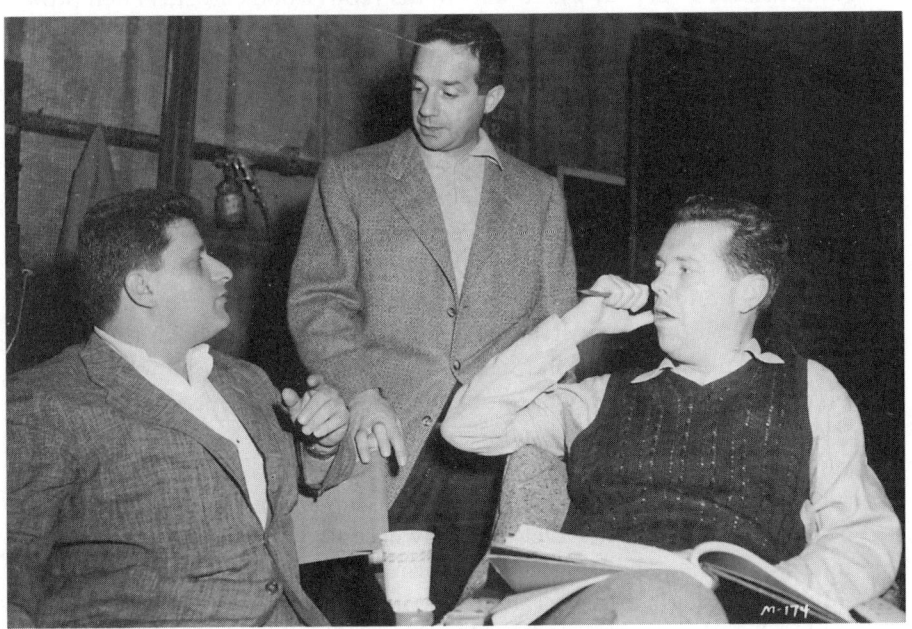

From left, Paddy Cheyevsky, Harold Hecht, and Delbert Mann conferring on the *Marty* set.

scene. The cameraman, Joe LaShelle, declared all was ready, and Del rehearsed the actors, made an adjustment or two, and I was about to roll the camera when Paddy interrupted and told the prop man to get him some bits of paper and some cigarette and cigar butts. He was concerned that the set didn't look like the outside of a New York corner bar. Of course, we waited while he and the prop man placed the debris in the "authentic positions."

The production was in the unique position of having a cast whose salaries were modest, a fairly small crew, and not much in running expenses. There were only five sets, four of which all fit on one sound stage at Goldwyn Studio. The fifth was the dance hall set, which was in downtown Los Angeles. After seeing the rehearsals on the actual sets, I proposed to Delbert and Joe LaShelle that we move right through on the schedule, shooting only the obvious close-ups and two-shots required, and then come back and shoot any additional shots necessary. This was feasible because we had a wonderful editing team who kept up with our shooting. Hecht and Klune agreed.

The plan worked, cutting time off the original schedule. And it gave Delbert a very favorable start to his Hollywood career. When production companies consider hiring a director, they like to see "On Schedule" and "Within Budget" after the director's name.

Never have I seen a company of staff, crew, and cast meld together as they did on this picture. There were very few parts, and in many instances, the actors and actresses who played them in the TV version were brought out to play them in the picture, although Ernest Borgnine and Betsy Blair, the leads, were new.

I liked the producer, Harold Hecht, and I want to think he saw to it that Del and Paddy were given a decent living allowance. If they were, one wouldn't know it, because about all you could say for the motel they holed up in was that the facilities were clean. The motel was strictly tourist class and certainly not notable for anything except maybe its low price. It was near Sunset Boulevard and Highland Avenue and within walking distance of some non-notable restaurants. The same could be said for the modest hotel on Vine Street they moved to later.

I don't think either Del or Paddy accepted any dinner invitations until we finished shooting, and even then, Paddy stayed in Hollywood only long enough to see a rough-cut of the picture. Whenever I tried to lure them out for a little fun, they'd beg off to "stay home and work." Come to think of it, I don't believe they even rented a car. I used to pick them up at the hotel every work-day morning and deliver them

Marty (1855)

back to their hotel in the evening. Del was also an ex-Army Air Corps pilot, so we had something else to talk about besides the picture.

I don't know whether Ernie Borgnine was thoroughly living the part of "Marty" or whether he was born for the sole purpose of being himself and coincidentally "Marty." One didn't have to be very perceptive to see how the two became one, and very real, indeed.

Another contributor who helped make *Marty* an Academy Award–winning movie was Betsy Blair, who lent her own sort of magic to the part she played. It was only after we were well into the shooting that I learned she was married to Gene Kelly (with whom I was destined to work on three pictures).

Very shortly after we finished shooting, Del, Hecht, Paddy and the editors ran a rough-cut of the picture, and I was invited to attend. When the lights came up at the end, there was silence. Finally, Hecht said he'd like to buy a drink across the street at the Formosa. Hecht and I were walking ahead of the rest, and when we were almost to the front door, he asked me, "Do you think they'll like it, Paul?"

"Who knows, but you'll sure find out!" was my expert opinion.

There was comparatively little editing to be done, and not much in the way of overall post-production work. During this time, Del's wife, Ann, came out from New York to be with him. Over dinner, when they told my wife and me that they were returning to New York and television there, I unhesitatingly advised them they were wasting the air fare, that Del would soon be getting Hollywood offers he couldn't refuse.

While I thought *Marty* would be well received, I didn't guess it would win *three* Academy Awards!

The Mad Hungarian

He was seated at his desk in his rather plain office. He was wearing a suit and tie, and though he was cordial enough, it was clear he was simply going through the motions of interviewing me, because he knew all about me before I appeared. I knew, for instance, that I had come to him highly recommended by Tenny Wright and others at Warner Bros. Here I sat in the presence of the king of the studio, and he was sizing me up for work on *The Helen Morgan Story*, his latest project. He of *Casablanca* and *White Christmas* fame. Meet Michael Curtiz, the Mad Hungarian.

Curtiz was probably the greatest money-making director in the industry at that time, and he worked solely for Warner Bros. Studios. In looking over his credits, it appears that he directed many more pictures per year than any other "A" director. This made him a rich man, one who owned acres of choice land in the San Fernando Valley on which sat a plush home, a stable of horses, servant's houses, and a regulation-size polo field. At the time I knew Mike, his wife, Bess Meredith, was a semi-retired, highly successful screenwriter and something of a recluse. I've heard it said that her knowledge of the business of making movies had much to do with Mike's success. From the beginning, I not only got along with him but found him quite easy to work with—if you were willing to overlook a few of his eccentricities Then, too, the studio had marvelous department heads, highly creative people on staff who were responsive to Mike's slightest request. They made it easier for me, too.

Marty Rackin had been a writer on the Warner Bros. lot for some time, and Jack Warner gave him a shot at producing this picture. As an ex-newspaperman from New York with a lot of connections to those in the entertainment business there, he was able to lure some pretty big "names" for cameo roles in the picture. A tall, lanky, very personable guy with a great gift of gab but lots of sincerity, he was liked by everybody on the set. Everybody, that is, but Mike Curtiz!

For some reason I never knew, Mike Curtiz took a dislike to Marty, and that was that! Marty spent less and less time on the set, stopping by mainly when some old friend like Walter Winchell was working, and then Marty would come to say hello.

One evening after looking at the dailies, Marty asked me to his office for a drink. It happened frequently and I soon found myself as a sort of go-between, keeping him abreast of things. I also listened as he lamented his seemingly thankless set-up at Warners, where his pay was the same as he was getting as a contract writer. I could see that here was a man of ambition and determination. I told him he'd never find happiness until he left the studio and went out into the independent field.

The next time I saw Marty, he was head of Paramount Studio. That was five years later.

One quick anecdote about Marty and I'll get on with *The Helen Morgan Story*. Marty had a story and a script called "Horse Soldiers," and he took it around trying to get a deal with a studio. The way I heard it, he told John Ford that if he (Ford) would direct, John Wayne wanted to do the starring lead. Then Marty hung up and got Wayne on the phone:

"Duke, Pappy Ford loves the script and told me he wants to direct the picture if you'll star." By the next morning, Marty had a deal.

If *The Helen Morgan Story* wasn't Paul Newman's first big Hollywood movie, it was among his earliest. Working with him day after day, one didn't need much insight to realize that it would be only a short while before he would be a big star. He put everything into his role, came to work completely prepared, and was always the thorough professional. He was courteous to one and all, though not terribly friendly with any of us. But never have I worked with a more innovative actor.

Between Newman and Ann Blythe, another fine professional and responsive artist, I think Mike Curtiz really earned only half his salary. I had heard about his display of temperament and abuse of actors but it certainly wasn't evident with these people. However, he did bully some of the "little" people around him. This was especially true of his cameraman (yes, that's what they called the cinematographer in those ancient days). Ted McCord was as tough as a two-dollar steak, but he'd be almost in tears when Mike would light into him, usually over nothing. McCord must have known something about photography, because 20th Century–Fox and Robert Wise hired him away from Warners to shoot *Sound of Music*.

One thing that Mike frequently did upset both McCord and me. At the end of each day, it is customary to get a good rehearsal of the first scene to be shot the next morning That way, the cameraman can have everything ready to go when the actors and director show up. McCord took great pride in this preparation.

There were days when Mike would show up, call the actors for a new rehearsal and completely change the staging—and hence the camera setup and the lighting. Supposedly, he'd re-thought the scene during the night and changed his mind. More than once I saw Ted get so mad he'd accuse Mike of letting Mike's wife, Bess, change the staging of the scene (with the aid of plans or diagrams). Then while Ted was re-lighting, Mike would needle him to hurry up! McCord and Curtiz did several pictures together, though I don't know how or why.

I don't know anybody in or out of the industry who has had more outlandishly funny stories told about him than Mike Curtiz. In fact, I heard that somebody had compiled a book on this subject some years ago. I know a few, and one of my favorites is about Mike's frustrating first attempts at learning to drive.

Like many foreigners new in this country, Mike didn't learn to drive for several years. I suppose when he was poor, he rode the streetcar or the bus. Then when fortune and Jack Warner deemed it time, he could afford a car and driver. The day came when he thought it would be fun to drive himself, so he phoned the head of the Warner transportation department and told someone to buy him a nice car and he would give him a check. The guy had a Packard convertible sent to the studio, and Mike fell in love with it. He was given a few driving lessons and turned loose. In short order, the guy got a phone call, and it was Mike screaming what a lousy car had been picked out for him. Steam was pouring out of the engine, and it was making loud banging noises. The guy picked up the car to drive for a day or two. It ran perfectly, though it did require water, and he took Mike for a ride to show him how well it performed and then returned to the studio. Next day, Mike called and yelled even louder. Once again the guy couldn't find anything wrong. Another time or two so the guy got smart and followed Mike, observing the temperamental director's driving. In no time at all, the problem was clear. After Mike started off in low or first gear, he never once bothered to shift into second and third! The car had overheated.

After Mike's comical attempts at getting the most out of studio-car transmissions, after *The Story of Helen Morgan,* and after many fruitful years together, Mike Curtiz and Warner Bros. parted company. Why? I never did bother to find out. Maybe Curtiz wanted to have more freedom to select his vehicles and the stars who appeared in them. Maybe he wanted to slow down and have more leisure time. Who knows? It was in the cards for me to be hired as the assistant director on Mike's second independent picture.

Sam Goldwyn, Jr., was embarking on what I think was his first venture in the business, producing a Western titled *The Proud Rebel* starring Alan Ladd and Olivia de Havilland and featuring some of Hollywood's finest actors. David Ladd, about 10 at the time and acting in his first picture, played the part of Alan's mute son.

Sam showed great and proper respect for Curtiz, and there was no doubt that Mike liked Sam personally and professionally. Sam hired one of the top production managers in the independent field, Clem Beauchamp, who, throughout our long association, was a joy to work with.

Off we went to Utah, where most of the picture was to be shot. The first and main location was near Cedar City where we were housed in the only motel near the shooting location. While comfortable enough, it lacked conveniences such as a telephone in each room.

At first, Mike was somewhat uncomfortable working with so many total strangers among the crew, although he had Ted McCord and me to kick around when he felt the need. But before the week was out, he was raising hell with one and all and at least once a day there would be an extremely unpleasant outburst. I could see that these people plainly didn't like it. They were each tops at their respective crafts and knew they didn't have to take Mike's verbal abuse. They could easily get a job at equivalent overscale wages elsewhere.

One evening late in the week, we came back to the motel after a difficult day, and I noticed a line had formed outside the single phone booth at the motel. Listening to the chatter, there was no doubt that several of these talented and top-salaried people were calling their unions and other connections and making themselves available for employment elsewhere. Jumping ship, as it were. I told Clem I thought we stood a chance of losing some of our crew because of Curtiz's behavior. He agreed, and because I knew Mike better than anyone, he asked me to talk to him.

Curtiz usually invited me to have a drink with him in his room, to unwind and talk about the next day's work, so it wasn't as if I were making a special trip just to tell him he'd better change his ways or lose the crew. He had a drink ready for me when I knocked on his door and without hesitation, I got right to the point:

"Mike, I don't think you realize that you are working with quite a different breed of people than you were at Warners, where you were the king. Down to the last person, this crew consists of the very top people in each craft, and they don't have to take any crap from anybody to make a living. Each one of them is much in demand and commands over-scale pay."

"What are you talking about, Paul?," he asked.

"Mike, you just can't treat these people like they were morons! When you blow up and yell at them, they don't like it *or you*. Right now, they're lined up at the only available telephone, looking for another job, and we can't afford to lose any of them," I explained.

If I'd stabbed him in the heart, he couldn't have had a more shocked look!

"I can't believe I was that bad with them, Paul. You know I don't mean it when—"

"Tell that to them, Mike, not me. I know you well enough but they don't. You'd better control yourself or you'll be making this picture all by yourself," I said, hoping to close the subject.

"I'm that bad?" he asked.

"That bad, Mike!" I affirmed.

On the set the next morning the crew was busy getting ready for the first shot when Mike told me to bring everybody together. He wanted to talk to them. With his Hungarian accent and inimitable way with the English language, the gist of what he had to say went something like this:

"My assistant tells me I have been son of a bitch to some of you and I should be better to you; so I want to tell you that if I haven't been so good to you, I will be better and I'm sorry. That's all, thank you."

Things went along just fine for about an hour and a half, but then something happened to set him off and he began castigating somebody unmercifully over some trivial thing. Almost in unison, we all started to laugh at him and he realized what an ass he was making of himself.

A day later, we were trying to make a shot of the fading sunset when the camera technician announced that the Technicolor camera required reloading. The technician was a big man, an ex-professional football player. He had worked on many movies with Mike and knew him very well. Those huge, bulky, three-strip Technicolor cameras took awhile to reload, and Mike kept trying to hurry this very stable and competent man along. He succeeded only in making him angry. The big man stopped reloading the camera and unloaded on Mike all the hostility for Mike that had been accumulating in him. He used every expletive I knew, and some I didn't. Finally, he called him a "has been," probably the most hurtful thing of all.

Mike was speechless as the technician continued to reload the camera and the beautiful sunset disappeared. It was as if Mike's fabulous career was disappearing below the horizon.

The next morning, all was forgotten and Mike was his old unpredictable self. When he was intent on a scene, he hated to have to stop for lunch or dinner. He would resist as hard as he could when we'd have to break for a meal or else pay rather dearly for a meal violation. Unless there was threat of a storm or loss of light or the like, I'd just call the break and suffer his wrath.

Mike took great delight in calling everybody "lunch bums" just because they got hungry once in awhile. What most of the crew didn't know was that the Mad Hungarian brought sandwiches that he would eat where nobody could see him. Consequently he consumed very little when he lunched with us.

Besides being beautiful, sweet, charming, lovable, and considerate of everybody she worked with, Olivia de Havilland was also a gutsy lady. We were shooting a dramatic action scene in which she comes to town driving a pair of spirited horses pulling a farm wagon. Little David Ladd runs from behind a parked wagon into the path of her horses, and she has to rein in on them, bringing the horses to a sudden, rearing stop. Olivia then jumps off the wagon and plays a scene with David. Mike wanted Olivia to drive the horses rather than use a stunt double.

Now, to make sure that the horses can't go forward beyond a certain point and possibly injure David, the wranglers and special effects experts had secured a cable to the wagon and to a solid anchor in the ground behind it. On the first take, the wagon came to the planned sudden stop—except nobody had thought to put a safety belt on Olivia, who pitched forward off the wagon seat and fell in between the excited horses.

Although she was thoroughly shaken up and bruised, Olivia insisted on changing costumes, touching up her makeup and hair, and doing the scene again. Fortunately her bruises were where they wouldn't be seen by the camera. For the second take she was equipped with a proper seat belt, which, unseen by the camera, she releases after the jolting stop so she can jump down and play the scene with David.

Both Olivia de Havilland and Alan Ladd had worked with Curtiz on several pictures, so while they were wary of him, they had great respect for his judgment because they knew he directed good pictures. He had a fine sense of what is entertaining and knew how to present it in good taste.

We had been shooting back at the studio for a week or so when Clem asked me to tell Mike that he had to stop using as a toilet the little alcove just outside of every Hollywood sound stage. The studio police department, backed by the studio manager, had evidence that Mike was the offender, and we'd have to take our sets and our director to some other studio if he didn't stop.

Over a drink in my office at the end of the day, I couldn't keep a smile off my face while I told Mike that he'd have to stop relieving himself anywhere on the lot other than in one of the men's rooms. Of course, he got very indignant, denied it, and left my office in a huff.

Now that I think of it, United Artists (later Samuel Goldwyn Studio), was my favorite place to work, and intermittently I spent many happy years plying my trade there. They had outstanding department heads, good facilities, and excellent equipment. Looking back, though, I'll admit that the bathrooms were few and far apart.

Toward the end of the location shooting, we were working on the Western street near Kanab, Utah. Everybody was tired and anxious to go home after a tough stint on location. We were making the last sequence, and it involved father and son, Alan and David. There was nothing difficult about the scene but Mike kept shooting take after take, and at Mike's insistence I kept pleading with David's welfare worker–teacher for "just one more take." But ultimately, from the sidelines, she gave me an adamant nod and I escorted David off the set, telling him that he was through for the day. When Mike blew his top at me, it was just too much to take and I guess I spoke to him more than somewhat rudely. We finished the day without speaking. I wrapped the company, and we returned to the motel to pack to go home.

Sam Goldwyn, Jr., had asked me to ride with him in his rental car to Las Vegas, spend the evening there, and catch a plane to L.A. the next morning. When he came to pick me up, there was Mike sitting in the front seat, looking neither to the right nor to the left. By now the snow was really coming down as Goldwyn took to the highway, and I soon realized that I was in for the ride of my life, the way he was taking those mountain curves. I felt uniquely grateful, though, for the hazardous conditions, thinking he was too busy driving to attempt a "reconciliation" between the monster in the front seat and me.

It wasn't until we were in darkness and out of the snow that Sam and Mike began planning the evening—where we were going to stay, where we would eat supper, what shows to see, and so forth. Like a pouting child, I asked Goldwyn if he'd drop me off at the airport, telling him that I'd better get on home.

The next voice I hear is Mike's: "Paul, I want you to be my guest in Las Vegas. Everything, and if you feel like doing a little gambling, that's all right, too. We'll have some drinks and have a good time, and you can't spend a nickel!"

Many years later, I blush with embarrassment when I remember my infantile answer: "I'd really rather catch a plane on home, Mike."

When we resumed shooting on a sound stage the following Monday, it was as if nothing ever happened between Mike and me. Damn! Even though I hate Las Vegas, I truly wish I hadn't been so petty that Saturday night in 1956!

It was while we were making *The Proud Rebel* that Mike learned my wife and I had bought a large house in North Hollywood. It required considerably more furniture than we possessed for the large playroom-den beside the swimming pool.

"Saturday, why don't you come up to my place and see if you can use any of the things we have stored there. They're mostly antiques, but maybe there are a few things you might like. Bring a truck or a trailer and just take whatever you like. My man will help you load," offered Mike.

Instead of horses, with which he had parted some years earlier, Mike's stables were filled with furniture. True to his word, many of the furniture pieces were lovely antiques, mostly from Europe. Encouraged by him, we loaded up a station wagon and a large trailer. Some of those lovely pieces grace the small house we presently occupy.

I never saw Mike Curtiz again, and he went on to direct only three or four more pictures, the last of which, I think, was a good one called *The Comancheros*. It was well known that Mike was in great pain with cancer during the location shooting and lasted only because John Wayne took the helm on the days Mike couldn't make it.

Mike was a handful, to be sure; but his talent made his quirks seem as nothing. And, besides, it wasn't as though the man couldn't laugh at himself. A story he once told me proves, I think, that he could look back at his own pride-inspired pratfalls and smile.

In the early thirties, Jack Warner heard about this young genius director in Europe and after seeing a couple of his pictures, sent for him to come to Hollywood, and provided a one-way steamship ticket. No matter that it was second or third class, Mike was enthralled at going to the Promised Land of fame and fortune. In New York harbor, the great ship slowly approached the docks, and fireboats were shooting giant streams of water into the sky. Tug-boats screamed their welcomes and a military band blared its own special greeting from the dock.

Passengers crowded the ship's railing. Many, including Curtiz, were seeing America, the land of the free and the home of the brave, for the first time. Somebody commented that there must be some important dignitary aboard and it suddenly occurred to Mike that *Jack Warner has arranged this welcome just for him*, and he tells all within earshot as much!

It wasn't until most of the other passengers disembarked and the band had put away their instruments and departed that the passengers on Mike's lower deck were allowed to set foot on land. Then Mike realized that his time for celebration was yet to come.

I am very glad that I had the chance to know and work with this complex artist.

Defiant Ones (1958)

When Stanley Kramer directed a picture, Clem Beauchamp was the production manager and I suppose because we had such a good working relationship on *Proud Rebel*, Clem called me in to be interviewed by Kramer for the job of assistant director. As I recall, Kramer's regular assistant wasn't available, for which I was most thankful, because I got the job.

Kramer made good pictures, but he would only make one when he knew he had a good script. Then he would throw his whole being into making it into a good movie. He dealt with controversial subjects in an open, sensitive manner and with exquisite good taste. As in *Judgment at Nuremberg* and *Guess Who's Coming to Dinner*, he sensed the best way to present the story.

Tony Curtis, far left, plays a scene as Sidney Poitier looks on, seated third from left. Director Stanley Kramer is on Sidney's left. I am hunkered down on the far right.

It was essential to the story of *Defiant Ones* that Tony Curtis and Sidney Poitier, handcuffed together and hating each other, appear to be escaping from prison against all odds and under the most miserable conditions possible. Which is pretty much what we, the staff and crew, endured while shooting the picture. Much of it takes place outdoors in the dead of winter, at night, and in the rain—whether made by God or our special effects people. If the actors were cold, we were colder. The only way I could have been made more miserable is if I had been handcuffed to the cameraman, whom I loathed. I looked at a tape of the movie recently and found myself shivering as I watched it and remembered.

On the last day of shooting we were on location at a high altitude on the Kern River in central California when it began to snow. Secretly, I think we were all grateful for the snow, especially Sidney and Tony and the stunt doubles who had to be in the Kern river. It left us no alternative but to pack up and go home.

When Mother Nature wouldn't, we made it rain.

Defiant Ones *(1958)*

Kramer had a way of extracting whatever hidden values there were in a script and putting them up on the screen. And he did so with ease. The same could be said of his actors; they appeared to add some dimension to their roles that really didn't seem to be there when I read the script.

It was my misfortune not to have the opportunity of working with Kramer again. I'm going to go through the rest of my life thinking it was only because I was never available when he was ready to make a picture and his regular assistant was.

I don't think that any of us in the company doubted for a moment that we had each helped make a very good movie. It was nominated for an Academy Award, so somebody else must have thought so, too.

Teenage Thunder (1958)

Anybody who thinks they know what the future holds for them is, in my opinion, a fool. And if they happen to be in the movie business, they are super-fools! The phone rang and it was Jack Marquette, who was the camera operator on *The Helen Morgan Story*, the picture I worked on at Warners the year before. He suggested that we meet. It turned out that Jack had formed a production company consisting of some key people he had worked with in recent years; a sound mixer, a property master, a key grip, gaffer, all the main crafts it takes to make a movie.

Not only had Jack a promise of their services, but they'd also invested money, and in some cases equipment, in various amounts. Affiliated with the new production company was Howco International, a North Carolina–based company owned and operated by J. Francis White and Joy Houck, who also owned and operated a large string of theatres in the South. They were not only going to release the cheap movies that Jack and his company delivered to them, they were also putting up some of the financing. This was the sort of arrangement any ambitious movie producer only dreams about!

If Howco said they wanted a science-fiction movie, a horror movie, mystery, teenage movie, or whatever, Marquette Productions would deliver as ordered.

Looking back, I suppose I should have fallen off the chair with glee when Jack asked me if I wanted to direct the first picture which was to be about teenagers and drag racing. Instead, I inquired, "Have you got a script I can read?"

On the first reading, it was apparent to me Jack and his writer had come up with a pretty good story that required only a little work to make a good program picture for very little money. Before he even asked, I told him I regretted that I was unable to defer my salary for a chance to participate in the profits. He still wanted me to do the job.

A young actor, Chuck Courtney, had already been hired to play the lead, which was just fine with me; he was boyish and exuded enthusiasm. The guy in the black hat turned out to be Bob Fuller, an extra who had never uttered a line on the screen in his life, and who only a couple of years later starred in three television series.

How we wound up with Fuller is kind of a fun story. Jack Marquette, J. Francis White and Joy Houck all wanted me to use another actor, Cookie Burns, but didn't insist. Burns was just fine with me until Chuck Courtney called, begging me to come right over to his house in Burbank for something "that will only take fifteen minutes" out of my busy life. Being a good sport, I did his bidding.

Placing me at a strategic spot on the front lawn, Chuck said: "Just stand there and watch!" and he took a position by the curb. Without so much as a nod from Chuck, a car containing a good-looking fellow with dark hair roars to a stop near him, and damned if Chuck and the driver don't play out the gas station scene from the script, including the fist-fight.

Getting up off the street and brushing himself off, Chuck handled the introductions: "Meet Bob Fuller. He is the guy you've been looking for. You just found him, Paul. Is he or is he not?"

Convincing Jack Marquette was easy, and Fuller was set for the part. As for the rest of the cast, I carefully picked experienced actors and actresses, except for the teenage girl lead. For that part, instead of casting a sexy beguiling beauty, I hired an average-looking but attractive girl with a good speaking voice and the ability to act natural.

I felt that the dialogue needed adjusting to the actors. So for a few evenings before we began shooting, I invited the cast to come to my home, where, in a large playroom by the pool, we rehearsed and, where needed, reworked the script. I even got a stuntman friend of mine to stage and direct the couple of fights involved. We were ready to make movie history—in six days, as I remember.

I never did know the cost, but it was well under $100,000, including a $5,000 charge when Joy Houck and Francis flew out to California in Joy's private plane.

My first meeting with those two Southern gentlemen was one to be remembered. I think Jack's hiring me to direct the picture was conditional on my being acceptable to Houck and White, who wanted to meet me. Houck phoned me and invited me come to "the old ladies home" in Hollywood, which turned out to be the Knickerbocker Hotel.

The door opened and there stood this bespectacled, rosy-cheeked, paunchy gentleman who looked like he might have been a high school principal. J. Francis White was the last guy you'd peg for being a multimillionaire movie man. He hailed from Charlotte, North Carolina, and was in total contrast to Joy Houck, a tall, good-looking, gray-haired, expensively dressed, shiny-shoed gentleman in his mid-fifties. If you were casting for the part of a Mississippi riverboat gambler, Houck would be your man.

It took me several minutes to get used to their Southern accents and join in the small talk that usually occurs on such meetings. I figured I was "in" when White suggested we have lunch. It took place at a restaurant across the street from the Brown Derby. Oddly enough, all the hired help seemed to know the names of the Southern company I was in.

The lunch conversation went along smoothly and easily, and it became apparent to me that these people might be very easy to deal with—as long as the deal favored them! I liked Marquette and I didn't envy him taking on these two shrewd gentlemen over the long haul.

Shooting, which was done entirely on nearby locations in the San Fernando Valley, went along smoothly until we came to the late night scenes at the drive-in restaurant. One of the shots called for Melinda Byron, my teenage leading lady, to come driving down the street and into the drive-in, where she stops the car, parks, and enters the restaurant.

We rehearsed the scene for Jack to light, which he did in short order, and we made a take. Melinda stopped the car right on the mark and we dollied into a close shot of her getting out of the car and all was well—except she was wearing big, black horn-rim eyeglasses that she hadn't worn in the previous or the following scenes, which we had already shot. Matter of fact, none of us had ever seen her wear glasses before this moment.

"But there's no way I could possibly drive the car without my glasses," she pleaded, in response to my insistence that she absolutely had to.

"Well, Melinda, then this is going to be a first for you," I said.

I had a walkie-talkie put on the seat of the car with me on another radio, and I shortened the distance she had to drive. With her car moving at about half speed toward the drive-in, and Jack compensating on the camera speed, and me steering her by radio, it looked like all was going to be okay—but I forgot to tell her to stop, and she ran the car into the side of the building!

We made a cutaway to another character, and when we cut back to the glassless Melinda, she's just getting out of the car, which is already stopped in the right place.

As for the damage to the drive-in, we paid the owner the money he needed to repair it himself.

The distinguished gentleman who played the part of Chuck's father in the picture, Tyler McVey, remains a close friend to this day. Chuck Courtney suffered a crippling stroke, and Bob Fuller died recently. I wonder about the other actor-friends.

It was flattering to have Marquette ask me to direct one of their next two pictures, a science fiction story and a horror story, but after reading the scripts, I had to beg off, knowing they were beyond repair.

Marquette Productions and Howco International, after two or three more pictures, had a falling-out and ceased doing business with each other.

But Howco and Paul Helmick would be keeping company again.

Rio Bravo (1959)

After four years and with considerably more experience in the world of moviemaking, I found myself once again in the company of Howard Hawks. This time it was a full-blown, shoot-'em-up, sheriff-against-the-world Western for which Hawks was noted, and the star was none other than the Duke himself, John Wayne.

A few friends in the business questioned the wisdom of my stepping down from directing my first feature picture, however small, and going back to being an assistant director. I took the position then that you can be working and be in the business, or you can be wishing you were working and be out of the business. As long as the job is in the same category in which I was experienced, why not take it and gain even more experience and contacts? Perhaps if I hadn't been firmly

Rio Bravo (1959)

attached to the role of responsible family man, I might have taken a different position.

Once Hawks and the writers, Leigh Brackett and Jules Furthman, got the story licked, it came time to do the casting of the lesser parts. Hawks had already set Angie Dickenson and had her taking lessons from a card shark on handling playing cards. She also underwent voice training, which consisted of going into a sound-proof room and shouting her lungs out. This was to deepen her voice and make it more interesting and, I suppose, sexy—à la Bacall, Lombard, Ann Sheridan, and others. Oh, and Paula Prentiss.

When it came to the part of Dude, the drunken ex-deputy sheriff, it seemed natural to bring up the name of Dean Martin, who had recently split with Jerry Lewis and was a smash hit in Las Vegas at the time. He wasn't known for playing serious parts that required serious acting, true; but I urged Hawks to at least have him in for an interview.

If he thought Dean Martin was capable of doing the part and wanted it badly enough to promise to stay sober for six or seven weeks, maybe it could work out. Also, we had a firm start-date with Wayne and had run out of candidates to play the part.

Dean flew down from Vegas the next afternoon and I don't think he was in Hawks' office ten minutes before I knew he had the part. He either kept his promise to abstain, or was drunk all the time, including the interview. Everybody liked being around him and working with him, including Wayne.

I also suggested to Hawks that it might be worth while to cast the other parts with television stars. I reasoned they would sell enough additional tickets to make it worth the money they might cost. He readily agreed. This is how we wound up with Ward Bond *(Wagon Train)*, John Russell *(The Lawman)*, and Ricky Nelson *(Ozzie and Harriet)*, who was *the* teenage idol at the time.

I had recently worked a few shows on *Ozzie and Harriet* as the assistant director, and I knew the Nelsons well. While Ozzie and I didn't quite see eye to eye, we parted company on good terms. Thus he was amenable when I approached him about Ricky making his feature picture debut in our movie. Of course, Ricky was thrilled at the idea of working with John Wayne and Howard Hawks, star maker.

Hawks told me he "found" Walter Brennan while he was shooting *Come and Get It!* He needed a guy to say a line, and the assistant director brought him three men out of a crowd of extras. Hawks told them each to say the line. When he came to Walter, who said the line to Hawks' liking, Hawks said, "Now take out your false teeth and say the same line."

"Ah gee, Mr. Hawks, I can't do that. Everybody would laugh at me."

"That's exactly what I hope they do. Now, take your teeth out and say the line for me," insisted Hawks.

So Walter Brennan, who was barely able to pay the rent and put food on the table, became a movie star and an Academy Award–winner on *Come and Get It!* his first picture. You don't have to look very closely to see that he subsequently played many parts *sans* false teeth.

One of the feature players was Claude Akins, and I don't think he had started his series, *Movin' On*, at this time. He was a versatile actor who was liked by Hawks the minute I introduced them.

Some years later, Claude was co-starring in *Planet of the Apes*. He lived a couple of blocks from us, and we occasionally did happy hour at one or the other's house. At the end of shooting one day, Claude saw fit to wear his ape make-up to our home. After greeting my wife, startling her, he proceeded down the hall and into our 12-year-old daughter's bedroom, where she was busy with her homework. He stood looking over her shoulder until she sensed a presence, took one look at his ape face and let out a loud scream. As well as she knew him, it was some time before he convinced her the man behind the make-up was her friend Claude.

Working with John Wayne for the first time was quite an experience. He was a disciplined actor, and when Wayne was called for rehearsal of a scene, he came on the set in full wardrobe and with whatever guns, horse, or other props the scene called for. What's more, woe to any actor who didn't have his stuff together. If we gave him a 9:00 A.M. call, unless there was an act-of-God disaster, count on him to be there.

On a later picture, an assistant gave Wayne a call time of 9:00 A.M. and Wayne roared, "You know damned well that you're not going to need me at any nine o'clock. They've got this whole set to light, so why have me come and just sit around? It doesn't make any sense!" he protested.

"I'm calling the crew for seven, and I'm guessing they won't take two hours. When do you think we'll be ready?" the assistant respectfully replied. Back came: "Oh, hell!" and Wayne walked away.

At 7:00 A.M. the next morning when the assistant arrived on the set, there was the great man himself having coffee with the grips and electricians—coffee he had arrived early enough to fix for them. While he didn't do that every day, he was known to do it frequently.

Wayne showed a great and, I think, unique respect for John Ford and Howard Hawks. If either man told him to play a serious scene while standing on his head, I think he would have done it without question. If Wayne was addressing Hawks in front of other people during a rehearsal, it was always "Mister Hawks." I never got used to a man of Wayne's stature in the industry calling someone he knew well "Mister."

From the moment we met until the last of his movies I worked on, we never warmed to each other, and I don't know why. I can only guess that he never understood the close relationship I had with Hawks, who at all times treated me like a close friend (which I was) instead of the assistant director, the associate producer, or the second unit director. I think Wayne's attitude toward me began on *Rio Bravo*.

We were working on the Old Tucson Western Street set one sunny morning. Hawks had been closeted in a quiet room with Wayne, Bond, Brennan, Martin, and Ricky Nelson, refining the introductory scene in which Bond and Ricky meet Wayne outside the jail. When the meeting ends they walk up the street to where the camera was located. Hawks seemed somewhat perturbed. In front of Wayne, Hawks said to me, "We don't have a good line for Ricky when the Sheriff asks him if he isn't kind of young to be guarding a wagon train."

After a moment's thought, I suggested, "How old do you have to be, Sheriff?" End of conversation. Good or bad, Hawks said nothing until he started talking with Bond and Ricky. It was then that Wayne turned to me with, "Since when does the assistant director write the dialogue?"

I was speechless with embarrassment! A few minutes later they rehearsed the scene and out of Ricky's mouth came the line just about the way Hawks heard it from me.

In my working capacity I didn't have the chance to know many writers very well except Leigh Brackett. She was a middle-aged lady of 45 or 50 who looked like she put up jelly and watermelon pickles. In truth, she was one of the top writers of men's stories as well as other movie scripts. Leigh's husband was mystery writer Ed Hamilton. They lived on a farm outside a small Ohio town. She would leave her beloved husband and farm only when summoned by a producer in need of a good script. When she was in Southern California on an assignment, she lived at a hotel on the Santa Monica Palisades and got about in a rented car. This enabled her to come to our house whenever she felt like it, and we always welcomed her.

She and Hawks worked together hand-in-glove. With only a minimum of talk, Leigh seemed to grasp ideas that he'd come up with and make good scenes on paper. If a scene didn't work, she'd come running to the set and would usually solve the problem in short order. Her name is to be found in the credits of many Howard Hawks' pictures.

Meanwhile, we were back at Warner Brothers Studio for interior shots and were nearing the end of shooting on the picture. One of the scenes remaining to be shot took place inside the jail, where Wayne, Martin, Brennan and Ricky are holed up waiting for word, or else a showdown with the bad guys. Ordinarily, a suspenseful scene like this would be heavy with a "threatening" musical background score that Dimitri Tiomkin was so good at. Instead, Hawks chose the occasion to have an original song that featured Martin and Ricky, with Brennan on the harmonica. The only practical way to do a song wherein camera cuts to different people are required is to pre-record the music and have the actors sing and play to the playback when you shoot the scene on the set. In this case it would take two days to shoot. The least you can get by with is a cue-track playback. It happened that the musicians union had gone on strike, and we didn't have a playback because Tiomkin didn't make one before the musicians went out. Hawks asked me what I was going to do about it. So did Steve Trilling, the second in command at the studio.

When I phoned Tiomkin at home, he was rather abrupt in telling me to get lost. Didn't I know he was out on strike?

When I showed up at his home, hoping to persuade him to ask the union for a dispensation and make a track for us, he wouldn't even discuss it. I know for a fact that the score for *Rio Bravo* was the last score he ever composed for a Hawks movie.

Remembering that we had given lead sheets containing the words and music to the actors so they could learn the words, I called Ricky at home and told him of our dilemma and exactly what was required. I also hired a playback operator to report for work on the following day. The next morning when Ricky came to work, without our exchanging one word, he handed me a tape. I, in turn, handed the tape to the playback operator. Nobody ever asked and I never told where the tape came from.

While he didn't particularly like to work after dark, Hawks thought darkness, shadows, and nighttime lighting effects enhanced the action of stalking, searching, or any scene that involved threat or menace. As a consequence, we spent many long nights shooting on the Old Tucson Street a few miles outside Tucson, Arizona, where we made three Westerns, all with John Wayne. I remember we had just finished midnight supper while making *Rio Bravo*. We were shooting a long shot requiring several lighting units that included some large arcs known as *brutes*. Suddenly, in the lighted area the air was full of flying bugs that turned out to be locusts or grasshoppers. We thought if we kept the lights off a few minutes they might disappear, but after several blackouts they just seemed to multiply when our lights came on again. Hawks finally gave up and told me to send everybody back to the motels and, also, to arrange that the bugs weren't around the next night. Needless to say, the local crop dusters came in for an unexpected pay-day and pay-night for standing by. But the critters disappeared by the next night just as rapidly as they had appeared.

One of the most memorable days I ever spent on location anywhere was the Sunday Hawks invited me to drive down to Nogales, Mexico, with him, Russ Harlan and John Wayne. The latter had a good friend (I think his name was Carlos Aruza, a bullfighter) who was the featured star at the bull fights that afternoon. About bullfighting, I'm glad I saw one if only for the pageantry and the color. I assure you it was, and will be, my last.

On the way back to Tucson, we stopped at a cattle ranch owned by Stewart Granger and Jean Simmons, where we had been invited for cocktails. Jean Simmons was just as lovely looking as she appeared on the silver screen. Granger was introducing a breed of French cattle onto the American cattle scene and insisted on showing them off to us.

Then it was back to Tucson in time for mint juleps at the exclusive Rocky Mountain Oyster Club, famous for its food and drink. We were the guests of a Colonel What's-His-Name who had something to do with luring movie companies to Arizona. With the mint juleps were served Rocky Mountain Oysters as hors d'oeuvres. I'm not sure how they are prepared, but I do know (1) they are delicious, and (2) they are bull's testicles.

After a simply great supper, it was on to Wayne's suite, where John Ford (who loved Arizona and being around movie-making, even if it wasn't his movie) joined us for a poker game. Because of his bad eyesight (he was blind in one eye and wore a patch), we played with his cards that were considerably larger than ordinary. As the evening wore on, the stakes got larger and the drinks flowed more freely. I had the good sense to limit my intake to a couple of drinks. Late in the evening, one hand came down to just Wayne and me, and he blew up, calling me a lousy poker player because I called and raised him on a five-card-stud hand, which he thought I had no business doing. Ford took exception to his remarks on my behalf and said some vile and unpleasant things to his favorite leading man, thus making the evening even more memorable and not endearing me one bit more to the Duke. Especially since the pot was mine.

There is probably no country on earth where John Wayne was and is, even today, not a top movie star and hero. Though Wayne and Hawks were close friends on and off the set, Hawks delighted in telling how in Japan, theatres displayed Ricky Nelson's name above Wayne's on the theatre marquees

What I wouldn't give to relive those days and nights! I'll bet Hawks, Ford and the Duke would, too.

Porgy and Bess (1959)

I have found that in writing this book, it is helpful to sit down and run a video tape of each picture I worked on before I attempt to put my recollections to paper. In preparation for this chapter, I approached Sam Goldwyn, Jr., who, I'm certain, would have been pleased to oblige me with a videotape copy of *Porgy and Bess* if he could. Unfortunately he could not.

As best I understand it, the Gershwin estate has the last word on what happens to anything created by George and Ira Gershwin. Ira must have made a deal with Sam Goldwyn, Sr., the producer of the movie, that allowed Mr. Goldwyn to produce a film version of the opera subject to approval of the finished product by Gershwin. Knowing Sam Goldwyn, Sr., and having great respect for him as a producer of fine pictures and an astute business man, it is difficult for me to believe he would ever allow anybody else control of his product.

The story I have heard most frequently is that the Gershwin people didn't like the way the picture turned out and shortly after its release invoked their legal rights and had it withdrawn from public showing. And I'm told that's where the matter stands as of this moment.

When offered the job of first assistant director on this prestigious picture, I was more than somewhat astonished to learn that it was to be directed by none other than Otto Preminger himself, and that he had requested—insisted, even—on me. Would I come to the studio and meet Mr. Goldwyn and the production manager, Doc Merman?

I should stop right here and relate some facts about a fire at the studio. Some months before, the sound stage at Goldwyn studio on which the principal set, Catfish Row, was built, mysteriously burned to the ground. Making matters worse, many costumes and props stored in a basement beneath another stage were destroyed by fire. The news accounts describing the fire hinted at arson, and there were protracted investigations into the cause of the fire. Thus, for *Porgy and Bess,* it became a matter of starting all over. However, the first thing replaced was the director, Rouben Mamoulian, a very capable and talented man. Then the production staff was changed and eventually the cameraman.

Mamoulian wasn't at all happy about being replaced, nor was the assistant director, and they both took the matter before the Directors Guild. Preminger and I were summoned to appear before the guild council. I had read the script and faced up to a very long schedule, which meant suffering Preminger day after day. My heart wouldn't have been broken had the guild disallowed Otto and his Sancho Panza to do the picture. However, the guild ruled in favor of Preminger and me, so it was on with the show.

The stage was rebuilt. The pre-recordings (playbacks) under the supervision of André Previn and Ken Darby were well under way. The Catfish Row set was about finished. There were the matters of deciding on final locations in the Stockton, California, area and the casting of minor parts. Then too, there needed to be final fittings of the sensational costumes designed by Irene Sharaff.

One morning, I was summoned to Preminger's office, where he told me I was to accompany him over to the stage where a long table and chairs had been arranged. Sidney Poitier, Dorothy Dandridge, Sammy Davis, Jr., Pearl Bailey, Diahann Carroll, and one or two other players were present. Preminger greeted one and all and introduced me to those I hadn't already met. He said that for this reading of the script, I would be reading the descriptions and everything but the dialogue. He would do the dialogue of actors not present.

I don't recall ever being so embarrassed and nervous. At the time, I was adjusting to either bi- or tri-focal glasses, and between the poor light where the table was located and my self-consciousness, I was miserable. Looking back now, I wonder if Otto wasn't getting back at me for the wild horseback ride I forced on him in Canada when we were doing *River of No Return*.

The cameraman (cinematographer) Leon Shameroy, came aboard with his gang, all old friends of mine from 20th Century–Fox. I was fortunate enough to get my choice, Mike Salamunovich, as the key second assistant. On this picture especially, his job was important because it was a time when black people, whatever their occupation, were striving for greater recognition and equality and were keenly sensitive to how they were respected and treated. In his position, it fell to Mike to coordinate things so that performers were ready when required. That meant having close contact with all who appeared in front of the camera. From the beginning, it was obvious that one and all in the cast loved him.

Looking back, I believe it was Pearl Bailey who asked for a place where, in between shots, the black people, those who wished, could go and have private discussions. Across from the stage entrance was a rehearsal hall, which was made available to them. When there would be sufficient time between shots, I would tell Pearl, who would then call a meeting.

I wonder if those actors and actresses suffered qualms about appearing in a movie whose portrayal of black people might be said to pander to stereotypes.

Almost from the beginning, Preminger and Mr. Goldwyn were at odds with each other, and I suppose the reason Goldwyn didn't fire him and pay him off is that paying off Mamoulian had already cost Goldwyn a small fortune. Otto had graduated from a Vienna law school, and Goldwyn probably instinctively knew that Otto was not a man to be fired easily. Mr. Goldwyn was quite elderly at that time, and I think he might have felt *Porgy and Bess* would be the last of several fine movies for which he was responsible. While I had little contact with him, I felt truly sorry for Mr. Goldwyn when Otto had him barred from the sound stage under a legal threat that if Goldwyn showed his face on the stage, Preminger would walk and everything would grind to an expensive halt.

This deteriorated situation was a far cry from the friendly relationships exhibited at a lavish "start-of-picture" party held for the staff and cast, the elite of Hollywood, and selected members of the press. The party was given by Ira and Mrs. Gershwin one summer Sunday afternoon. The bubbly flowed freely, as did the unscripted b.s., and I recall observing Otto and Sam strolling together about the garden, greeting guests and being quite cordial to each other. The Gershwins were gracious hosts and mingled freely with their guests. They seemed rather pleased with the casting of the major roles. All was at peace with the world this beautiful afternoon, which makes me wonder.

If the Gershwins were so displeased with the finished product that they, and their heirs, would halt its release, I'm prompted to ask, didn't they read a copy of the shooting script? Didn't they listen to the prerecordings of the music? Had they not screened some of Preminger's previous pictures so they might have an idea how he would treat their prize jewel?

I either read or heard that one big objection they had was that Porgy, the cripple, got about with his goat pulling him on a cart. That was well described in my script. Another objection was that they would have preferred lesser artists filling the roles and doing their own singing as opposed to the way it turned out. I ask, who would have put money in an expensive undertaking such as this movie without star "names" filling the major parts? More about this later.

The entire company, including the dancers and chorus, stayed at an old hotel in Stockton, California, for the location shooting. This included the picnic scene, the ferry boat ride, the rape scene, and Diahann Carroll's lovely rendition of "Summertime." We took over the entire hotel and many members of the cast had their families stay with them for an unexpected holiday. The hotel management opened up a lounge on the first floor for our use. Some of the singers and dancers were also fine instrumentalists, and on any given evening there would be entertainment in the lounge as good as could be found in any big city. Except for Saturday nights, the impromptu show broke up early.

When it came time in the early morning to board the ferry that took us to work on our island, all the cast and singers and dancers would be present and on time. Occasionally a crew member would miss the boat. This was my first—but not my last—experience of having people going to and from work on a ferry boat.

Strange, but when I try to recall incidents on pictures I worked on "a few years ago," memories of some pictures come to me easily while others draw almost a blank. In the case of *Porgy and Bess* I was able to call upon the memory of Mike Salamunovich, the second assistant director on the picture, who recalled most vividly the almost daily verbal sparring sessions in which Otto and I would engage. They usually occurred toward the end of the day and often I wondered if I'd just done my last day's work on the picture, especially when Otto's secretary would call down to the set and say that he wanted to see me in his office before I went home.

At first I'd approach his luxurious quarters bristling for battle, only to have him ask me to fix us each a drink, and then maybe he'd want to talk about something that had nothing to do with the picture. It only worked a couple of times, but if he had pissed me off enough on a particular day, I'd wait until he got a couple of brandies (his usual drink), and at the precise right moment, I would casually mention that I heard that Mr. Goldwyn sneaked on the stage that afternoon. The mere mention of such a bold violation would have Otto ordering his secretary to get his lawyer on the phone, no matter where he was or what he was doing! This became my cue to thank Otto for the drink and make my exit. I had wrought the evil I had craftily conjured up. I knew Frances Goldwyn, always protective of her husband, would never let any such disturbances get beyond her.

Toward the end of the schedule, Otto sent for me one afternoon while the crew was lighting a shot, and when I entered his office, there sat a certain cameraman with whom I had recently worked and could not stand. We had had a classic personality clash, and Otto knew about it. Smiling his broadest smile, Otto announced, "You two are going to be working together on my next picture."

Without a moment's hesitation, I grabbed the gent's slimy hand and shook it enthusiastically. Turning to Otto, I told him, "I'm going to have to pass, Otto, but thanks anyway."

"Have you got another picture?" he queried.

"No, but I can only take you about once every two years," I replied, and turned and strode out of his office.

Besides being a great entertainer, Pearl Bailey, affectionately known as Pearlie May, was also a sensational cook. I was privileged, along with my wife, to be invited to the after-picture party she put on at her Apple Valley ranch one Saturday afternoon and evening. It wasn't what could be called a lavish affair but was a Western-style barbecue, complete with riding horses. She and her husband Louie Belson, the renowned big-band drummer, made every guest comfortable and welcome.

The meal was served family style at long tables in a ranch cookhouse and was prepared entirely by Pearl and a few of her helpers. It consisted of traditional Southern dishes with a Western influence. It was a great American-style banquet.

My wife and I remember that the guest list included the cast and their children and a few members of the staff, like Preminger, Shameroy, Ken Darby, André Previn, Doc Merman and, of course, their ladies. It was about a two-and-a-half hour drive to Apple Valley, and we remember Sidney Poitier whizzing past us on a motorcycle.

Another party we were privileged to attend was hosted by Dorothy Dandridge at her home in the hills above the Sunset Strip. The house was a moderate-size, single story, white bungalow. This evening party was a rather dressy affair attended only by the principals in the cast, some of the staff, Dorothy's mother, and a few of her friends. Dorothy was one of the most beautiful women I have ever seen. Her husband evidently thought so too, for his eyes never seemed to leave her. The most memorable thing about the party was that everything inside the house, at least the rooms that my wife and I were in, was white. The only holdouts to be found were 36 keys on the grand piano!

Thunder in Carolina (1960)

Sometime during the last week of shooting on *Porgy and Bess,* an old acquaintance, J. Francis White, called me from the Knickerbocker Hotel (he called it, the "old ladies' home"). He asked me to meet him for lunch.

From the sound of his voice, even with its thick drawl, I figured he wanted to talk about something besides the national debt, and I told him I would join him the following day. When it came, I told Otto that I would probably be a little late returning from lunch because I had to attend a business lunch with a producer for whom I had directed a theatrical feature. From the incredulous expression on his face, I think he figured that I was merely being loose with the truth.

After telling me how well *Teenage Thunder* did and was still doing, J. Francis White got to the meat of the meet.

"Ever hear of the Darlington Southern 500 Stock Car Race, Paul?" he asked. "It's the biggest event in automobile racing outside of the Daytona 500," he added.

"What about the Indy 500, Francis?" I inquired.

Ignoring my question, he continued, "Some friends and I are going to make a movie of the next race and I want you to direct it."

"Francis, I wouldn't know the first thing about doing a documentary," I unhesitatingly replied.

He patiently explained, "It's not a documentary at all. We've got a good story about car racing and the script is being written by a good writer you're going to like. We're going to use some 'name' actors this time, and we're not expecting to make this picture for the budget you had on *Teenage Thunder*, Paul."

"Have you got anything I can read?" I asked. I think he was shocked that I dare ask such a question when here he was, giving me the chance of a lifetime.

"Come up to my suite with me and I'll give you an outline and what little script I have so far. The racing boys I'm in this with think it's a good story, and so do I," he explained.

"I hope I do, too, Francis! Everybody likes a good story!" I said.

Maybe I just imagined it, but when I returned to the set, it seemed to me that Preminger viewed this humble assistant in a new light after I volunteered that I couldn't decide whether to take the job until I read what was on paper and, more important, know whether I liked it. What a dilemma!

There was nothing unusual about the story or the characters. The lead male role was, of course, a rogue. He was a down-and-not-quite-out race driver who somehow never found the right woman.

I was delighted when Rory Calhoun signed on to do the part. The rest of the principal roles were filled with adequate actors who seemed bent on making me look as good as they possibly could in the 18-day shooting schedule. During the race, which lasted only four and a half hours, we shot several dialogue scenes with these people by bicycling them from one camera set-up to another. While one camera was shooting a dialogue scene, a second camera and crew were moving to a new pre-determined camera setup. Other cameras shot the race itself.

Even though this was an important step in my career, I accepted the offer with reluctance; my dear mother was quite sick in a hospital at the time, and I didn't want to leave her. Had it not been for the big auto race, I probably could have gotten Francis to postpone the start date awhile. At my mother's urging, I took on the job and left for Charlotte, North Carolina, where I stayed at Francis' beautiful home for two days of meetings.

The first morning at breakfast with Francis and his wife, I noticed a toaster sitting on a little table beside Francis. It had to be, if not the original, one of the first five built. It was that old. This toaster had sides that folded down, and for those who prefer their bread toasted on both sides, you turned the bread over. Here we have a gentleman who is worth $27 million, and he's living out the remainder of his long life with a toaster that probably came into being only a week or so after electricity was invented. I later learned that the beautiful car he used to pick me up at the airport was his wife's car, and I had yet to ride in his car, which I assumed pre-dated Jack Benny's Maxwell.

On the day I was to go down to Darlington, Bob Colvin, the president of the race track company, and three other track owners came to Charlotte to fetch me and have a get-acquainted lunch at Francis' private club. Instead of letting myself be subject to their inquisition, I bombarded them with questions about racing traditions, superstitions, and unusual drivers they had known, and occasionally I made notes as they talked.

Little did Francis or anybody else except Howard Hawks and Leigh Brackett know that in the short time we had together, Francis' writer and I were not on the same wavelength on several important scenes. His dialogue especially bothered me. I had sent copies of the script to Hawks and to Leigh Brackett prior to a five-hour meeting with them during which they loaded me with notes and ideas of characterizations. I think it was during this meeting that Hawks offered this piece of sage advice: Make three good scenes and don't bore the audience in between. Although I never saw Hawks' 1932 movie *The Crowd Roars*, I imagine there was a certain amount of that movie that crept into our current effort.

Every spare moment was spent writing or re-writing, and it was all I could do to stay ahead of the shooting. Many was the night the actors got the next day's scenes at 11:00 P.M. It was a couple of weeks before Francis White confronted me about the almost nightly long-distance calls to and from Hawks. He said he was afraid that working all day in the heat and writing at night would render me unable to get through the picture. Little did he appreciate what garbage might have resulted if we hadn't thrown all that added effort behind the picture. I reminded him that I told him going in that he had the wrong boy if he wanted a documentary.

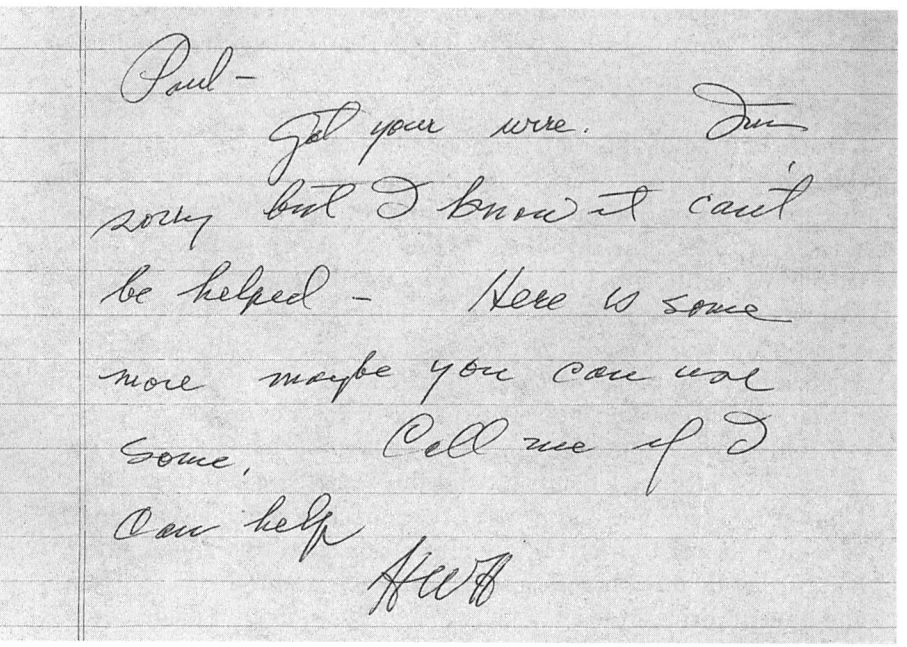

Howard Hawks sent me this note after Francis White told me to quit working all day and re-writing scenes at night. Needless to say, I didn't.

Driving down to Darlington in Colvin's big station wagon, somebody asked me what I had been working on, and when I said *Porgy and Bess*, there came a lull in the conversation before somebody else asked, "Isn't that all about niggers?" No doubt about it, I had arrived in the Deep South!

"It's an opera written by George Gershwin, and it's about black people living right here in this state a few years ago. We made a wonderful movie about the opera," I explained.

Long pause, then Bob Colvin spoke up, "You're not planning to use any of them in this picture, I hope. We wouldn't like that at all, Paul."

I took off my gold wristwatch and handed it to the gentleman sitting next to me in the car.

"Read what it says on the back," I said.

"Many thanks, Paul. Sammy Davis, Jr.," he read and handed the watch back to me.

"I haven't any plans to use blacks in this picture, but if you're telling

Thunder in Carolina *(1960)*

me that I can't, you might as well let me out right here because I don't need the job that bad and I've got a round-trip ticket home."

End of conversation.

When you are making a picture that includes an event that actually takes place over four hours, you need more ingenious ways to indicate time passages than dissolves and montages. I realized this problem existed and needed to be solved. So I wrote a couple of scenes of a driver's wife who is too nervous to go to the race and instead listens to it on the radio while chain-smoking cigarettes in her motel room. A maid comes to clean the room and noticing the growing pile of cigarette butts in the ashtray, remarks, "You must have a man in the race, Ma'am."

Sometime later, after we started shooting, I took some delight in asking Colvin who would be cleaning motel rooms in Darlington.

"A nigger cleaning woman," he replied.

"Thanks," I said.

I wasn't terribly surprised to learn that there were no little theatre groups that might have an aspiring black actress for the bit part, so with a lot of help from Connie Hines, the race driver's wife and our leading lady, I recruited one of the maids who actually cleaned the motel rooms we stayed in. She wasn't exactly at ease with the lights and the cameras, but we got the job done. Not one of the money people or the producer ever said a word about a black appearing in their picture.

The day after I arrived in Darlington, the production manager, Rex Bailey, who had arrived a few days earlier, awakened me with the news that my mother had died. The producer, Francis White, had already arranged for me to be on the next plane home with only my promise that I'd return as soon as I possibly could after the funeral. I thought that was not only decent but tremendously "big time," considering all he had riding on the picture and that there was an inflexible start date.

The crew and other cast members came from Chicago and New York as well as Hollywood. The movie was being made in the jurisdiction of the New York Cameraman's Union, who insisted that we use a New York camera crew. I wanted to use one of the Hollywood cameramen I had worked with on TV commercials. I raised such a big fuss that Francis finally agreed to pay for a New York cameraman (who would be used as a second cameraman) so I could have my Hollywood guy.

The New York local said no. Their man would have to shoot the movie. Like a spoiled brat, I told Francis just to pick someone and I'd have to make the best of it. So the Union sent a man named Joe Brun. After our first hour together, I knew he was more than up to the job. Despite the tight schedule and my inexperience, there was nothing I could come up with that he couldn't cheerfully handle. For example, we were getting ready to shoot a fairly wide exterior shot of a residence at night (night for night). About an hour before dark, I got the idea that it would be nice if it were raining. The interior scene immediately following would play better if it were raining, with the sound of the rain on the tin roof of the garage.

"Joe, if we could get the Darlington Fire department to come here and give us a little water, what do you think about shooting this night scene in the rain?" I challenged.

"Let's see what we can do," he replied.

No question. With the accompanying rain falling on the darkened area and beating on the tin-roofed garage, and the girl with her short rain jacket and wet hair, it was indeed a better scene, thanks to Joe Brun.

A friend saw this poster in a small-town Kansas theatre and brought it to me.

Thunder in Carolina *(1960)*

We asked the race car drivers to remain in Darlington with their cars and crews after the big race. We wanted them to work in the shots I needed to intercut with the actual race footage. While I expected the race car drivers to be gutsy guys and include the usual number of showboaters that one finds in the world of sports, I had a hard time convincing my producer and the money men that we must have at least one highly experienced and camera-wise stunt driver with us. One of the most convincing arguments they offered against the idea was that the race car drivers would be offended if we brought in a "Hollywood type" to do their work, a race car driver's work.

"Not to worry," I told them. "The guy I have in mind will furnish his own tutu and ballet slippers!"

After whining, pouting, and stamping my feet, I finally won out, but the bosses insisted the stuntman must also play a part. Foiled again! Cary Lofton, recognized in the industry at that time as the very best car and motorcycle stuntman, was also the very worst actor in the industry. Salting my wound was the hard fact that he loved to act and thought he was pretty good. More salt in my wound: The only part I had for him was that of a drunken race car driver who gets killed in a fiery crash. As you surely have noticed, even good actors and actresses have a tough time playing drunks.

Cary came back a week early on his own to help me work out a few things. He also loved to mingle (drink) with the race car drivers, many of whom knew of his reputation and spectacular stunts.

The time came to shoot Cary's big confrontation scene with Alan Hale, Jr. (*Gilligan's Island),* and I could smell the ham smoking as Cary stepped in front of the camera. After only one rehearsal, I could see it was no use, so we shot and printed the first take, much to Cary's disappointment.

That strip of film should be screened before classes in acting to show students what not to do.

The craft Lofton really excelled in was stunts , and when he came roaring out of the third turn and down the backstretch during a time trials scene, we had two cameras whose lenses were glued onto his car. At precisely the place he told us, his car blew a front tire, crashed into the wall, rolled over four or five times, and finally came to rest on the car's top within a few feet of where Cary had said it would.

I had given strict instructions that no one was to go near the smashed car until I told them. Only the camera crews and two other guys standing inconspicuously on the sidelines knew what I was up to.

One of them had a three-gallon can of gasoline and the other a torch and lighter. Once I knew Cary was okay, I told him to get the hell out and away from the car. I told him it was going to catch fire and might explode.

"Not with my lucky safety belt in it! Bring me some cutters," he insisted. We rescued his safety belt.

Once we were away from the car and behind the camera, I signaled to my torch men and the camera operators. They made a beautifully fiery scene, and when the two pieces of film were put together, the car appeared to burst into flames as soon as it came to rest on its top. Ta-da!

So while we're all standing around telling each other what a great job we did, into our midst burst J. Francis White, who had witnessed the "accident" from across the track. One brief glance told me that he was less than joyous.

"Paul! You realize that you just destroyed a five-thousand dollar race car!" he excitedly drawled at me.

"Francis, I swear these firemen are the best I ever saw! Did you see how quickly they got in there and put out that fire? That car is barely singed," I returned. "I'll save the money someplace else, but believe me, this picture needs a good kick in the ass. All we do is talk about how dangerous this business is. When we show one of our drivers 'buying the farm,' the paying customers will understand why the wife really is terribly worried about her husband," I explained. Tossing a hateful look at Lofton, I continued, "Even if the son of a bitch is nothing but a stinking drunk who had it coming."

When Butch Cassidy and the Sundance Kid appear in certain scenes in the picture, a scene works perfectly *in slow motion* because that's the kind of movie it is. Recall Paul Newman showing off with that choreographed bicycle routine, in tempo with great music. Inspired directing, no less. But when a director expends a half-hour of film and has worked hard to get his audience into a frame of mind where they believe what they're seeing and hearing on the screen is probably true, you shouldn't destroy the illusion by spending five minutes in slow motion screen time for the villain to hit the water after being thrown off the Golden Gate Bridge by the hero. This is why, if you happened to see our car-racing movie, you don't see any slow motion shots. Except for one, which was not intentional.

There was a young, would-be rookie driver who hung around the camera and me every day and was in there trying to help wherever he

Thunder in Carolina *(1960)*

could. He'd borrow a race car and drive in a multi-car scene when he could, and I felt I could depend on him. I called him Soapy, but his name was Neil Castles. I should explain that by this time, Cary Lofton had returned to Los Angeles to go on another job. Soapy begged to do the job.

The scene called for a car in the middle of a racing pack of cars to lose control on a turn, bounce off the rail and roll on its wheels down to the infield while other cars dodged around it. After the drivers ran through the scene at slow speed, we made some adjustments and got ready to make the shot. Calling Soapy over to the camera, we explained that we didn't need to do the stunt at high speed, that we could make the cars look like they are traveling fast by adjusting speed on the camera, and Joe Brun explained how that was done. But Joe did need to know the speed the cars would be traveling.

"Sixty-five," Soapy told Joe and the other drivers. Joe computed the camera speed and told his assistants.

Twice we tried shooting the scene, but Soapy couldn't get the car to come off the rail the way we wanted. A couple of the older drivers seized the opportunity to needle Soapy, and he was getting angry. On the third try, with Soapy setting the pace, the pack entered the turn much faster than 65, and Soapy's car actually rode on top of the rail for several feet before falling back onto the track where the other cars did a great job of missing him. It was a spectacular shot, if ever I saw one! Except it was done at the wrong car speed and hence the wrong camera speed. I couldn't bring myself to ask the drivers to do the shot again, so I printed it, moved on, and hoped for a miracle.

When we screened the film, it looked like a speeded up scene from Toonerville Trolley Cartoons to me, but it didn't seem to bother anybody else nearly as much as it bothered me. I took the shot to the best specialists available back in Hollywood, but nobody knew how to fix it. That was in 1960. Today, with the great technical advances that have been made, it should be easy to solve the problem.

The Darlington Southern 500 Stock Car Race is no small potatoes, I soon found out. They have over one-hundred thousand people in attendance and several thousand spend the whole holiday weekend camping out on the track infield. Motorhomes, trailers, tents, vans—whatever. Once parked there, they are not let out until after the big race. Consequently, the prostitutes and the bootleggers do a thriving business.

In addition, there's the big parade in town, and everybody turns out for that event. I was able to effectively incorporate it into the story.

Not only that, I made a shot of two little boys sitting on the curb together watching the parade. One kid is white, the other black.

But the biggest challenge was to coordinate the minister's invocation prayer with the huge Marine Corps Band and Choir playing and singing "The Battle Hymn of the Republic" so everything ended on "Amen." Then Ray Melton, the track announcer, issued his instructions, "Gentlemen, start your engines!"

In addition to the regular camera crew, we had seven or eight more for the race. Joe Brun and I spent hours laying out each camera's position and what they were to cover during the race, such as crowd reactions, accidents, flag signals, lap number sign boards, and so forth, while Joe, the sound crew, and I shot scenes with the cast.

We even had a car officially entered in the race. It carried one and sometimes two cameras in different positions. They were operated by the race car driver, who had instructions to make daring passes and mix it up with other cars. Also, we had to make the background projection plates for use back in Hollywood when we put our actors into the race scenes. We even did over-shoulder shots with the driver wearing different helmets and jackets to double the two main characters, Rory Calhoun and John Gentry. We went so far as to change dashboards and repaint hoods for those shots.

When the race was over, the winner and his car and crew were escorted to the winner's circle where there was a grassy mound the winner drove his car onto. He was immediately surrounded by news reporters and press photographers, his adoring fans bearing flowers, the beautiful race queen, and the race officials bearing the trophy. At the height of the enthusiasm, imagine everyone's surprise when I elbowed my way close to the real race winner and with a loud-hailer megaphone announced that we were now going to shoot our "movie race winner and his movie race car" accepting the plaudits, flowers, kisses, and the trophy—oh, and would the audience please act like they had just done, only more so! "You will all then appear in the movie," I promised. All this while, our crew members were removing the astonished genuine winner and his car out of the winner's circle.

Did you ever see a movie in which a perfectly sober actor or actress takes maybe a few sips of a drink and all of a sudden, before you know it, is drunk? No dissolve, montage, or anything else to indicate a time lapse. Well, we had just such a scene. In our story, an afternoon lawn party beside a lake is given by a rich sponsor for drivers, their ladies, and race officials. Our assistant hero shows up with his wife, and while she mingles with other drivers and their wives, he is set upon by a

Thunder in Carolina *(1960)*

beautiful sex-trap who emerges shimmering from the pool in a scanty swimsuit and leads him over to the bar. They have some conversation and booze, and we hear a couple of strange-sounding chords. Cut to a lovely young lady in a summery silk dress sitting in the shade of a tree. On her lap she has a zither, which she gracefully strokes and begins her song, a Civil War ballad. Intercut with couple at bar, famous drivers, audience, and cut back to our man as the bartender hands him a new drink. The song ends, and when we go back to our scene, the assistant hero is drunk.

I met the young singer before starting the picture, when I was interviewing local people for bits and extras. She was a charmer, an orphan as I recall, whom some local business men adopted and were presently putting through school and giving her a musical education. She certainly has something to tell her grandkids.

We had another cocktail party sequence coming up and needed a place to shoot it. Francis White found what he thought was a suitable

```
        J. FRANCIS WHITE

                              6/23/60



           Paul:

           "THUNDER" has gone into orbit--doing
           even better than even our last ad indicates.

           The news is getting around.  We open on
           the Fox Mid-West circut out of Kankas City
           in August.

           July is jammed with bookings  in Georgia,
           Tennessee, and Virginia. The Paramount
           circut here did such tremendous business
           that all of their affiliates now know about
           the gross.

           Hope the enclosed copies are readable.

                                   Regards,
```

J. Francis White often sent me notes like this one, which, I believe, I received while in East Africa.

place in Florence, a town just south of Darlington. It was a rather ritzy upstairs Elks club, available for me to see only in the morning. Besides, it had to be early because I was scheduled to be shooting at the track. Francis picked me up in his ancient Plymouth station wagon. On the way back, a front tire blew out. We were on a road where there were no signs of civilization, and I'm already late getting to work. Seething, I said nothing while helping Francis change the bald tire. Twenty-Seven great big ones and he's riding on bald tires!

The Darlington Raceway partners, all rich men with money invested in the movie, were all at my beck and call, no matter how menial the task, and indeed I did use them. They were not used to the fast pace of making movies and I think I sometimes prodded them a bit too hard. One guy in particular, who I knew only as "Scrunt," frequently made fun of a big straw hat I wore. By the time we finished the picture, the hat was all sweaty, smelly, and falling apart.

These partners had a little home-away-from-home where they conducted the occasional soirée and where they decided to put on a little going-away party for me. When I arrived with Francis White, daggered to the wall by a long hunting knife was my hat. Blood had dripped from underneath the hat and dried on the wall.

For a year or so after the movie's release, Francis sent me press notices, and occasionally he would tell me how much the picture pulled in over a weekend. It must have made money for the investors.

I wonder if my hat still hangs on the wall, and does blood still drip from it?

Hatari! (1962)

Once again, the phone rang, and I heard Howard Hawks' distinctive voice summoning me out of my temporary oblivion and into action.

"If you're not doing anything, why don't you meet me at my house at nine-thirty tomorrow morning? I think I might have something interesting," he said.

We rolled through the gates of Paramount Studio in Hawks' car and were soon being introduced to a group of five expensively suited executives who had been waiting for Hawks in the spacious office of the then–head of production, Jack Karp. He was a New York business man if I ever saw one. Karp was most pleasant but rather reserved. I'd like to think it was a "first" when Howard Hawks introduced me as his "associate." I'd been promoted!

Coffee served and the cordialities over, Karp told his group that Hawks had an intriguing idea for a picture with John Wayne, and perhaps he'd like to tell them a little bit about it. This was akin to turning the Fuller Brush Man loose in a room full of housewives and janitors!

As Hawks delighted in the telling, so his attentive listeners sat spellbound as the plot unfolded. I was just as awed as anybody else in the room. As much as movie-goers seemed to like what we finally made, I later thought, what a hell of a great movie it might have been had we only made the yarn that Hawks spun.

I just thought of something, and I've got to digress here a moment to relate a little-known story about Edmund Goulding, another fine director, writer, and storyteller. One night at Ciro's, a popular Hollywood night club in the 40s and 50s, Goulding, in his cups, saw Darryl Zanuck seated at a table with a couple of friends and went over to say hello. Zanuck liked him, and because Goulding was an amusing fellow, Zanuck asked him to sit down, whereupon Goulding proceeded to weave a story which he made up as he spoke. Zanuck must have liked the story, because the next day, Goulding got a phone call summoning him to Zanuck's office that afternoon to tell the story to Zanuck's people. When she hung up, Goulding didn't have the slightest idea what story she was talking about. He barely remembered where he had been the night before. Somehow, though, he recalled somebody who was at Zanuck's table and after much effort tracked her down. Over the phone, she sketched out enough of the story he told that he could remember the rest. It was made into a very successful South Seas picture, the name of which escapes me.

Hawks' African story told, and the meeting over, he and I went to lunch. There wasn't the slightest doubt he had a deal, and his agent, Jack Gordean, was turned loose to settle the details. Thus was born *Hatari!*, a very memorable adventure and more than a year's worth of most happy work for me.

In praising Hawks' ability as a storyteller, I certainly don't wish to diminish the work of the writers of *Hatari!*, Harry Kurnitz for the story and Leigh Brackett for the screenplay. I think Hawks got the basic idea from someone he met in Europe.

It didn't take us long to realize that it's one thing to write about a group of people whose business it was to catch, cage, and ship wild animals, quite another to photograph them doing it. Here was the problem: As long as movies have been made, whether photographing cowboys chasing Indians, chariots going all out, even pedestrians strolling down a garden path, the camera has had to remain fairly steady; otherwise you make your audience dizzy or maybe even seasick. The camera can move two or two hundred miles per hour in any direction, but the platform has to remain reasonably steady. Realizing that we would have to photograph our catches of animals on the terrain where the animals were to be found, whether rough or smooth, and most often at high speed, it became obvious that a very special camera car would have to be developed. With the success of the entire picture riding on these "catch" scenes, once a satisfactory camera car was built, a backup car would be needed in the event of accident or breakdown. The problem was turned over to Russ Brown, the head of Paramount's technical department, and he came through handsomely.

Don Robb, a Paramount unit manager, was assigned and the decision was made for us to go to East Africa on a survey trip. I went armed with my 16-millimeter movie camera, a still camera, an audio tape recorder, and lots of film.

Before we left Hollywood, Don hired a professional hunter as our guide. A reputable safari outfitting company, Kerr and Downey, had highly recommended doing so. Like most professional hunters in Africa (don't dare call them "white hunters"), Eric Rungren was an Englishman who had been in East Africa many years. His claim to fame was that he held the record for killing the largest tusker (elephant) up to that time. He also had part of a shoulder eaten by a leopard. In Rungren's safari hunting car, Don and I set out on a survey trip of much of Tanzania (known as Tanganyika at that time), parts of Kenya, and much of Uganda. Either native uprisings or infestation of the dreaded tsetse fly kept us from looking in other countries where African animals were plentiful. With us were Rungren's two "boys," natives who were his gun-bearers, camp-makers, cooks, tire-fixers, and anything else that Eric wanted them to be.

Riding along mile after long mile, Eric was pleasant enough company, and listening to some of his hunting stories was fascinating, even though most of them were about those he called his "stupid, egotistical, American clients." It soon became apparent to me that this guy wasn't terribly fond of Yanks and compensated for it by being overly fond of himself.

Occasionally, we came upon herds of animals and we would drive alongside them where the terrain permitted. There was a large hole in the roof of the car, the edges well padded. I could stand and photograph the herds with the movie camera. This was done to demonstrate the importance of a steady camera platform and that, indeed, the animals were there in all their natural glory. Eric was very good about getting us where they were.

There was one main set called for in the script. It was described as a large, rambling house where the characters lived when they weren't on safari catching animals. There were animal pens and sheds, and a few other out-buildings. For this location, I favored a place known as Momella. There were three other possibilities that I showed Hawks (on film, of course), but he trusted my judgment. Momella was located eight miles over mostly paved highway from Arusha, a rather attractive town with a motel and hotel that could house our people. There was even a small movie theatre where we could screen the film we exposed. If the Indian merchants didn't stock something the cast and crew asked for, it was soon on their shelves. Don arranged for the rental of several furnished private homes for Hawks, Wayne, and others in the cast.

After seven weeks of traveling, Don and I returned to the studio full of enthusiasm and optimism. We had successfully negotiated with the government in Tanganyika's capital, Dar es Salaam—whose cooperation, especially the Game Department's—was essential.

They seemed pleased that we had engaged the services of Willy de Beer, the highly experienced animal catcher from South Africa.

Don arranged for a large moveable safari camp for the second unit, which I was to direct.

Meanwhile, Hawks and Leigh Brackett had developed the script considerably, and Hawks even added a couple of characters to the cast. Carl Anderson, one of Hawks' favorite art directors, was put to work, and the Paramount lot buzzed with *Hatari!* activity.

John Wayne had completed a picture he produced, directed, and starred in, *The Alamo*. He had a considerable amount of his own money invested in it. When it was shown to several friends in the business, including Hawks and me, it wasn't very well thought of, and Wayne knew it. Hawks realized Wayne would be happy to escape deep into Africa where he would be away from the *Alamo* picture, his company, Batjac Productions, and into an entirely different and fun environment.

While in Africa, Don and I listened to a variety of opinions about the best time of year to begin shooting. Based on these opinions we had about come to a decision (quite wrong) when we happened to fly with a talkative private pilot. After learning our planned start date, he told us about the smoke. It seems that after the long and very wet spring, the tall grass dries in the summer sun and is then set afire. So extensive is

Hatari! (1962)

Top: Hawks' home away from home in Arusha, Tanganyika. A most comfortable abode that came with several servants. *Bottom:* The living-room of the house. Russ Harlan is seated in the chair; I'm slouched on the couch. Hawks took the picture.

the burning over East Africa, it is difficult for a pilot to navigate in some areas because of the smoke. The pilot made it quite clear that we would be well-advised to start our movie after the big smoke and finish it before the torrential rains came. We took his advice.

Paramount supplied excellent crew members for both the first and second units, and they also welcomed the people we brought in from the outside. Russ Harlan, the cameraman, had all of his people. I

Joe Brun, center, poses for a picture in Ngorongoro Crater, where the opening scene was shot.

brought in a few people I could count on, including Russ Saunders, once an all-American football player at USC, who had been my assistant director on several commercials. He was like a first sergeant on safari, and everybody liked and respected him.

As for the cameraman with my unit, I really wanted Joe Brun, with whom I'd just worked on the race car movie. Since Brun was a New York cameraman neither Hawks, Harlan, or Paramount had ever heard of, my chances of getting him were slim, if not nil. However, when you are preparing to make a movie about an unusual subject (especially if it takes place in a foreign country), it is a good idea to review whatever film is available on the subject. So, we were screening what seemed like miles and miles of film pertaining to Africa and wild animals. One day the film library arranged for us to view an RKO movie called *Savage Splendor* and both Hawks and Harlan thought it was well done. Much to my pleasant surprise, when the end credits came on the screen, my

French friend, Joe Brun, was listed as the cameraman. Yes, he was available, and glad to come aboard with us.

One day, Hawks asked me if Cary Lofton, the car stuntman friend we both knew and liked, was going to Africa with us. Meaning: "If you haven't got him, get him."

"And what about a stunt double for Wayne?" he asked, adding, "I don't want to use any of his people, if you were thinking about it."

When Wayne called me and I had to tell him that we had already set Ted White as his double and that we were not taking a transportation captain and couldn't use his man, the message did not endear me to him one iota. I did not feel the least bit good about being the associate producer on the picture. No doubt, had Wayne insisted, he could have had anything and anybody he wished on the picture, but that wasn't his style.

I had directed commercials for Kaiser-Jeep Corporation and had a close contact with the man in charge of publicity, Con Ritchie. Together we worked out a deal whereby for far less money than it would cost us to rent trucks and cars in Africa, Kaiser-Jeep Corporation would furnish all the brand new vehicles we needed. They would be delivered in Mombassa, Kenya, along with spare parts and an expert mechanic to maintain them. They even gave the vehicles a special zebra-striped paint job. In turn, we would furnish them with three, one-minute TV commercials to be aired on the national network programs they were sponsoring at the time. These were to run in conjunction with the release of *Hatari!* and were to advertise our product as well as theirs. I made up the commercials as we went along, shooting footage featuring performance and ruggedness, which is what Jeep wanted the commercials to sell. The vehicles really were not very dependable and had it not been for the proficient mechanic Kaiser-Jeep Corporation sent along, I might easily have suffered regrets.

Hawks arrived in Africa a week or two before we started to shoot, and after settling him in the comfortable home that had been rented for him, it fell to me to show him around. We were tooling down the highway with him at the wheel of a new Jeep station-wagon when I noticed him suspiciously eyeing the red and white metal signs that were attached to every wood utility pole. On each sign was just the one word, *Hatari!* which in Swahili means "danger." The signs were meant to warn the natives who might be tempted to cut down the poles for firewood that they could be electrocuted. I let him seethe for a mile or so before telling him that I had nothing to do with the signs, that I wasn't advertising the picture prematurely.

When the first unit cast and crew were settled comfortably in Arusha, I joined my second unit camp at Longido, an area in which game was plentiful at that time. Willy de Beer and his very special people, who did the catching and caging of animals under Willy's supervision, were already there and getting familiar with the vehicles

Top: Cary Lofton looks on as Hawks gets onto me about something. *Bottom from left to right:* Jerry DeTois (the South African who doubled John Wayne in most catching scenes, and also Willy de Beer's real-life catcher), Ted White, and me.

from Hollywood. Willy drove the "catch" truck, which was a specially equipped pick-up truck. It was fast, powerful, and had special suspension. It also was equipped with a seat which could be mounted on either front fender for the man with the rope. The truck was radio equipped, of course, as were all our picture vehicles and the camera car, so I could talk to everybody during a catch and they could talk to me.

The camp was first-rate in every respect, and I think everybody in the crew knew from the start that we were in for a rare and wonderful experience that few of us could dream of. The food was well selected and well prepared, and our tents were made very comfortable by one attendant being assigned to each tent. He took care of our clothes and personal belongings. To Africa I brought along a record player and a supply of favorite records. (Later, when audio tape cassettes became popular, I traveled with them.) If, while we were out shooting during the day, a dust storm would blow through camp, I could be sure my man would keep my records clean, along with everything else. While his English was sparse, he seemed to anticipate my every need, even to washing and gassing up my Jeep after we had been out shooting all day.

The camp natives getting ready to put on a dance, which were great fun to watch. Can't remember what I was so worried about.

When the picture was finished and his job was over, he retired to his village, where I visited him before I returned to the States. I added a little to his retirement fund for his kindness and thoughtfulness.

Another key person in my African life was Keith Mosely, our spotter pilot, who took off very early in the morning in his Piper Cub airplane and looked for game herds that were within a reasonable travel distance from camp. There were times when it became necessary for him, together with our five or six professional hunters in their Land Rovers, to move a herd to better catching ground. He would radio its position to us, waiting in camp, and we would get in our vehicles and follow the professional hunters. We were in touch by radio all the time, and some of the conversations were priceless. Hawks even spoke of using some of these transmissions for radio commercial spots when the picture was released, but I don't think we ever did.

Once we had the game in sight, we would ready the cameras, though we always traveled with one or two Arriflexes at the ready in case we chanced upon the unexpected. Then, of course, it would be all business.

Howard takes a rest while his son, Gregg, has the time of his life riding on the camera car.

Hatari! (1962)

Top: When at Christmas I couldn't catch land animals I caught the ocean variety instead. *Bottom:* Keith Mosely, our game-spotter pilot, with his trophy bluefin. Mosely was a wonderful pilot and a dear friend.

At lunch, out would come the box lunches that had been prepared for us in the camp kitchen. As I recall, they usually tasted pretty good. The natives liked them, too. Members from the Warusha tribe, an offshoot of the magnificent Masai, would mysteriously appear from out of nowhere. They came for our lunch leftovers which they never ate in our presence. Then out would come Russ Saunders, the assistant director, with a football, and the touch football game would begin, the teams made up with a mixture of Warusha warriors and our crew. Our hunters interpreted and passed Russ' instructions to the natives just as his coaches might have instructed him at U.S.C. Then there were the spear-throwing contests, which were great fun. We had an American assistant cameraman, Bert Eason, who could out-throw anybody the natives put up against him. When I announced that it was time to put the football away and get back to work, I was soundly booed.

When we finished work on Saturdays, Keith would fly me to Arusha for meetings and supper with Hawks. For these trips, we used another plane which we had standing by for emergencies. At Christmas time, we gave everybody a few days to go to Nairobi or Arusha. Keith and I went deep-sea fishing off the Kenya coast.

From the beginning, our plan was for me to develop a team capable of photographing the catching and the caging of an animal. We used the actors' doubles in these scenes. Then, after Hawks had seen and approved the film my team shot, his first unit with the actual cast members would take over our camp while we moved to Arusha or Moshi and waited for him to integrate the principals and dialogue into the scene. When possible, we would have something for the second unit to shoot while we waited to go back to camp and catch another animal. Then Hawks would return to Arusha and continue his shooting of scenes that did not involve a catch. This scheduling was haphazard, but generally it worked.

Hawks didn't like anything about our giraffe catch so he re-shot the whole sequence using some of the real actors and some doubles. I think, looking at the production stills, that John Wayne rode in the catcher's seat and dropped the loop on the large animal himself, no small feat—even for the Duke!

Our agreement with the Game Department was that we would not hold any animal longer than three or four minutes after we caught it, and we were true to our word. They watched our operation closely, at least in the beginning. I think it is safe to say they learned from us about more humane methods in the capture and treatment of animals, and they put the knowledge gained to good use in their subsequent capture and moving of animals from over-populated areas to sparsely-populated areas.

Only a few species of animals were exciting or dangerously difficult to catch. Even the cape buffalo, considered the most dangerous of all African animals, wasn't a dramatic capture. In one of our Sunday meetings, Hawks and I came to realize that, though the picture was to be called *Hatari!* which means "danger" in Swahili, there sure as hell wasn't anything very dangerous-appearing in the film we'd exposed so far. True, I'd yet to capture rhino and the Game department was not forthcoming with their blessing. Urgent pleas were made in Dar es Salaam, the capital, and the Game Department finally agreed to their tranquilizing one rhino living in an overpopulated area some miles distant. *They* would move the rhino by flat-bed truck to Willy's animal compound. Since I wanted to have Mount Kilimanjaro in the background, the plan was to later move it to another area where we would be able to photograph the catch.

Hatari! (1962)

I was at Hawks' house in Arusha one Sunday morning when I got a call telling me that the truck hauling the poor beast had arrived at Willy's compound. The animal was lying on its side and was in bad shape from the long trip. It died before it could be unloaded. The Game Department was sorry. So were we.

I thought it a good idea to be as informed and equipped in the area of tranquilization of wild animals as possible. The San Diego Zoo, I learned, was as knowledgeable in this regard as any in America, so I solicited their cooperation, offering to share with their zoologists anything learned by veterinarians in Africa in our employ. (We never had occasion to use either their knowledge, the medicine we took with us, or an African vet.) Anyway, it placed me in contact with a young veterinarian-zoologist who, on my second or third trip to San Diego, I made a date to meet, along with his wife, for supper at the Del Coronado Hotel.

At the appointed hour, an attractive young lady in the cocktail lounge introduced herself to my wife and me, saying her husband would be a little late because one of his "patients" was sick. When he finally showed, he ordered a drink, gulped it down, and promptly ordered another. It was quite plain to see that he was despondent over something. After another drink, he was close to tears, and I presumed to ask what was wrong.

"My animals hate me, that's what's wrong," came the reply. "No matter how nice to them I am or how much I show I love them, they run when they see me coming," and the tears began welling in his eyes.

We sat there helplessly in silence for a few minutes. Until something flashed in my little brain.

"When you treat your sick patients, how do you usually do it?" I queried.

"Depends on what's wrong," he replied, looking at me as he would a child.

"I mean, do you have to use a hypodermic needle on them much of the time?" I asked.

"Of course. They get antibiotics and other medicine just like humans," he replied, rather impatiently.

"There's your answer. Stay out of sight while one of your assistants or your nurses gives them the shots," I stated simply; "they'll love you." It took only a second or two to sink in.

"Damned if I don't think you're absolutely right," he exclaimed.

When we sought permission to go down into the sacred Ngorongoro Crater, permission was eventually granted with the stipulation it

Men at work.

was only for eland and some other clove-hoofed animal in which I was not really interested. Nevertheless we decided to go. While our camp was being moved to a new location, we headquartered our outfit at the Lake Manyara Hotel, which was situated on the edge of a lofty escarpment overlooking the lake. At sunset, huge flights of pink flamingoes numbering in the thousands would take off from the shallow lake in a scene that could only be found in Africa.

The floor of the giant volcanic Ngorongoro Crater is about two thousand feet below the rim, and access was on a dirt road that went down steeply with many switch-backs. We proceeded to explore when we arrived at the bottom and were pleased to find that the crater, about nine miles across, appeared to provide plenty of good running ground for our vehicles. There wasn't much game to be seen from where we parked in the shade of some large trees. We were soon joined by the Ngorongoro game warden, who lived in a comfortable house on the rim of the crater.

He was a pleasant enough English chap who seemed quite interested in our operation and equipment, particularly in the catch truck driven by Willy de Beer, a man rather famous in East Africa. We talked awhile about the great variety of wild game in the crater, and when he mentioned the plentiful rhino, I assumed my "doubting Thomas" posture.

"Don't rhinos make it dangerous for tour vehicles to drive across the crater?" I inquired naively.

"Once in a while one will charge at a car and give them a scare, but they always stop several meters from it," he explained.

Incredulous, I asked, "Several meters? They *always* stop?"

"I never heard of one not stopping, and I certainly would have if it ever happened," he stated simply.

"I'd sure like to see that, sir, if you've got the time to show me," adding, "Not that I don't believe you."

Back came, "Well, I guess I could—"

"Great! You ride in the front seat with Mr. de Beer so you can tell him where to go and I'll hop in back," I said as I led him to the catch truck and opened the door for him.

It really wasn't necessary but I nodded to Joe Brun to get the cameras ready on the camera car in case I called on the radio.

It wasn't long before the truck slowed to a crawl and then stopped. Some distance off stood a large rhino peacefully grazing on the short grass. He gave us a glance and went back to grazing.

"Could we get closer?" I asked.

We were soon within several yards of the beast—whereupon he started after us, quickly closing the gap, and Willy began moving away at just the right speed. The rhino began to chase us in earnest and putting on a sudden burst of speed, he was upon us; I could almost touch his horn. I was on my knees in the bed of the truck, hanging on, when he hit the truck side which had been lined with old tires to protect the animals. On the third try he flipped a tire, which hit me full in the mid-section, though not hard enough to hurt much. Willy sped up the truck and then stopped when we were a good distance from the rhino.

The game warden jumped out of the truck and was most apologetic in explaining the rhino's misbehavior: "I guess we're going to have to give that old fellow a tape measure. I hope you're all right!"

All right? I was ecstatic at the possibilities.

"That old boy wanted to go for a ride in the truck with us," I said, adding, "Rather unsettling on the nerves."

"A nip or two of Scotch up at my place on your way home will fix that," and he elaborated on the invitation. "Drop by on your way home."

"Thanks, but not today. Got a meeting I can't change, but maybe tomorrow," I replied. "That is, if you'll let us come back and maybe photograph a rhino."

"Just as long as you don't try to catch one," he answered in the sweetest ten words I'd heard in weeks.

Once on the rim of the crater where our longer distance radio would work, I talked to our unit manager, Jim Henderling, who was back at the hotel.

"Do whatever you have to, but get a case of Scotch delivered to the game warden's house on the rim of the crater tonight," I begged.

And he did, because when we passed the game warden's house about 10:00 the next morning, there, with only slightly bleary eyes, was the warden, who joined our troupe. No doubt he received our little gift.

He could not know we had been late into the night working out a plan. Willy felt certain that with some luck, he could get a rhino to charge the little "herding" jeep, the vehicle used to urge an animal into position near the "catch" truck. The herding jeep would be driven by the stunt double for Hardy Kruger, Cary Lofton, while Ted White doubled Bruce Cabot in the passenger seat.

This was surely my good luck day because shortly after we had finished lunch and gone back to work, we spotted a very large rhino who wasn't at all happy about our intruding into his privacy and showed

Somebody took this photo while in the "catch" truck. I am on the far left.

Hatari! *(1962)*

Top: A rhino gives chase as stunt doubles Ted White and Cary Lofton hit the accelerator. *Bottom:* As we in the camera car gasp, the beast just misses goring Ted.

it by charging the jeep as if he'd read our minds. On the third try, he hit the jeep, almost tipping it over, and when Ted White, the stunt double for Cabot, grabbed his leg and writhed in pain, I thought for sure the rhino had got him. With the four cameras still rolling, I called on the radio, asking how bad it was. The stunt guys were highly insulted and replied, "Don't you know good acting when you see it?"

We spent the rest of the afternoon making shots that could be used in the sequence: medium long shots of the vehicles in action, the running rhino photographed through the windshields, everything anybody could think of.

I told the game warden to go with the shots we had in the can, as Mr. Hawks would be coming back with John Wayne and the other actors and actresses to complete the sequence. I hoped he'd be as helpful to him as he was to us. This gentleman understood more than I'd given him credit for; he said he hoped it would be soon because with only a little rain, the foliage would turn a different color and wouldn't match what we'd shot. As a result of his warning, we spent the next day making background projection plates just in case.

"We can stop worrying about calling the picture *Danger* in Swahili, Howard, because a rhino damned near did in Ted White this afternoon. And we've got it all on beautiful Eastman Kodak color film with no less than four cameras," I told Hawks on the shortwave radio that evening.

"We put a special rush on it before sending it off to the laboratory in London, so you should see it in four or five days. Meanwhile, I think you'd better drop whatever you are doing and get up here, because the game warden said if it were to rain, everything would turn a different color. I can show you exactly what, where and how it all happened."

My words fell on deaf ears because, though he called me to tell me how great our film was, his unit didn't arrive until nine days later. When they did, and after he had time to exercise his fine writing skills, he created perhaps one of the best openings a movie ever had.

If I've written anything to discredit the Ngorongoro game warden, it wasn't my intention. To this day, I believe that he was a man who, instead of being negative and authoritative, realized that we were spending hundreds of thousands of dollars and showing his beautiful country to millions of possible tourists. We deserved reasonable cooperation, and he was smart enough to know it and acted accordingly. Perhaps the same could be said of his bosses in the game department, because when we were located in our new camp, permission came down allowing us to catch rhino.

We didn't have to travel far before we came upon a large rhino with perfect horns. With their usual expertise, Willy and his people did a fine job of making the catch and the crew was never better at getting everything on film. This time, though, I kept one camera running while the animal was released. I did it in case I had to prove that the animal was in no way harmed but merely "inconvenienced." It didn't occur to me at the time we made the shot that Hawks would use the scene of the voluntary release as the scene of "this rhino got away," which is what the action looked like on film.

Hatari! *(1962)*

The time came when there was no more work for my unit to do, and it was disbanded. Everybody went home and I moved in with Hawks, who had a few more weeks of shooting remaining. Unknown to me, the number of baby elephants in the cast had grown from one to three. Watching Hawks make scenes with them and the humans in the cast made me wonder if he had been staying out too long without a hat under the African sun. When I watched Elsa Martinelli take the elephants into a slimy, muddy, little lake for a bath, I discussed the matter with the cameraman, Russ Harlan.

We were having dinner one night at his house and seated at a beautifully set table when Hawks turned loose his pet mongoose, Squeaky, and I knew Hawks had gone "round the bend." The little creature had a wonderful time turning over wine glasses, trying bits of food, and seeming to enjoy being center stage. We got to talking and Squeaky disappeared. After a few minutes, I felt something foreign inside my trousers as Squeaky worked his way up. Jumping up from the table, I

From left to right: **Michelle Geridon, me and Elsa Martinelli, a brave and delightful actress.**

Hawks, Henry Mancini, and me.

grabbed my leg with both hands in an effort to stop his progress up. I pleaded for help while Hawks, his 10-year-old little boy, and the supper guest, actress Michelle Geridon, sat laughing and enjoying every moment of my dilemma. Never before or after have I seen Hawks enjoy anything as much. Taking pity, Michelle suggested I remove my trousers, which I did, and she shook Squeaky out. Never again in Africa did I sit down for a meal with Hawks without tucking my trousers inside my socks.

We brought several animals back to Hollywood for interior scenes, including the three baby elephants, a cheetah, Hawks' mongoose—Squeaky—and Red Buttons' mongoose, along with one of Willy de Beer's men to care for them. It was a very sad day when Red was told that mongeese were not, under any circumstance, allowed in this country, and had to be destroyed. I think Hawks, too, was quite

Hatari! *(1962)*

disappointed. It seems that many years ago, the Hawaiian Islands were overrun with snakes, and someone got the idea of importing mongeese to eliminate them. They did, all right, but not without over populating and killing almost every living thing on the islands.

Back at Paramount Studios, the interior shooting went along smoothly, except that now the three baby elephants were no longer cute little creatures to be taken for walks around the lot. They especially delighted in chasing people on bicycles.

One evening we were having our usual end-of-the-day cocktail which had been deftly made by Hawks' good friend, actress Charlene Holt. Hawks, seated at his desk, was unusually pensive, and I knew he had something on his mind. In response to my asking, he said he was soon going to have to face a relationship scene between Wayne and Elsa Martinelli, and how can you make any kind of a believable love scene with a beautiful young creature like her and an aging, ex-leading man like Wayne?

"Why not make her as unromantic-appearing as he is?" I offered.

A few days later, he shot the scene with Martinelli in the bathtub with her face covered with cold cream and her hair up in curlers.

When Hawks met Henry Mancini and decided he was the man for the movie, he told him that he hated violin music and he'd prefer that no violins be used in the score.

Thinking it might be fun, Hawks shot a sequence in Africa with ostriches chasing people around the compound. That scene was in the rough cut that was shown to Mancini before he started to work, and film editor Stu Gilmore had done his best to make it work. But Hawks told him to take it out. One day, weeks later Mancini called and asked Hawks to come to the projection room and look at something. Unknown to us, Mancini had written and recorded a score for the ostrich chase that was absolutely delightful and featured a single violin. The ostrich sequence was reprieved.

The big thrill came for me when Hawks and I walked on the recording stage in time to hear the beginning of Henry Mancini's score for *Hatari!*, which in my opinion is evidence of his genius. The main title music was absolutely thrilling. I know Hawks felt the same.

Man's Favorite Sport (1964)

Hatari! was in the post-production phase, I believe, when Howard Hawks bought an original story called "The Girl Who Almost Got Away" and hired John Fenton Murray to do the screenplay. Even without the finished screenplay, Hawks' agent made a deal with Paramount, and I found myself employed without the usual down time between projects.

To illustrate how chance plays such a large role in this business, consider this: Hawks and I were sitting in the dubbing room, correctly identified as a re-recording room, where the dialogue, sound effects, and music tracks are combined onto a single track for marrying onto the edge of the film. A lot of time is consumed while recording engineers and technicians are setting up reels, and Hawks was reading a *Saturday Evening Post* story, which he finished and handed to me.

Man's Favorite Sport (1964)

"This fellow is a pretty good writer. Why don't you see if you can get hold of him? I'd like to talk to him," he said.

Steve McNeil lived in Oregon on the coast, and he and his wife got by on the money he made selling the occasional story to a magazine. He was a well-met, humorous sort who seemed to know the right things to say, because almost overnight he found himself making several times in one week what he made in months writing magazine stories. Here he was in Hollywood with an office and a typewriter at Paramount Studios, writing material to please none other than Howard Hawks!

Here's the irony: When we were in that dubbing room, it was one of the few times I ever saw Hawks without something to read. As an avid reader, he almost always had a pocket-book or some reading material with him, but this time he was reduced to reading an old magazine he found there. And thus began Steve McNeil's Hollywood experience, short-lived as it was.

(Another aside: Hawks did not allow Murray and McNeil to work together. Instead, he'd have them write sequences from ideas that one of the three had come up with. Hawks would stuff pages that each writer had given him into his briefcase and eventually they would be refined and appear as the finished product on the silver screen.)

One day a few weeks into the preparation phase, Hawks went across the street to the executive offices. When he returned, he made a phone call to Jack Gordean, his agent, who, in less than an hour after they first spoke, called him back. When Hawks hung up, he told me we were moving to Universal after lunch. Before the sun had set (and it was wintertime), we were installed in new offices at another studio! I think our names had even been painted on our parking places.

As I recall, Paramount and Hawks didn't agree on the selection of a leading lady, and when Paramount insisted on their choice, Hawks told them he didn't wish to make the picture there. Remember, at this stage of his career, studios were only financing and releasing his pictures. Hawks owned a large percentage of the profits. In addition to his nominal salary, of course.

Universal had many talented people and several of them were known to Hawks from other days and other studios. I liked them all and made many friends there, especially the studio production manager, Jim Pratt. Here was a man who started out as a laborer on the back lot and progressed through many other jobs before he became a big boss. He was a smart and likable Irishman.

Paula Prentiss was set as the leading lady opposite Rock Hudson. Paula was able to pull off the inimitable Hawks comedy scenes in her own special way. Howard somehow got his good friend Edith Head to do the costumes in addition to her regular chores at Paramount. One afternoon, Edith called and asked Hawks to come to her office to look at sketches. He asked me if I'd care to join him and Paula. The sketches looked great, of course, and Paula was pleased. For some reason I can't explain, I thought about a certain hat that the game warden of the Serengetti Plains gave me as a present, a beautifully made Sherlock Holmes sort of headwear. When I mentioned it, Hawks, who had seen it, immediately responded, agreeing that it might look good on Paula. The following day, I turned it over to Edith, who not only had it copied but built a great costume around it. So much for that.

Hawks and I used to lunch at a place just down the street from the main gate, and one noon Rock Hudson asked to join us. He was great company and a fine relief for both of us. It became more or less automatic for Hawks to pick up the check, though on occasion I paid it. After a few times, Rock insisted on paying, only to find he was wearing his costume and his wallet was in his dressing room.

"Remember, tomorrow it's my turn," he promised. Tomorrow and pick-up-the-check-time came, and he told the waitress not to dare give either of us the check, that it was his treat. After this display of goodwill, he reached for his money, but it was not to be found. Overwhelmed with genuine embarrassment as he searched and re-searched his pockets, we delighted in letting him suffer awhile before Hawks finally paid the check.

Before the sun had set, Rock presented us with a hand-drawn gift certificate he had arranged for at the same restaurant. It more than covered our lunches for a week. I wish I had that piece of paper framed and hanging on my wall now. A more likable guy I never met.

One morning, Hawks was shooting on the back lot when my phone rang and the assistant director said that Hawks wanted to see me right away. When I arrived, I could tell from his protruding lower lip that all was not well.

"We're trying to make a picture here, and no sooner do we get a scene going than somebody with a loud-speaker messes up the sound track! Tom said some guy was talking to a bunch of people on an open bus. That better stop or I will," he said meaningfully. Tom Conners, who Hawks liked very much, was the first assistant. He worked on *Hatari!* with us, and he was the same guy who started me directing commercials.

Back in my car and I headed straight to the production office.

Man's Favorite Sport (1964)

"Let me put it this way: If your picture brings in half as much money as those studio tours are projected to earn in a year, Universal will be very happy, Paul," Jim Pratt explained.

This happened not long after Universal had instituted its now-famous tours, and the system had not been refined yet. So we resolved the problem to Hawks' satisfaction with alert flagmen, red lights, and the studio's promise that the tour guides keep quiet when we were on a take. Today, of course, the tours are as popular a tourist attraction as Disneyland, I'm guessing.

Before we started the picture, Hawks showed up one day with a magazine picturing the new Buick Riviera. I had to agree with him that it was a stunning car and probably one that he would be driving in the immediate future. He told the secretary to get our "tie-in" man, Jack, on the phone, and when she did, I heard Hawks tell him that if he received a reasonable discount on a Riviera, the car would be featured in the picture. While Hawks was waiting for Jack to call back with an answer, Edith Head came in with some sketches. Alas, they'd have to wait while Hawks showed her the picture of the car and extolled its virtues. When he was through, of course, she had to have a Riviera exactly like his.

A few days later when the cars were delivered, it fell to me to teach her the nuances of hers, things like where the headlights switch was, how to turn on the wipers, and so forth. A few hours later, I had just arrived home when I had a frantic call from her saying that she heard a loud buzzing noise while she was driving home on the freeway, and something must be terribly wrong with the car! Not knowing what it could possibly be, I called a Buick dealer only to learn that it was a warning signal that sounded when the speed exceeded the limit the driver set on the speedometer. Edith's happened to be set at 60.

Let me observe that Edith Head had more diplomacy in her little finger than Margaret Thatcher, Madelene Albright, and Claire Booth Luce combined. She had to, to clothe some of the egocentric leading ladies she dressed over the years!

There really wasn't a lot for me to do as associate producer, so I used my time working out the bugs on several of the physical gags in the picture. That and directing—and I use the term loosely—the fish sequences, which required a very small crew and a large amount of time and patience. I, who prided myself on directing wild animal-catch scenes, found myself reduced to catching fish! The ups and downs of the business, I suppose.

The Great Race (1965)

I read in both the "trades," the *Hollywood Reporter* and *Daily Variety*, that Blake Edwards was going to make a big movie with the title *The Great Race* at Warners. I didn't know whether it was about the human race or some horse race, but knowing his step-father, the unit manager on the picture, I phoned Jack McEdwards to see if they needed a second unit director. Damned if he didn't call me back, saying that Blake was interested in talking to me. Blake was a man who made good entertainment, had a wonderful sense of humor, and knew his business. I was absolutely delighted to go home with the script, knowing I had the job. I'll never know how much my old chums, Clem Beauchamp and Russ Harlan, the production manager and cameraman, respectively, had to do with it, but they probably helped.

The Great Race *(1965)*

For those who are so unfortunate as to miss seeing the picture, it is about an automobile race around the world, starting in New York and finishing in Paris in the early 1900s. Hence, it involved many locations, both domestic and foreign. I soon discovered that Blake wanted me to accompany Clem and Ferddie Carrere, the exceptionally talented production designer, on a survey trip to Paris and Austria in search of a castle and a palace that fit the story. Germany would have been a more likely place to look, but Tony Curtis, one of the stars, had given the German government reason never to let him out if, per chance, he ever managed to get in. After Blake and Martin Jurow, the producer, got our reports and saw my film, they deemed the trip a success. But about three weeks later, I was told to re-pack, that we were going back to Europe to search France for castles and palaces. As long as we had to end the picture there (because of the Eiffel Tower), it made better sense to find a castle and palace in France.

Tooling through the French countryside in a huge, black Cadillac limo that Warners provided, took a bit of getting used to. The driver was an Egyptian who had been General Eisenhower's driver during the post-war years and was now a man without a country. However, he knew the best eating places in all of France. I'll bet he weighed at least 250 pounds. Had Jack Warner an inkling of what just one of our lunches cost, he might not have survived the shock.

Ferddie Carrere knew something of Mr. Warner's frugality. It seems Jack Warner had a strict rule that no employee, under any circumstance, including a studio fire, was ever to leave their office "without turning out the lights!" One Sunday, early in the evening, Ferddie was working at his drawing board in his upstairs Art Department office, whose windows faced the Warner Avenue street and sidewalk. Naturally, his office lights were lit, and when Warner, who was making the rounds of his studio, looked up and saw the lighted windows, he re-entered the lot and charged to the Art Department to find out the name of the negligent employee who occupied that office. There was Ferddie, hard at work on his own time on a Sunday, slaving away for Warner Bros. Mr. Warner introduced himself and Ferddie showed him the sketches he was working on and offered a drink of Scotch. Before the bottle was finished, they were on a first-name basis!

In *The Great Race*, there is a sequence where the two featured competing cars race across Siberia in winter. Blake wanted to film vast, bleak fields of drifted snow and dispatched me, along with unit manager Jack McEdwards, to Alaska. There are two ways to double a picture's cost:

(a) Shoot it on water or (b) shoot it on snow. If running shots are called for, the costs will escalate. Blake must have been aware of this, but my job was not to reason why, but to do or die. And die we might have, because we were in Anchorage on the Good Friday afternoon the big earthquake struck. Until the light was gone that day, I shot both movie and still pictures of the extensive destruction.

We had planned to fly to Nome the next day, but with the airport runway all wavy and cracked, commercial flights were suspended. We decided to head for home by whatever means we could. It was our good fortune that through a councilman with whom we had become friends, our retreat south happened to be on the governor's plane, which was heading to Seattle. I prayed that no big aftershock would occur before the big bird gained lift-off speed.

Gearhart, Oregon, and the surrounding areas had many of the location elements we needed, featuring a clear-water lake and miles of abandoned railroad track available within a reasonable distance from adequate housing. After getting a very favorable weather forecast for the period the second unit was scheduled to be in Oregon, and a guarantee of perfect, sunshiny weather from the Oregonians who touted the area, we arrived at Gearhart ready to make pictures. I don't think we had an aggregate of 10 hours of shooting weather the two weeks we were there. Between the rain and almost constant overcast, we exposed very little film. Little wonder that the studio ordered us to abandon the Oregon location and return to the studio.

It was explained to me the afternoon I was told that my services were no longer needed that, between Blake's being so far behind schedule and over-budget and my not coming through with any film, Jack Warner decided to eliminate the second unit.

The Great Race is a splendid picture, and I'm only sorry I couldn't have contributed more to the making of it.

Redline 7000 (1965)

Loving cars, speed, and competition as he did, Howard Hawks' yen to make another movie about car racing proved too strong for him to resist. Hawks delighted in telling stories about the making of *The Crowd Roars*, a picture he directed back in the early thirties, and I know he enjoyed coaching me via long-distance telephone when I directed *Thunder in Carolina*. There were devoted fans and car-racing cult people who liked *Redline 7000*, but there were many Hawks fans—like me—who wished he had fought off his urge. Less than halfway through the shooting schedule, Hawks himself realized that this movie wasn't going to be one of his winning efforts.

When I first joined him at Paramount for this movie, he made it clear that "I'm no longer going to pay people like John Wayne million-plus salaries while I do all the work and take all the chances for practically "living expenses." Well, he certainly had a point—though you can hardly call something like $200,000 living expenses!

Paramount, not Hawks, paid all salaries, even if a movie was never released. But, of course, Paramount had to recoup all costs before Hawks' substantial percentage kicked in. That must have been what he meant about salaries he "paid."

"Car racing is pretty much about young people, and there are plenty of good, young, talented people in this town to choose from. And you won't have to pay them a fortune, either," he reasoned. He called out the open door to Joan Waugh, his secretary, "See if Eddie Morse [casting director] can come over."

He got his young people, all right, and he worked long and hard trying to mold them into the characters he envisioned. I think he succeeded with some, like James Caan. With others he didn't.

Hawks more than once told me that audiences were not interested in seeing "nice" women up there on the screen. It was his contention that a girl of questionable virtue is much more interesting to the audience. He had no use for the girl-next-door types. Look at the characters played by Angie Dickenson in *Rio Bravo*, Jennifer O'Neil in *El Dorado*, Marilyn Monroe in *Gentlemen Prefer Blondes*, and Roz Russell in *His Girl Friday*, to name a few. When Hawks took off and lectured on some aspect of his moviemaking, I'd just listen, nod, smile, or make some innocuous comment now and then. But when he got onto his "wicked woman" theory, I had a classic retort—though I never expressed it: "The world is a better place because Richard Zanuck bypassed you for *The Sound of Music*."

No question, Hawks was absolutely right. If you want to read about good or nice women, you don't buy the *National Enquirer* at the grocery store. So it came as a delayed surprise to me as day after day I watched the dailies and, like flowers opening and blooming in the spring sunshine, the characters of the three femmes revealed themselves. Even in the vintage moral code year of 1965, I kept waiting for Hawks to show us the hitherto unseen darker side of at least of one of them dames. While none were exactly convent candidates, we never learned of their lurid past, although one was allegedly willingly deflowered on screen.

I honestly don't know why I was never invited to direct the second unit of *Redline 7000*. I like to think it was because I was busy with *The Great Race* at Warners, but I have a deep down suspicion that Hawks was interested in trying new blood in the form of Bruce Kessler, a young friend of his, an ex-race car driver who had also been the script clerk on *Man's Favorite Sport*. Bruce had made a very good short about Lance Reventlow's new race car. (If your memory needs prodding, Reventlow was the heir to a cosmetics fortune.)

Hawks generously gave people chances to upgrade themselves, whenever he thought they had a chance of succeeding. During the period I knew him, there was Russ Harlan, who went from being a camera operator on previous Hawks pictures to cinematographer on *Red River* and subsequent Hawks movies as well as several other big pictures. Then there was Chris Nyby, a film editor whose first feature directorial credit was, I think, Hawks' *The Thing*. And Hawks certainly boosted me from relative obscurity to a respectable standing in the industry. I won't even try to list the young actors and actresses to whom he gave opportunities and encouragement.

Since no one knew exactly what shots were needed to make the story work, I think Bruce did as creditable a job as anyone could. In hindsight, maybe it would have been better if Hawks had told the action part of the story that he wanted to tell on film, and then have the second unit design and shoot the shots required to make it work. It would have been a lot less costly.

It occurs to me now that what I was helplessly witnessing was the failure of my hero, who I never thought of as fallible when it came to making movies.

Hawks, Charlene, and I went to dinner before the preview showing at a theatre in the beach town of La Jolla. Howard Koch had recently become head of Paramount, and after the preview, we met with him in the lobby of the theatre. It reminded me of the way a family might gather outside the chapel after a funeral service. Koch asked if we could meet him at his house for coffee the next morning, a Sunday, and Hawks agreed.

In his own diplomatic manner, Koch, sipping coffee, made some excellent editing suggestions, but it seemed to me like administering the Heimlich maneuver to a dead man.

Two years later Hawks came up with a big, successful picture for Paramount. This time he wasn't the least bit reluctant to pay the Duke his stipend, or my old friend Robert Mitchum's!

Previews are useful, certainly; but audience reaction is not always a reliable indicator or quality, as Hawks knew full well. He made a movie for Warner Bros. that he thought not only good but very funny, and he was looking forward to the preview. The studio executives all went to dinner together in a private room at a famous restaurant and then drove straight to the theatre. During the showing, there was very little reaction from the audience, certainly nothing like the executives expected from a great Hawks comedy. When the lights came up, they moved into the lobby with the solemn audience. Jack Warner consoled Hawks with comments like, "Don't let it get to you, Howard. You're bound to miss once in awhile."

Only when the group reached the front of the theatre and walked outside beneath the marquee did they learn the news that had subdued the audience. There was a newsboy hawking an *Extra* which had a grim, black headline announcing that America's dearly loved Will Rogers had died in a plane crash in Alaska.

When Hawks' picture was re-previewed a month later, the audience laughed it up as a whopping success.

Lest you think I'm pooh-poohing preview audiences, I'll share another story. In 1934, when I was working at United Artists for Darryl Zanuck's 20th Century Pictures, *Clive of India*, a tremendously bold and expensive movie, was previewed. The cutter, which was what film editors were called in those days, was an ex-boxer (Zanuck was partial to ex-fighters and often gave them jobs), Alan McNeil, and it was up to him to see that the several cans of film, eight or nine picture reels and an equal number of sound reels, got safely from his cutting room to the theatre's projection room. It wasn't until toward the end of the running that McNeil discovered that one whole reel, about ten or eleven minutes of film, was missing, and he knew he was in big trouble with Zanuck who, of course, was furious. The preview cards were sensational and the audience never missed the missing reel.

They took the picture to another sneak preview, this time with the missing reel not missing, but the preview cards were only lukewarm, some saying the picture was too long and draggy. The release prints were made with only small sections of the missing film back in. McNeil was a hero.

A Guide for the Married Man (1967)

I have only to think of Robert Morse giving advice to Walter Matthau on how to cheat on his lovely wife without getting caught, and I get a smile in my heart. Morse and Matthau together spell my kind of fun. So I was glad when 20th Century–Fox, my alma mater, called me to come to the studio to meet the director of the picture, Gene Kelly, and interview for the job of assistant director. Apparently, Doc Merman, the assistant studio production manager, remembered me from *Porgy and Bess*, made when Doc was in the independent field.

Sure, it was a step down from the positions I held on the last few pictures and commercials, but I didn't have any jobs in sight, and the parochial school tuitions and all the other expenses that go with raising a large family went on, whether or not Daddy-Bear worked. As it happened, the job led to a long and happy association with Kelly and Frank McCarthy, the producer.

The way Frank Tarloff constructed the script, there were good parts for just about every popular comedian available at the time, and we used 18 of them in vignettes. For my taste, none of their sketches could top the scenes between Morse and Matthau.

What sort of a guy was Gene Kelly? What was he really like? Was he as nice as he appeared to be? I found him to be pleasant enough, but then, I was at the interview for him to decide if he wanted me for a job that meant working closely with him for several weeks. He struck me as a highly disciplined man who probably worked hard when he worked and played hard when he played. He made me feel good about having to take a cut in my salary to work with him, and I drove home eager to read the script. My assessment was right. Gene Kelly turned out to be genial enough, and generous with that famous smile as long as he thought you were working at your best to make a good picture.

This was not an easy picture for any of us because there were many sets and local locations required. Fortunately, we had a unit manager, Harry Caplan, who knew his business well. The cameraman, Joe McDonald, one of the best 20th Century–Fox had under contract, was aided by a top-notch crew, and he was often ready to shoot before the actors had time to change wardrobe and freshen their make-up. Joe was one very nice guy, too, whose only fault was being a chain smoker. Shortly after finishing the picture, Kelly and I visited him in the hospital just a few days before Joe Camel claimed him, too.

The studio had sold off its back lot as prime real-estate a few years before, and the land was now being developed as Century City. Several of our shooting sites were there. I recall that only a few shops on the huge mall were occupied and the set dresser had to dress storefront windows, some entire stores, and a restaurant. In the scene Art Carney talks on the phone to Lucille Ball, there is a great deal of construction activity visible in the background where workers were building what is now Century Towers and the Century-Plaza Hotel

While preparing, late one afternoon, Gene wanted to check out a location on Rancho Golf Course. Without allowing me time to make any prior arrangements, Gene and I jumped in his car, and after reconnoitering the course, Gene drove through an open maintenance gate and onto a road that seemed to criss-cross the course. By the time we looked,

A Guide for the Married Man *(1967)*

and talked, and retraced our way back to the gate, we found some zealous nitwit had locked it securely with a sturdy chain and padlock. If it hadn't been for the barbed-wire fence surrounding the premises, we wouldn't have been quite so concerned. Spending the cold November night in Gene's convertible had no appeal for either of us. We were two happy fellas when Gene finally found a worker with a key to the padlock who didn't know it was time to punch-out and go home to the wife and kiddies.

Things went along extraordinarily smoothly for wintertime shooting of a picture with so many exterior scenes. Three or four days before Christmas and, coincidentally, the end of our shooting schedule, Gene came to work feeling like anything but his usual "up" self, and I knew something was wrong. He got through the morning, but about 2 P.M. he told me he was going home and readily agreed to let me have somebody drive him. I think his doctor saw him very shortly after he arrived home. He had a high temperature, and the illness was diagnosed as a bad case of the flu.

I wasn't very happy when Frank McCarthy called to tell me that he and the powers-that-be had decided they wanted me to finish the picture in Gene's stead. Frank Tarloff, the writer, would be on the set to support me. There was considerable money involved if the actors, the staff, and the crew had to be "carried" over the holidays.

I would have readily agreed if it had been almost any other director but Gene. He had such a deep devotion to this movie and so delicately handled the material, I had to tell Frank that the only way I would do it was if the studio agreed that Gene could re-take anything I shot that he didn't like. Frank called back with an affirmative and asked me to meet him at Gene's house to get Gene's input on how he wanted the remaining scenes handled. I don't know why the nurse even bothered to lead us to Gene's bedroom, because he was so sick that he showed no signs of knowing we were there.

The slight adjustment in my check for the week didn't compensate me for the phone call I got from the studio general production manager, raising hell with me for printing so many takes on different shots. When we were both young, this guy and I were friends who worked together on several pictures. I couldn't complain, though, because I was still on salary when we went to the preview in San Francisco. Frank McCarthy's doing, I'm sure.

While I was uneasy taking over for Gene, it was hardly the first time he had sacrificed his interests for the good of the studio. When he was a rising young MGM star, he, unlike some in the studio's stable of stars, would do whatever the boss, Louie B. Mayer, asked him to do—and without argument. In the days when the studio was turning out well over a hundred pictures a year, Gene would arrive at his studio dressing room and find a sheet of paper listing the four or five pictures in which he would be acting that day. The paper set the time and place where he was to report for each picture and the dialogue he was expected to memorize, presumably while he was getting into the wardrobe that had been labeled and laid out for each picture.

    I wonder how many millions of theatre tickets he sold for MGM over the many years he was under contract there. Still selling them, no doubt!

El Dorado (1967)

"You don't have to tell me the story, Howard. Just tell me whether I'm inside or outside the jail this time." Thus spoke the Duke in response to Howard Hawks' phone call inviting John Wayne to make another Western with him. Two good friends, they had great respect for each other.

Rio Bravo was such a successful movie that Hawks decided to do an encore. I was invited to come aboard as his associate. Another friend of his, the Old Tucson Street, was engaged along with our orchestra of talented people: Leigh Brackett on screenplay, Carl Anderson on art direction, Edith Head on costumes, John Carter on sound, Earl Olin on props, and Eddie Morse on casting. I should also mention the chef from *The Wild Goose*, Wayne's yacht, because he too was an artist who delighted us with each meal he catered.

We had a problem when we tried to cast a counterpart to Dean Martin for the role of the drunken deputy. Sure, *El Dorado* was what might be called a sequel to *Rio Bravo*, which is why Wayne asked if he, as the sheriff, would be in or out of the jail. It seems to me every actor in or out of town was considered for the drunken deputy part, whether he was a "name" or not.

Let's face it: In 1967 when you thought of an actor to play the part of a drunk, you thought of Robert Mitchum; but when I urged Hawks to at least have Mitchum come in to talk, I thought I'd end the day in the unemployment office. It was only after another week of futile searching that once again I brought up Mitchum's name. This time I told Hawks that the only time Mitchum misbehaved was when he worked with directors who were indecisive and didn't know good from bad.

"The way you work, Howard, you two will get along just fine. I promise. He'll inspire you to make scenes you haven't thought of yet," I over-stated.

The very first shot in which Mitchum appears shows him as a drunk coming out of a bar and crossing the street to the jail. It really didn't require a rehearsal and was lit with Mitchum's stand-in crossing to the jail. When the scene was shot with Mitchum, Hawks printed the first take, obviously pleased as he tossed a nod in my direction.

A few days later, we had just sat down to lunch when Mitchum arrived on the set with an absolutely stunning-looking young thing whom he introduced to Hawks, Wayne, and me as his new drama coach. They joined us for lunch, and it turned out she was a senior at the local college. We thought it would be great fun to have her around, but unfortunately her classes interfered with her new career, short-lived as it was.

Hal Rossen had been a top cameraman at MGM some years before and was the preferred cameraman when it came to photographing MGM's leadingest leading ladies. He was married to one of their stars, but I can't remember which one. The point is, he and his brothers had been close friends with Hawks, and after Hal had been retired for several years, Hawks wanted to jump-start him back into the business. Had Russ Harlan been available, I doubt whether Hal would have gotten the job, because of the somewhat tricky night shooting involved. Rossen was slow and indecisive, frequently changing the lighting on long shots of the streets. It was evident to me that something had to change before we were hopelessly behind schedule and over budget.

Hawks lived across the hall from me at the motel, and we usually had a "daycap" together. (On the night shift, we would work until

Eldorado (1967)

daylight and then sleep most of the day.) Much as I dreaded doing it, I told Hawks what he didn't want to hear about his friend Rossen and warned that something should be done before it was too late. I also reminded him of the penalty clause in his contract with Paramount. After we finished our daycap, he kicked me out of his quarters with the admonition that I had fixed it so he wouldn't sleep a wink all day.

In the late afternoon, he asked me what I thought should be done to speed things up. He even suggested that we get better, more attentive stand-ins.

"I'll talk to Hal nice and gentle, but you have to back me up if he resents my picking on him. I've got some ideas I think are constructive that should appeal to him," I offered.

So we added an excellent background gaffer (chief electrician) and three other electricians who worked on lighting the backgrounds and who were on a different radio frequency than the foreground gaffer and his crew. This made a substantial difference. I believe I convinced Hal that he wasn't working his crew to the pace they were used to and liked, thus putting the onus on them and not so much on himself. All was happiness again.

Well, not quite.

Since I last worked with him, Hawks had acquired a taste for Palamino horses and purchased three of them, real beauties. He "rented them out" for use in the picture and had them brought over to Tucson along with the cast horses. (Cast horses are gentle and dependable for non-equestrians, or horses trained to do certain things, or a horse preferred by an important actor or star such as Jimmy Stewart, who had a particular horse he preferred to ride.) All three Palominos were rather small, and when Hawks asked Wayne to pick the one that suited him best, Wayne, being the respectful, disciplined man he was, reluctantly mounted the largest. I could tell Hawks was pleased at seeing Duke on his beautiful horse. Wayne being a large man, wasn't at all happy about how he must look on the mount. No sooner was Hawks out of earshot than Wayne began bitching to the wranglers, his ire finally coming to rest on me.

"You've got to talk to him. I can't ride something that looks like it belongs on a kiddies' pony track! Hell, I bet I weigh as much as that Palomino. Let Jimmy Caan or some other actor ride it," he told me.

It struck me that the horse was equally indignant with the casting but was more concerned about a swayed back than his image.

Get a tape of *El Dorado* and see what you think. Was the Palamino too small for Wayne?

Even if the race car picture wasn't one of his proudest achievements, Hawks was mighty pleased that through it he made the acquaintance of James Caan, who until then had appeared in only three or four movies. Caan would appeal to young audiences, so important to the success of any movie. I'm sure that the way Hawks developed the character Caan played made him even more appealing: Caan would have a black top-hat and a good story to go with it, the inability to shoot, the blind approach to certain danger, and the orphan syndrome. Everybody was pleased to have Caan aboard, and he held his own in scenes with Wayne and Mitchum.

Toward the end of the location schedule, we were hampered by overcast days more frequently. There were days when we accomplished very little since we had already shot what few cover sets the small sound stage could accommodate. The unit manager, John Coonan, and I talked to the weather people and the forecast wasn't encouraging. Then I was told by a local about how a couple of years ago, the company filming *HUD*, a Paul Newman picture, endured several weeks of steady rain before giving up and going elsewhere. I was determined that wasn't going to happen to us.

Having told Hawks about the lousy weather forecasts and the *HUD* experience, I volunteered my studied opinion,

"Why gamble when we don't have to? Tomorrow is Sunday, and we can be shooting back at the studio Monday morning."

While the look Hawks gave me wasn't exactly withering, I felt he was trying to control his impatience with me.

"What about the scene of Mitchum getting a bath? Don't ask me to move it inside the jail, because it wouldn't be any fun at all unless it's outside, in front of the jail. You ought to know that," he said, trying to close the discussion.

"We'll build the front of the jail and fifty feet on each side. I've already discussed it with Carl and Rosson (the art director and cameraman, respectively) and they're all for it," I continued, reminding myself of a nagging wife.

It wasn't raining, but it sure looked threatening when the charter plane took off from the Tucson Airport. In my little black heart, I prayed that we would be hearing about the great floods that would be ravaging Arizona by the time the plane had reached cruising altitude.

He shot the bathtub scene inside the jail on a set we already had of the jail interior.

Some time later I was having a mid-afternoon nap in my office when the phone buzzed. It was the assistant director, Andy Durkus, calling from the stage.

Eldorado (1967)

"Mr. Hawks wants a guy to take a fall out of the bell tower onto the church floor. Do you know of a stunt man we can get in on a rush-call this late in the day?" he asked. The casting office called my good friend Joe Canutt, who came right over.

Joe Canutt was the stunt-double for Charlton Heston on all his pictures. He was also one of two sons of Yakima Canutt, undoubtedly one of the greats of the stunt world. Joe told me once that he and his brother, Tap, were never anxious to work for their father when he was directing second units because he gave them the most difficult and dangerous stunts to do. He cited *Ben Hur* as an example. I never told Joe, but I thought it was because the more dangerous stunts naturally paid the most money, and Yak wasn't taking any chances on having to support his sons, one way or another!

Later, when I walked over to the sound stage, there was Joe in a Mexican bandit costume. He was wearing a big mustache and talking to Greg Hawks, Howard's 11-year-old son who was brought to the studio every afternoon after school. Howard's life pretty much revolved around Greg, probably because Greg appeared rather late in his life.

"Have you met Mr. Hawks yet?" I asked Joe.

"Not yet," came the reply. I ushered him over to where Hawks was seated in his high leather chair.

"Meet my very good friend, Joe Canutt. He's here to do the fall from the bell-tower," I added as they shook hands.

"Pleased to meet you, Mr. Hawks," Joe said, and paused before adding, "That grandson of yours is sure a good-looking boy. I was just over there talking to him and—"

Hawks interrupted, "That good-looking boy is my *son*, not my grandson!"

"Of course. Sorry, Sir," Joe said as he withdrew.

Had Joe not been the son of Yakima, whom Hawks had known and worked with for many years, I think Howard might have had the bell-tower raised another 50 feet and had Joe land on his head.

Funny Girl (1968)

Everyone I knew who ever met Johnny Veitch liked him. Bright, handsome, always well groomed, impeccably mannered, he rose from location manager on *Rio Bravo* to general production manager of Columbia Pictures.

"If you're not doing anything, I wish you'd come by this afternoon. I've got something you might be interested in," he said one day in 1967.

The "something" turned out to be the job of unit production manager on Columbia's big musical, *Funny Girl*. I didn't find out until later that the job had been held by two different big-time production managers who fell from grace with the producer, Ray Stark. Or maybe they quit. Anyway, the job interested me, and I hoped I would pass muster with Stark and William Wyler, the director.

John Veitch's boss was Ben Hersh, who was soon to vacate the job to Veitch in order to move on to a more important job elsewhere. It was Hersh who took me up to Stark's office and sold me to him, exaggerating wherever he felt the need to.

I found my own way to Wyler's office after Stark "cleared" me. Wyler's very attractive blonde secretary, Mary Jane, greeted and announced me. As long as I knew them, she called her boss "Willie."

Seated behind his completely bare desk was the great William Wyler, the mind behind some of Hollywood's most successful pictures, both financial and artistic. I started to sit down in a chair in front of his desk, but he stopped me, gesturing to an empty chair on his left side.

"Sit here," he said. I did.

"Anybody they pick is fine with me. I do not care for production people, but I guess we have to have them, and as long as you do your job and don't get in my way, you're fine with me. Anything you want to say?"

"Well, yes, sir. Just one thing," I replied.

"What's that?" he said impatiently.

"Where did you make your kill?" I queried, pointing to the bracelet he wore on his right wrist. My question evoked sudden interest as he looked from bracelet to me and back again.

"What are you talking about? I never killed anything, and what's my bracelet got—" he tried to ask but I interrupted him.

"Mr. Wyler, anybody who knows anything about Africa knows that you don't move your elephant-hair bracelet from your left wrist to your right wrist until you've killed your elephant. That's why I asked you where you made your kill. Anybody can wear one on his left wrist," I explained.

He took the bait: "How do you know so much about Africa?"

We spent at least another half-hour talking about East Africa, the places we had been and the hunters we both knew. Going to Africa with his family on photographic safaris had become a favorite vacation of his, and he would be anxious to show me his pictures some time.

I would love to be able to write that he moved the bracelet from his right to his left wrist, but I honestly don't remember, and it is too sacred a memory to be wrong about. I can say with clear conscience that he and I got along rather famously, although I sure gave him a few occasions to be upset with me.

The picture is about the life of Fanny Brice, the very successful Broadway musical comedy star of the 20s. Francis Stark, the wife of producer Ray Stark, who was my big boss on the picture, played Fanny Brice's daughter. Ray Stark is one of the most dynamic people I've ever met and anything but relaxing to be around.

This was going to be a challenge for me.

While we were in the preparation stage, I made several trips to New York, either alone or with some of the staff. It was on one of these trips that I was made aware of how close we came to not making the picture at that time. To get to the lavatory on the plane, I had to pass by a partially enclosed section where, at a large table covered with papers and scripts, sat Mike Frankovich, the head of Columbia Pictures. He glanced up at me as I passed by. I'd met him once during a brief meeting in his office with several other people present. I returned to my seat and began wondering if he recognized me, and if so, what sort of a nitwit I was not to acknowledge him with at least a nod. I took the bold step and moved forward and stood by his table. He looked up and smiled.

"I didn't want to interrupt your working, but I thought I shouldn't just pass by without ... ," I said.

"Going for a meeting with the Board. I'm not sure but we may not make your picture. We're afraid of the war between Israel and Egypt, with Streisand a Jew and Sharif (Omar) an Egyptian," he told me. "It's a tough call," he added.

"Mr. Frankovich, Columbia Pictures doesn't have enough money to buy the kind of publicity for the picture that the war generates. Just hope it keeps up until the picture is ready. Sorry to bother you, Sir," and I returned to my seat, wondering how my unsolicited opinion would sit with him, and where I might be working next.

Barbra Streisand already had a fairly strong hold on New York, what, with her musical outings, the stage play *Funny Girl,* and her albums. Now she was arriving in Hollywood, destined to overwhelm and captivate it, too. Next stop, the world. But I'm jumping ahead.

Stark and Wyler put on an afternoon garden party, the purpose of which I'm not certain, at Stark's beautiful estate. I suppose it was to introduce Barbra to the creme de la creme of the town and to gather the key players and staff together socially before they established the togetherness that goes with making a big picture. It was an extravagant affair guided by the gracious hostessing of Francis Stark, who as I've said, is the daughter of Fanny Brice.

My wife and I happened to be standing near the entrance when John Wayne and Bob Mitchum arrived. I walked over to them, smiling pleasantly.

Funny Girl *(1968)*

"What are *you* doing here?" questioned Wayne, surprised but I think pleased to find me in company other than Howard Hawks.

"I only do cowboy movies when I can't land a nice clean musical with dancing girls," I replied. "And what are *you two* doing at a fancy affair like this?"

Harry Stradling, Sr., was considered among the best cameramen in town, and Stark and Wyler very wisely chose him to photograph Barbra and the movie—one and the same because *she* was the movie. With his Bronx accent peppered with a sort of twang here and there, he left no doubt about where he hailed from. As for the movie business, he told me that when he was a little tyke, his folks owned a nickelodeon in Yonkers, New York. I'd say he really grew up in the business.

The time came to make tests on how best to photograph Barbra, and we had top make-up men and hair stylists to work with her and Harry to produce the best results. After an hour or so of trying different approaches to photographing Barbra, we heard her telling Harry that he didn't have her key-light placed properly, and she went on to make some other suggestions. I began mentally going down the list of other cameramen who might be available. Not to worry. Harry took it all in good grace and had the key-light moved wherever she suggested, each time shooting a little film and keeping notes. These tests went on for two or three days until the team, including Barbra, achieved the wonderful results seen in this, her first movie.

On another trip to New York, this time with Ray Stark, we found the perfect locations for the "Don't Rain on My Parade" number. Almost all of them were in New Jersey. With the Jersey Central Railroad in bankruptcy and inactive, I found it quite easy to make a deal for use of the ornate, turn-of-the-century train station where Pullman cars were already on the tracks. Cleaning and applying a little paint was about all that Gene Callahan, the production designer wanted or needed to do.

Gene Callahan was a Southerner who made his mark in New York. A talented designer but an articulate whiner, he wasn't very easy to get along with. Columbia had a fine accounting system that made it fairly easy to control costs, and because Gene's tastes leaned toward the costliest, he and I were constantly crossing swords. When I would see costs for a set edging toward the amount estimated and budgeted, I would refuse to okay his purchase orders, telling him to find less expensive materials. I'm sure he appealed to Ray Stark many times, but Stark always backed me. I loved Callahan's work, though, and didn't hesitate to tell him so. Consequently, there were times when we found ourselves being civil to each other.

Another problem with Gene was his habit of leaving our sets partially built or dressed until the very last minute before shooting was to start. When we were deep into our schedule and working at the studio, Gene proudly showed Wyler and the key people the set for the nursery scene in the Long Island mansion. This was the evening before we were to shoot the scene, and it was the only set that was ready. For some reason, Wyler didn't like anything about it and told Gene as much. Gene pleaded and whined until Wyler shrugged his shoulders and went home.

Early the next morning I was having breakfast with my wife.

"What did Mr. Wyler want last night?" she asked.

"What are you talking about?" I said.

"When he called you around midnight. What was so important that it couldn't wait until morning?" she persisted.

"You must have been dreaming, Sweetie. I never talked to him or anybody else." I was growing impatient.

"You certainly did! I answered the phone and handed it to you and you must have talked for ten minutes. All you said was "Yes, Willie, I'll take care of it, Willie. Okay, Willie. Don't worry, Willie," she mimicked me.

It finally dawned on me that I *had* received a phone call but I was so deep in sleep it didn't register in my memory. I began to realize the seriousness of the situation and its possible consequences. Desperation suddenly overcame me.

"What did he *want*! What did he *say*! Don't you remember *anything*!"

Her reply: "You're going to wake the children. Why don't you just get in your car and go to work? Maybe it'll come to you driving to work."

Callahan frequently visited his outside suppliers before coming to the studio, so on a hunch I phoned him and asked that he come to the studio first, just in case. Willie showed up about 8:15, took one look at the nursery set and turned to me: "I thought you were going to see that this was changed. It's the same as when I saw it last night," he said.

"Was *that* what your call was about?" I felt my face glowing red.

"I should have told you, Willie. Never try to talk to me on the phone when I've been asleep without first telling me to stand on my feet, because I never remember anything, even if I say I do. I'm sorry, but—"

Funny Girl (1968)

"This set is not right and I don't want to shoot it. Do something to change it," he directed to Callahan. Then to the assistant director, "I'll be in my office or the cutting room when there's something to look at."

We were shooting on a new nursery set about 2:00 that afternoon. I was still employed.

That wasn't the most embarrassing moment I suffered while working on the picture; here is one incident I'll never live down. For the "Parade" number, the choreographer-director of musical numbers, Herb Ross, wanted a helicopter shot of a period train moving through the countryside. The camera pulls from a close-up through the train window of Barbara singing her heart out to a high, long shot of the train steaming through the countryside. This meant we had to find approximately a mile long stretch of tracks without trees or telephone poles on one side of the roadbed. Getting the old train with a steam locomotive was easy, and borrowing the New Jersey governor's helicopter enabled us to survey unused or infrequently used Jersey Central tracks. Their supervisor provided us with a map of the tracks we could use, and I gave it to the helicopter pilot. Within a couple of hours, we found a perfect location, which the pilot carefully marked on the map.

Preparation for the shot required a lot of organizing on the part of the assistant directors, Ray Gosnell and Jack Roe. Communications links were required, including playback on both the train and the camera helicopter. There were extras dressed in period costumes, meals, and so forth, and so on. I don't recall why, but these efficient assistant directors had me in the rear Pullman car to give cues.

On the survey trip, I had noticed a large number of buildings in the area we had selected, but they were in the opposite direction from our camera angle, so I didn't give them any thought. I assumed they were just part of New Jersey industry.

Herb Ross was in the helicopter with cameraman Nelson Tyler and the photo pilot, Davey Jones. Herb, the perfectionist, called for several takes, and between the train frequently having to take on water and the chopper frequently having to take on fuel, we became familiar to the neighborhood and attracted attention. After four or five runs, Joe Brady, a man who was assigned to me by the governor, told me there were some officials waiting at the road crossing who wanted to talk to whoever was in charge.

"Tell them I can't come right now, but I will when we get the shot," I told him as the cue was given to make another run.

With the run completed, but still no print, the train backed up to the start point for another take. Brady approached me again.

"You'd better go talk to them, Paul. The one guy is getting pretty mad!" Joe said.

"Okay, if you say so," I agreed and got in the car with him.

As we approached the road crossing the track, I saw at least five Army officers in full uniform standing together, three command cars, and two military police jeeps.

"Are you in charge of this outfit?" demanded the two star General.

"Well, yes, sir. May I ask what's wrong?" I countered.

"Do you know where you and your outfit are at this moment?" he snapped.

"Not exactly, sir. We have this map the railroad gave us, and—"

"You are trespassing on U.S. Government property. This happens to be the Picitinny Arsenal, the most important and restricted piece of government real estate in the whole country." He gave a warning look at the other officers. "If Washington ever heard about this ..."

The general wanted to confiscate our film. On the promise that I'd have a print of every foot of film we exposed in his office by nine the next day for him to see, he relented and told us to get the hell out of there—now. I pleaded for just one more take, throwing in that my job was at stake, and I had a whole bunch of children to feed. Damned if he didn't say okay. It turned out that Ross already had three prints.

Since I am in a contrite mode and ready to express humility, here is another slight mistake in my judgment of human nature that still makes me blush when I remember it. In the Jersey Central Station was a restaurant that wasn't doing much business because there was no regular traffic and only a few employees remained. We would have to buy the restaurant out for the period we would be shooting there, which was only reasonable. This wasn't a large restaurant, but it had a good size kitchen area. The man who leased the restaurant from Jersey Central despondently told me the story of how his once-thriving business was now almost extinct. With the demise of the station he was nearly broke.

Unfortunately, I got the idea that it would be a kindly and noble thing if I would have him cater our company lunches. After I explained our requirements—the type of menu he would have to serve and the amount of help he would need to provide quick service, and all the other things that go with movie crew catering—I told him to think it over and that I would talk to him the next day.

"Nothing to it," he replied, adding, "I'll just have to rent a few more tables and chairs."

The first day came, and it was a total debacle: There was not enough help to serve what little and unappetizing food they had, and for those who dared to special order, preparation took forever. Among the company, I was a ruined man and beyond redemption, while the man I was trying to help turned out to be a disgrace to the human race. But the word got around to the cast and crew that I was only trying to help this man out by giving him our business, and they somehow found it in their hearts to forgive me. Needless to say, I had an experienced movie catering company feeding us for the remainder of our stay there.

Shortly before we began, the Jersey City riots erupted, and Jersey City was deemed a good place to avoid if possible. Unfortunately (or, as it turned out, fortunately), the location manager and I were unable to come up with suitable housing in Jersey City. So we put most of the staff, some cast, the dancers and the crew in a 12-story, first-class motel located right across the street from the cruise-ship piers in Manhattan. The motel had a fine dining room and even a swimming pool on the roof.

With the riots came the threat of our cars and buses running into trouble getting from the western end of the Holland Tunnel to the Jersey Central Station and then back again. I was also concerned about protection for our people from the rioters while we were working in the railroad station. Even at that time, most states had a film commission that existed mainly to urge the movie companies to make pictures in their states. The commissions provided incentives and assistance where possible. New Jersey had such a commission, and when I told the governor's office my concerns, they sent me a man named Joe Brady, who was more than up to the task. Later, I used him on other projects. At all times when we were working, state troopers patrolled the station and railyards, albeit in an inconspicuous manner. I put Brady up in our motel, where he was readily available to help us if necessary.

The other problem was getting everybody to and from work during peak traffic hours without having to go through Holland Tunnel, where accidents frequently occurred. Watching the excursion boats circle Manhattan Island gave me the idea of transporting our people by boat. We wound up using the Circle Blue Line, which was able to pick us up and deposit us at a dock right across the street from our motel and was cheaper than a bus and cars. The weather was very hot and everybody loved this idea. They could get coffee and Danish pastries on the boat on the way to work, a cold drink on the way home. I was back in their good graces again.

Willie Wyler had a reputation for being a perfectionist. He often demanded take after take of a scene when only he could tell the difference between the second and thirty-second takes. Throw him together with a super-perfectionist named Barbra Streisand, and the consumption of raw stock movie film soared. "I should buy stock in Eastman-Kodak Company," I thought when I watched them working together the first few days. Soon I began to realize that I was watching two artists who were tuned to the same frequency and milking each other's talents for all they could.

Back at the studio and shortly after we started shooting, I received a call from Mrs. Wyler, who asked me if we could provide a car and driver to chauffeur Willie between their Malibu summer place and the studio. But it couldn't be just a regular driver because Willie insisted on only one speed, fast! If the guy didn't go fast enough, she warned, Willie would simply drive himself to and from work in his big right-hand-drive Rolls-Royce, his mind totally on the day's work ahead and not on his driving at high speeds over the canyon roads. I knew just the man, Joe Sawyer, a fellow I'd used on several pictures and an ex–race car driver. After a day or two, he exchanged the studio sedan for a front-wheel-drive Olds Tornado, a fast and better handling car, because Willie wanted to go faster. They even put a lamp and a desk in the back so Willie could make notes on the way to work. Cheap insurance, I thought.

Whenever I would go to the set where the company was shooting, I would come away feeling slightly depressed. The more I got to know Willie Wyler, the more I liked him. Wyler was a chain smoker, so it wasn't very pleasant to see him seated in his chair, often right below the camera lens. His hand would be cupped behind his ear because of his deafness, and a glass of water would be close by in case his emphysema brought on a coughing fit he couldn't control, and spoiled a take. I remember once during the shooting of the picture when Willie, Bob Swink (our film editor), and I tried to quit smoking, but none of us lasted beyond three or four days. Willie lasted not even a whole day. The tobacco companies were doing their part to control the population!

We tried to hold the expensive sets and Columbia stages until at least the musical numbers were cut together in rough form. Herb Ross not only choreographed (assisted by his wife, the great ballet artist, Nora Kaye) but also directed the musical numbers. I'm guessing that

Funny Girl *(1968)*

Wyler had approval of what went into the picture, though, because one afternoon, Ray Stark asked me to attend a showing of the "Pregnant Bride" number in its rough assembly. Present were Swink, Stark, Wyler, Ross, Kaye, Gene Callahan (the production designer), and, I think, Barbra. Maybe the screenwriter, Isobel Lenhart, too.

When it was over, it was obvious that Wyler was quite unhappy with the piece of film, saying that it was much too long. There ensued quite a discussion, pro and con, and when there was a lull, Ray Stark asked me what I thought. "Why not let the preview audiences decide?" I replied. Then added, "A hell of a lot of money was spent on this number and I think it deserves to be seen." I have a feeling that Stark was glad he solicited my opinion, because not much else was said and we disbursed. I looked at a tape of the movie not too long ago and I think the number is about as it was shot.

It had taken me a long time and cost considerable money to get rid of an agent I had for all too long. When Paul Kohner offered to represent me, it was quite a different story. He was a highly respected, brilliant gentleman who was welcome in any office in Hollywood. He was a successful producer who had turned agent, instead of vice versa. He really cared about the well-being of his clients. As my stint with *Funny Girl* was coming to an end, I began getting calls from 20th Century–Fox about coming aboard as Gene Kelly's assistant on their super-musical *Hello, Dolly!* Much as I enjoyed working with Gene, I wasn't very excited about the offer and really had in mind finding something I might either direct or produce for myself. Besides, I was tired and had become interested in sailing and wanted some time off. When Kohner had the money up to the maximum he felt they would pay, which was considerable for 1968, I accepted the job graciously but reluctantly.

Hello, Dolly! (1969)

I think I was the first refugee from *Funny Girl* to get to 20th Century–Fox Studio for *Hello, Dolly!* and the people at Fox were waiting with questions concerning Barbra, of course. I was followed later by *Funny Girl* cameraman Harry Stradling, sound mixer Jack Solomon, and Irene Sharaff, the wonderful costume designer. There was a time when Sharaff frightened me, but over the course of the two pictures we had worked on together before *Dolly*, I lost my fear, and by 1969 I actually liked her and even brought her drinking water from Manhattan. Both the art and the set dressing departments at Fox were busy designing and furnishing Barbra's dressing room trailer in the motif of the Gay 90s. They seemed determined to out-do Columbia Studios' lavish accommodations for Barbra. The sound department was designing a

Hello, Dolly! (1969)

quadraphonic playback system for her to sing to, and the accounting department was hiring additional accounts payable people to dispense the millions *Hello, Dolly* was destined to cost.

The studio went all out in every department, assigning their best people and resources to the production. The New York Streets sets were absolutely amazing, complete with horse-drawn street cars and an elevated train with a steam locomotive. Construction was under the supervision of the production designer, John DeCuir, who did an outstanding job, and the art directors, Jack Martin Smith and Herman Blumenthal. It was great fun just to watch the sets grow day by day. As they neared completion, the temptation to make the sets better was a little too much for producer Ernest Lehman, and the production office found itself okaying substantial amounts for new buildings and other improvements.

A soft-spoken gentleman if I ever met one, Lehman also adapted the highly successful Broadway musical to the screen, sort of his specialty, his best known adaptation being *The Graduate*, I suppose.

From left to right: Jack Martin Smith, art department head; me; Gene Kelly; Doc Merman, studio production manager; and production designer John DeCuir, a very talented man.

When I see the "Parade" number on the videotape, I am still secretly embarrassed that the way the opening shot was designed by Kelly and Stradling (the cinematographer), there is only one moment for the expensive and impressive elevated train to enter and cross the top of the screen. The train had to start precisely on my radio cue and move at a consistent speed. For reasons I never understood, the engineer never got the timing right, and consequently the train never was shown to best advantage, much to Mr. Lehman's disappointment (which, great as it was, could not have been overwhelming as my own).

Unfortunately, Kelly's and Lehman's personalities didn't exactly mesh, due mostly, I believe, to Lehman's failure to relax and leave the making of the picture in the capable hands of Kelly and the staff and crew. Anybody would be hard-pressed to find better people for the job: Michael Kidd, the choreographer; Roger Edens on music; the wonderful supporting cast, including Michael Crawford; the unbeatable unit production manager, Chico Day; Stradling; and, of course, me.

I guess the first time the ill-feeling manifested itself was the night we were on the New York Street and Lehman showed up with a video camera and proceeded independently to shoot the musical number we were shooting! This was the first video camera I or anybody else on the set had ever seen. Lehman went to his office to run the tape and then came back to the set and made comments about the scene. Kelly thought it all "highly unprofessional," and he told Lehman as much and a little bit more.

A question I am often asked is, "What does a producer do?" I don't remember a single picture I have worked on where one producer performed the same functions as another. Some producers have a great influence on the product from inception to release. For example, as the producer on an Elvis Presley movie at Paramount, Hal Wallace, a very strong and successful producer of many big pictures, wouldn't allow Mike Curtiz to move a light fixture without his okay. Other producers find and acquire the rights to a story, get financing, and make a release deal with a producing organization such as a studio. They also sign the main cast and hire the director. Another might arrange the financing or put up the capital money himself just to see his name on the screen and say he is the producer of record. Unlike most other jobs in the industry, no specific iron-clad duties go with the title.

I saw a movie recently which benefited, according to the screen credits, from the vast expertise of *five* producers: an executive producer and three associate producers. The writer-director, actually one of

Hello, Dolly! *(1969)*

Who better? Gene Kelly teaching Michael Crawford a dance step as I watch.

today's better ones, had the temerity to credit himself as the producer-director. I forgot to check if any of his helpers had his last name, or the star's last name, or had the same name as the then-head of Paramount. It can be a good job to give one's brother-in-law.

When the New York Street set and Barbra's dressing room were complete, we started shooting. Barbra is one of the fastest learners I ever saw, and picking up routines Michael Kidd would first create using a dance-in for Barbra was child's play for her. The same technique was used when Barbra made *Funny Girl* and Herb Ross created the dance routines by using a dance-in.

Gene Kelly totally immersed himself in the job and took me with him. And I enjoyed every minute of it, difficult as it often was. When we would break for lunch, someone would phone Lois McClelland, Gene's very special secretary, and up to his office we'd hop, lighting on every third step, to the third floor where Lois would have Bullshots (bouillon and vodka) chilled and waiting for us. Then came the inevitable bologna sandwich on white bread, a little mayo, and mustard. I mean *every* day! Once in a while, Lois would pick up something like coleslaw or potato salad to go with the monotonous sandwich, but not often. When we were working in Garrison's Landing, New York, where Vandergelder's Yonkers set was built, Gene had an office behind one of the storefronts that served as a refuge. He and I went there for our midday refreshment and, you guessed it, those damned bologna sandwiches. Occasionally, if I had missed breakfast, I'd have the caterer set aside something more substantial for me.

It was during some of those lunch breaks as well as during the car trips looking for locations that Gene would occasionally talk about some of his earlier experiences. Like when he was a kid growing up and he had to do his share of the household chores along with his brother, Fred, and his sister. Fred was already a professional dancer and was teaching both Gene and his sister to dance. When their mother would make them set the dining room table, they would make up dance routines as they placed each item. Another time, he told me about some of his experiences while he was enlisted in the Navy and how it took a lot of fast talking to avoid having to fight hicks who wanted to brag that they beat up Gene Kelly. There was one jerk he couldn't avoid when he was in a San Diego bar with a couple of friends, and when he went to the men's room, this gorilla followed him in and locked the door behind them. It was all or nothing, and Kelly got lucky with the first punch. Somehow, the story reminds me of *From Here to Eternity*. Gene didn't stay an enlisted man very long once the Navy wised up to his potential as a public relations officer.

Traveling with Gene and looking for locations was invariably a challenge. Our old friend producer Frank McCarthy was preparing to do a movie that was titled *Tom Swift and His Airship,* and Gene and I were assigned to it. (Remember the Tom Swift books? They preceded the Hardy Boys books). The studio went so far as to order two specially built airships from a firm in Wichita, Kansas. The picture promised to be important and expensive, with several unique locations required. This meant a lot of traveling was required in the search for locations. On one occasion we went to New Jersey, where I had my friend Joe Brady, the governor's aide, pre-scout a few sites. When he was ready for us, back we flew, Kelly, a production designer by the name of Gene Allen, and myself. We drove all through beautiful up-state New Jersey, evaluating the possible locations. The first night, we found ourselves in a picturesque little town amid rolling hills. There was an old church with a tall, white steeple, and a small two-story motel where we got rooms on the top floor for the night. After settling in and washing up, we met in my room for a planning session. Gene seemed somewhat awed by the place, and he told us that this was the first time he had ever stayed in a motel. He also told me he once was an altar boy.

A few minutes later, he heard a noise from outside and walked over to the window. Looking down, he saw a kid shooting baskets in the schoolyard across the street. Gene headed for the door.

"Carry on without me," he said gleefully. "I can't resist the sound of a bouncing ball."

I wonder if that kid ever knew who the guy was who shot baskets with him.

I never made flight reservations without first telling Gene all the possible flights we could take and letting him pick the one he wanted. I don't think we ever actually took the flight he had selected; instead, as our departure time neared, Gene would get the urge to catch an earlier flight, sometimes on another airline. And the race would be on, running from the car to the ticket counter with our luggage, then running to get aboard the plane before they closed the loading ramp.

Once on a flight to or from New York, we were on the same plane as Lucille Ball, a good friend of Gene's. I changed seats with her so they could be together. Later, he told me how when she used a restroom on a plane, she would clean it thoroughly—so it could never be said that she left it a mess.

Oh, yes! the *Tom Swift and His Airship* movie was canceled because of the projected cost.

We were shooting *Funny Girl* when I asked Marty Erlichman, Barbra's manager from the very beginning of her career, what we could possibly do to get her to be ready at the appointed time, when everyone else was ready. Could we change our working times? Could we have a car pick her up at her house? Could we give her wake-up phone calls? Erlichman just smiled and said, "Paul, when she was just getting going and starting to get a name, I was able to arrange an interview and pictures with the *Life* magazine people. Even then, she kept them waiting."

It took a lot of teeth-gnashing on my part and quite a while before Barbra sat me down and told me the way it was:

"I can't come out of my dressing-room and onto the set until I am ready. I mean committed! I don't know if you or anybody else understands that, but that's the way it is!" she explained, and I found myself seeing the light and also the futility of my frustration. However she chose to conduct her career, she sure as hell must have done more things right than wrong.

I thought back to the scene of the tardy Marilyn Monroe with the studio production manager at 20th Century–Fox, played out in the rehearsal hall years before. The mills of the gods grind slowly, but they grind exceedingly fine.

One morning, quite early, the studio phone operator found me, wherever I was, and gave me a message to call Barbra at the number the operator also relayed to me.

"Can you come and get us? Our car broke down on the way to the studio and we need a ride," explained Barbra, and gave me an address in Beverly Hills. She made it sound like a hilarious adventure. When I arrived at the given address, out came Barbra, her faithful maid, her hair dresser, and the lady of the house with whom Barbra had become chummy during an unexpected, brief interlude in her busy life.

When we were shooting *Hello, Dolly!* at Garrison's Landing, New York, Ray Stark arranged a night showing of *Funny Girl* at the Columbia Pictures office in Manhattan for Barbra, Harry Stradling, and me. He even arranged a limo for us. I thought it was a very nice thing for him to do, and I know Harry appreciated it, too.

The tag (finale) of *Dolly* was shot at the United States Military Academy at West Point, which overlooks the Hudson River. There was a sizable crowd of onlookers that was well managed by the police. All in all, it was a very busy day for me and my assistants because the operation was so spread out. To escape the activity on the set for a few minutes when everything was almost ready, I chose to walk the block or so to the dressing-room trailers to get Barbra and Walter Matthau. When Barbra and I started walking to the set, Walter joined us. We hadn't gone very far when a lady approached and asked Barbra for her autograph, which Barbra obligingly gave her. The lady thanked her and then turned to Walter.

"May I have yours, too?" she asked.

"Certainly, my dear lady," he said, taking the extended pen and paper.

"What is your name?" he asked, intending to give the personal touch.

"Gladys," she said, and while he was writing, she added, "And what is yours, sir?"

Death, where is thy sting!

Matthau and Barbra were just getting over their infamous, much publicized battle that, had it not been for the masterful intervention of

Hello, Dolly! *(1969)* 201

Gene Kelly, could well have made the movie frightfully more expensive than it was. This new episode cost the studio for the loss of a whole afternoon's work while wounded feelings were soothed.

When I went to Barbra's dressing-room, I could see that she was not going to be able to work any more, and Gene and I, in concert with Chico Day, decided to dismiss the company for the day.

I found Walter sitting on a bench by the river, so I sat down beside him and then told him there would be no more shooting that day. He finally spoke:

"I guess I cost the company some money."

"A lot," I responded.

"How much?" he asked.

"Maybe forty-five thousand," I returned. "Chico, the unit manager, will figure it out down to the penny. Wanta give him a check for it?"

In answer to my question, he slowly turned his gaze away from the Hudson River to me and then back to the river.

In going through some old photographs, there's one of me handing my glasses to Gene. Apparently, we had the same vision problems, and now I'm wondering if the reason he wanted me on his movies was so he didn't have to carry his own glasses but could use mine when he had to read something.

The real reason I worked on Gene Kelly's last three movies: He could use my glasses to read with and didn't have to carry his own!

The Cheyenne Social Club (1970)

When your daily job for 18 months exposes you to wonderful music, people blessed with extraordinary talents, beautiful ladies wearing glamorous clothes, and you also get to go home for dinner every night, there is little else to be desired, one might think. Unless one has experienced the charms and delights of the Old West as it was, or might have been, when it was struggling to become all grown up.

Just being in remote areas of Arizona, New Mexico, Montana, Colorado, Old Mexico, Utah, and, yes, even parts of California, made me feel good. It still does. So I welcomed the call from Gene Kelly inviting me to join him in helping make *The Cheyenne Social Club,* which

The Cheyenne Social Club *(1970)*

was to star James Stewart, Henry Fonda, and Shirley Jones. It was to be made for National General Productions, Inc., who had many theatres but were fairly new at making their own product.

Gene suggested that I be the production manager in addition to being the assistant director. My agent, Paul Kohner, negotiated on that basis quite successfully. After reading James Lee Barrett's script, I felt the picture would be uncomplicated, and I was also free to hire whatever help I needed, so I felt comfortable handling both jobs.

Like the chicken and the egg conundrum, the order of things was mysterious: I'm guessing National General bought Barrett's script, then signed Barrett's friend Jimmy Stewart to star. Jimmy Stewart, in turn, got Henry Fonda to co-star, Gene Kelly to direct and produce, and Stewart's cameraman, Bill Clothier, to photograph. The latter gentleman and I became good friends, and he shot Howard Hawks' next (and last) picture. In any case, I was glad to be among the chosen, because it turned out to be one of the most pleasant assignments I ever had.

Gene Kelly hired to direct a western? You might think that would have made a good headline in *Variety*. But unlike the case when Otto Preminger was hired to direct *The River of No Return*, by the time we started shooting *The Cheyenne Social Club*, Gene had studied and he knew almost as much about the Old West as Louis Lamour. Well, maybe that's over-stating things a little, but he became well informed. He frequently asked questions and he listened carefully to the answers. And *Cheyenne* was a comedy. And about the making of comedies, Gene knew a great deal.

The production designer, Gene Allen, had earned a reputation doing many of George Cukor's movies. Together, we looked at the few Western street sets available, and I think we both wished this picture had a new and special look, something that hadn't been seen over and over, such as the Old Tucson Street set in Arizona.

Our wish came true. I was somehow introduced to a gentleman by the name of J. W. Eaves who owned a large ranch outside of Santa Fe, New Mexico. He had made his money in trucking and, along with some friends, in building a horse racing track. He was now semi-retired and living in a beautiful home on the ranch.

I well remember the morning he met me for breakfast at my hotel in Santa Fe to set up our agreement to build a Western street that Gene Allen would design. It would be built on Eaves' ranch on a site Allen selected for the best light. It would be mainly financed by Eaves, with

National General Productions picking up a balance which would be about what we would have to spend to rent an existing Western street.

We then convinced ourselves and Eaves that the Western street set would be more valuable if there was a railroad running into and through our bustling town-to-be. While I don't recall how it came about, we ended up with about one-third of a mile of track, a steam locomotive, and three or four cars. Naturally, I had our contract stipulate that the set could not be photographed for commercial purposes until well after our movie had been released. When that period was over, the Santa Fe Western Street set became a popular rental for other movies, including one I produced a few years later.

While the supporting cast and crew were housed in Santa Fe, Gene Kelly, Jimmy Stewart, Henry Fonda, and I stayed at a marvelous guest ranch, Rancho Encantada. Shirley Jones stayed there, too, during the few days she was required on location.

Rancho Encantada was a great place to be at the end of the day. There was all the privacy one could ask for, comfortable quarters and good food. I dwelt in one half of a single-story, Southwest-style building that had a large room and bath on each side. Gene occupied the other half. The rooms were tastefully decorated with colorful Indian artifacts and original paintings, and were connected by a long porch, where we discussed the picture, sipped after-dinner refreshments, and, when they occurred, watched the lightning storms as we looked out toward Los Alamos across the valley below. Gene's wife and two little kids and my wife with our two smallest children came to visit while we were there. Those were times to remember.

Betty Eagan, who owned and ran the ranch along with her two teenage children, was a great hostess, and even took us on a cookout at a nearby lake. We had so much fun at the lake that a few weekends later we had Gene's motor home–office brought in from the location to the ranch where Gene loaded it up with steaks and all the other essentials for a two-family cookout. I was the designated driver but knew little or nothing about the machine. Our wives and kids got along famously, and after a wonderful afternoon of fishing and eating and just goofing off, we headed down a long, hot and dusty road (we didn't know how to use the air-conditioner), Gene leading us in singing old songs.

Other times to remember were when we dined in the private outdoor dining area that was set aside for Stewart, Fonda, Kelly, and me. I listened to those two old friends Stewart and Fonda talk about their early beginnings in New York—the ups-and-downs, the apartment they shared together before Hollywood beckoned them, and the model airplane they were building together when Stewart got "the call" and left Fonda and the unfinished plane behind. I thoroughly appreciated how privileged I was to be in the company of three of our national treasures. My Mom would have loved just hearing about it.

The executives of National General were very pleased with the film they saw, and two of them came up to the location to tell us as much. When I told them that we were running about $140,000 over budget but thought we would pick up some time at the studio, they smiled and told me not to worry myself about it. These were words I thought I would never hear in my long career.

Jimmy Stewart had a horse that he rode in every Western for many years. While he didn't own the horse, the stable that did kept it just for him, I believe. It was an excellent "picture" horse, smart, dependable, and a fine-looking animal, and Stewart loved it. If you cast him in your Western, you cast the horse. I think that horse may even have been in his contract. Anyway, when the cast horses from Hollywood arrived on location, I think it fell to Buddy Van Horn, Stewart's very capable stunt double, to tell Jimmy that the old horse was ailing but was getting the best possible care. This came as a blow to Stewart, and he often visited the horse before it had to be put down. One of the reasons Stewart accepted this picture was because of his deep grief over the death of his beloved son in Vietnam, one of his wife, Gloria's twin sons, both adopted by Stewart.

James Lee Barrett was a fine writer, adept at dealing with the early West at its comic best. The premise of the story: Stewart, a plain, ordinary cowhand, inherits a large sum of money and a completely equipped and very successful business—a bordello—from his deceased brother. He has to travel a thousand miles to Cheyenne to claim it. This wouldn't be so bad if it weren't for his side-kick of ten years, Henry Fonda, who rides alongside him and stops talking nothings only when he sleeps.

A few years ago, an article appeared in the *Smithsonian* magazine extolling the talents of Gene Kelly but failing to mention his qualifications and accomplishments as a director. This prompted a letter from me to the editor correcting the oversight. It was published and read by Gene, who phoned to thank me.

Rio Lobo (1970)

When I was working on *Funny Girl* at Columbia, I got an offer to join a new company, Cinema Center Films. At the time it seemed like a pretty good idea, even though it meant taking a desk-type job. One of the reasons they wanted me was they thought I might be able to lure some proven directors into making movies for them. I was also to act as general production manager. The proposition sounded good, but there were more drawbacks than possible advantages.

Cinema Center Films didn't stay in business very long as it turned out, but they lasted long enough for Howard Hawks to deliver a John Wayne Western, *Rio Lobo*, to them. I assumed my customary position as associate producer on the new picture.

Hawks told me the first order of business was to find a Civil War era steam train and period railway station, a location with railroad tracks that ran through a forest of big trees, and hilly terrain. Of course, we must have complete control. Some assignment!

There had been just enough train mishaps and subsequent lawsuits in the United States to make it futile even to think of making the picture in this country, so together with unit manager Bob Besche, we headed for Mexico, the land where the expression *no problem* originated. Some friends of mine were working on a movie there and thought I might find the railroad locations a short distance from Cuernavaca.

Seated in the executive office of the big boss of Mexican National Railways, I explained my mission to him and a couple of his people and asked for their help. They went into a rather lengthy discussion in Spanish. I thought they were discussing whether or not to cooperate, but when they got out big maps I knew it was only a matter of where.

"We'll need one of your people who understands English and has the authority and know-how to get things done. Somebody who knows all about railroading to work with our people and me," I explained. "I'll put him on our payroll."

The boss went into a huddle with his people, and they seemed to arrive at a decision. One person left the office to make a phone call.

"We've got the perfect man for you. He's recently retired and needs something to do. Knows more about railroads than anybody. We call him 'Penicillino,'" the boss said.

I bit: "Why do you call him 'Penicillino?'"

"Because he can fix anything," he laughingly explained.

So, at the designated hour the next morning in the downtown railroad yards, we boarded a little motorized handcar with Penicillino and two helpers. From there we putt-putted our way some thirty miles through beautiful mountains almost all the way to Cuernavaca. Regular trains used the line twice a day and we would have to clear the tracks for them, but everything else was so favorable that I readily agreed to the site. Through our new-found railroad friends, we located the period freight train. We found the period depot only a few miles outside of Cuernavaca. Success on the first try!

Hawks had not yet found a male actor to co-star with John Wayne, and while I was in Mexico, I had the idea that a foreign star might be worth considering. I mentioned the idea to Hawks on the phone, and as usual, he said we might as well explore the possibility.

One of the hottest Latin stars in the Spanish-speaking world at the time, I was told, was Jorge Rivero. I had our Mexican casting director check Rivero's availability for the date we intended to begin shooting, and I was told he would be available and would do anything to appear in a Howard Hawks-John Wayne movie. I interviewed him and found him to be a great-looking young man, too humble for a movie star, I thought. I also found his English much in need of improvement. I felt he was somebody to keep in mind if we didn't find a more likely actor to play the part of a young, rebellious, soldier–train robber.

We found all the other locations required, and I asked Hawks to come and see them for himself. With him came Bill Clothier, the cinematographer, and Bob Smith, the art director. I waited for them in Cuernavaca.

Remembering my camera needed a new battery, I decided to walk to a downtown camera store. I had gone only a few yards when I was joined by a pleasant, young Mexican who asked if he could walk along with me, as he needed to practice his English. He, in turn, would show me the way to the camera store. With a smile, I thanked him and told him I knew where it was, but he was welcome to join me if he wished. Along the way, we came upon a formally dressed young couple and their wedding party just entering a church. I decided I'd like to follow them inside for a few minutes, which rather irked my walking companion, but in he came anyway. After a brief visit, we went on our way to the camera store where, before I entered, he extended his hand and announced that I owed him $10 for showing me to the store.

I quickly agreed to the amount and, in turn, held out my hand and demanded $5 from him. He looked at me angrily and asked me what for.

"What for? I don't give English lessons for nothing: I charge fifteen dollars a lesson, so hand over the five dollars you owe me," I demanded. He was still swearing at me in both Spanish and English as I entered the store.

Hawks had set Yakima Canutt to direct the second unit, which pleased me because I knew I was out of my league filming a stunt-action scene using ropes strung between trees to stop a downhill runaway train. The scene required a much more experienced man than I to pull this off safely.

Our casting director, Hoyt Bowers, and I saw and interviewed every English-speaking actor, and a few actresses, in Mexico. We were trying to fill the bit parts and smaller parts there. I think there was a

Rio Lobo *(1970)*

rule that American companies had to try to cast their pictures in Mexico before the government would issue work permits to actors and actresses from a foreign country. This rule didn't apply to stars and feature players, of course.

Hawks still had not cast the co-star. Hoyt liked Jorge Rivero when he met him, so we arranged for Rivero to go to Hollywood to meet Hawks. Hawks also liked Rivero, in spite of the actor's poor English. Meanwhile, Jorge had been taking English lessons on a crash basis in case he got the part. They didn't help much, if any.

Shortly before photography was to begin in Mexico, a circulatory problem (diagnosed as "not a heart attack") befell me, and I was out of action for about three weeks while my doctor worked his magic on me. When I returned to work, I had to take it easy for awhile. Hawks had his physical problems, too. He somehow hurt his lower leg on the train flat-car. This was a painful injury on the shinbone from which I don't think he ever fully recovered, although he was able to keep working. The hotel swimming pool was kept at a warm temperature as therapy to help his leg. When we got to Tucson, we rented a house that had a lap pool for him to swim in. I stayed at the house much of the time and helped whenever I could. As long as I knew Hawks, he derived great pleasure from leisurely swimming laps in a pool every day possible. This habit may have played a part in his decision to live in Palm Springs in both winter and summer for most of each year.

There was a tall, dark-haired girl to whom Hawks gave a small part in the picture. She took her acting quite seriously, and I think he had high hopes for her. But when it came time to do her big scene with John Wayne, it took hours to get a printable performance out of her. I think he ran out of tricks to bring out what acting ability she had.

One evening, which happened to be the night of the Academy Awards, he invited her to supper at the house. (We had hired a housekeeper who was also an excellent cook.) The guest, Sherry, arrived shortly before the awards began, and we all took seats in front of the TV. As best I can remember, she guessed no less than 90 percent of the individual awards correctly while Hawks and I got maybe 20 percent right. She was truly a student of the industry. Hawks called her "Storky," but her real name was Sherry Lansing. She is, and has been for a long while, chairwoman of the Board of Paramount Pictures, Inc., and has been more than somewhat responsible for several of their very successful movies.

That was the night that Wayne won the Academy Award for *True Grit*. Hawks had shot around him (did scenes that didn't involve him) so he could fly to L.A., collect his award, and return the following day to Tucson.

Luster Bayless, our men's costumer (and a fine one) got the idea that it would be fun if, when Wayne's car arrived from the airport, he saw us all wearing black eye patches (as he wore in *True Grit*). Then Chuck Roberson, Wayne's stunt double, thought Wayne's horse should also be wearing one. We photographed the whole thing, and it appeared on the national news that evening.

This was the last movie Howard Hawks was to make, although he had one or two stories simmering on the back burners right up to the time he died.

It was also the last time I would ever see him. We spoke on the phone about various matters, mostly deals he was thinking of getting involved in, shooting conditions in Jakarta, and other matters I can't recall now.

Late in December 1977, I was in Atlanta working on some pick-up scenes that Delbert Mann was doing for a movie-of-the-week. We'd finished for the day and I was dressing for supper and watching the news when I learned that Howard Hawks had died from a fall he'd taken a few weeks before.

Losing a great friend is never easy.

The Migrants (1974)

After a short stint as producer of a forgettable movie (1971's *Culpepper Cattle Company*) that ate up too much of my time and energy to merit rehashing here, I was being offered the job of unit manager on a TV movie that Lorimar didn't intend to make. Because CBS wanted Lorimar to try again after failing two years before, Lorimar called me in to have a go at it. Eddie Denault, vice president and general production manager, didn't have much hope of ever getting the story made because it concerned the dismal, hopeless plight of migrant laborers in their struggle to stay alive, and the growers and packers didn't want their dirty little secrets of exploitation revealed. But what CBS wants, CBS gets.

So together with the very capable director Tom Gries, we approached the problem. I listened to what he and another unit manager did two years before, and I decided I would take a different approach. In particular, there had been a certain meeting in a Florida motel with some angry growers who had a gun, an episode I wasn't too keen on repeating.

Much of the script involved itinerant workers picking various kinds of field crops, so it became a matter of my talking to the Department of Agriculture and finding out which states would have crops ready for picking at the time we hoped to be shooting. The best possibilities were on the East Coast, so Tom and I drove through three states before we arrived in New Jersey (whose license plates proclaimed it the "Garden State"). We had made an appointment to meet Joe Brady, the governor's liaison to the motion picture industry, and an old acquaintance who had worked with me on other pictures. The crops were great, and Joe promised us the state and all its resources and made a few phone calls to high places. When I told Brady what happened to Tom in Florida two years prior, he assured me there would be two state troopers with us at all times. It began to look like CBS was going to get their movie.

This movie, whether for theatres or television, was one that I really wanted to see made. With a very good story by Tennessee Williams, a teleplay by Lanford Wilson, and the director of *Will Penny* (maybe one of the best Westerns I ever saw), it *had* to be good, and I had to have my name on it. Tom also produced the picture, and when he became as convinced as I was that we could make it in New Jersey, he phoned the go-ahead to the network and the studio.

Migratory workers and their plight was by no means a subject of ordinary conversation, particularly with strangers, and the subject matter of our movie didn't arise during the short time Tom and I were there on the preliminary survey trip. It certainly did, though, when a few key people and I returned to make arrangements for housing, food, transportation, construction, and the countless other things that make a company function. I was calling on a grower near Vineland, New Jersey, when I happened to open my briefcase and there, big as life, was a script with the name "The Migrants" on the cover. If the grower noticed, he didn't say anything. But I lost no time in calling the studio and giving them the new name of our picture, "The Barlows," with firm instruction that any and all reference to the previous title be obliterated: "We are making a story about a family named Barlow and their experiences as they travel from place to place." We had new covers and flysheets the next day.

The Migrants *(1974)*

Other than a small motel with five or six rooms, the only possible accommodation in Vineland or the vicinity was a Holiday Inn. It was one of the better ones, probably because a very nice and efficient temporary manager had been sent from headquarters as a trouble-shooter to get it up to par. A real Southern gentleman, he was most accommodating and the epitome of courtesy except for the day our cast, including the leading lady, Cloris Leachman, arrived from New York and California.

It was almost noon when I arrived back at the hotel from a meeting and was met in the lobby by two or three anxious faces.

"You'd better go see the manager—now! He's waiting for you in his office, and he's mad, Paul," they explained.

"What's all this about? Everything was just fine when I left here a little while ago. What happened?" I asked, and wished I hadn't.

"Cloris Leachman went into the restaurant to get a sandwich and didn't like the air-conditioning blowing down from the ceiling on her, and each time she asked them to turn it down, they didn't do anything about it. They said they have to keep it cool for the business lunch crowd they have every day," volunteered one of my informers.

Another picked it up, "So she was standing up on the table trying to stuff paper napkins into the vent when they sent for the hotel manager."

The other tidings-bearer resumed: "And when he tried to calm her down and get her off the table, she called him some not-very-nice names."

To which the other added, "And everybody has to be out of the hotel by four o'clock. Everybody."

"Does Tom Gries know?" I asked.

"I'm sure he does," came the reply.

The manager was seated behind his desk when I entered his private office. He was obviously still genuinely offended and damned mad.

"I've been waiting for you. I want you people out of my hotel by four o'clock, and no later—all of you. I've never been so embarrassed in my life. That woman—I want every last one out of here, under*stand*?" He was now on his feet.

"Hold it, Wally. Hold it right there," I moved a step toward him. "Say that line again, just the way you said it," I commanded.

"What line? What are you talking about?" he said.

"The line you just said: 'I want every last one out of here, understand'—the way you said it the first time," I instructed; "Go on, say it!"

And he did, but I wasn't satisfied with the reading. "Madder. Like the first time you said it when I came in," I ordered.

And he did, and while I'd like to have gotten more emotion out of him, something told me to cool it.

"I imagine you do quite a bit of public speaking in your line of work, don't you, Wally?" I asked.

"A fair amount. I do considerably more back in Atlanta, though. I'm an ex-vice president of the Rotary and the past president of ... Why?" he asked.

"Do you think you'd be comfortable in front of a camera? This movie is going out over the air to millions of people. It's a television special first, and then it will go in theatres all over the world and—"

He cut me off. "Hell, Paul, nothing like that would bother me," he assured me.

"We're having an awful time casting the part of the overseer, Wally," I explained and continued; "It's not a very big part, but it's a damned important one, and we just haven't found the right man. I know you're pretty tied up here at the hotel, but if we promise not to keep you waiting, and we send a car when we're ready for you, could you possibly get away?" I asked, trying to contain myself. "Oh, I'm not asking you to do this for nothing, Wally. It pays three hundred a day, whether you're there two minutes or two hours. Can we shake on it?" I hoped my hand wasn't shaking when I extended it.

Wally is very much in the movie, and I was extremely pleased that I was able to persuade Ms. Leachman, who happens to be a very fine actress, to apologize to the manager-overseer. As for my casting Tom Gries' actors for him—what were the choices?

We finished the picture on time and within budget, all on location, and moved on to whatever the future held for each of us—Sissy Spacek to the stardom that was inevitable, Ron Howard to forgo acting to become an important director of good movies, and Ed Lauter and Cindy Williams to fill many commanding roles in both feature movies and television. Tom Gries died not long after making this picture, but not before seeing that I received associate producer screen credit.

Looking back, I think we might have done some pretty good things together had he lived.

Comes a Horseman (1978)

I finished reading the script just before the plane began its descent into Colorado Springs on this summer Sunday afternoon. It was another Western, which was just fine with me, but I was darned if I could see why they told me I'd be tied up on the picture for so long. The script simply did not read like a very tough picture to make, even with a high-powered cast. I would soon find out.

Only two days before, I had answered a call from a production executive in Canyon City, Colorado, where a company had been shooting for about a week on *Comes a Horseman*. I'd never heard of the man, but he represented Chartoff-Winkler Productions, people who made good pictures, so I listened. It seems that the first assistant director and the director were having difficulty working together, and they wanted me to replace the assistant. They had checked on me, and I came highly recommended. "Just name your price, but come right away," he said.

After speaking to the unhappy first assistant, a superb professional, to make certain that it was his choice to leave, I agreed to give it a try.

I found it would be very hard not to like the director, Alan Pakula, a genial man I certainly felt comfortable with on our first meeting. He suggested I spend the first day just going with his driver to all the locations that had been selected but had yet to be shot, to see what I thought about them. I privately thought this was an odd idea. After I had seen everything, we, along with cinematographer (Gordon Willis) would have supper together.

Later, when asked what I thought, I told him I liked them all except the location they planned for the big cattle stampede. It was in a valley with high wooded hills on each side and at the beginning of a rather steep slope. The idea was for the cattle to come running out of the woods, driven by unseen wranglers with noise makers who stop once they get the cattle running so they don't get photographed. There is supposed to be only Jane Fonda and James Caan to finally turn and stop the cattle.

"Cattle don't like to run any distance downhill. They will be walking or even grazing once they are away from the noise—I'd say less than a hundred yards. Then they will head for the woods up on the hillsides, and the wranglers will be half a day getting them rounded up again. It's not a good place for a stampede," I explained.

"But we're shooting it day-for-night (with filters to make it look like moonlight) and Gordon wants to show as little sky as possible, so we need the hills on each side," explained Alan.

"Then, if I were you, I'd change it to day-for-day and find a level location. Otherwise, we'll be forever shooting it, and still never get a shot of the whole herd running," I advised, and went on enjoying my supper.

We shot the stampede at the location they had selected and it took just three days short of forever. What I didn't tell them was that I'd worked on shooting three previous stampedes.

Gordon Willis was and is an artist. Confirm it by looking at some of the scenes in this picture. Whistler himself, even with his mother looking over his shoulder, couldn't have painted such beautiful landscapes. But when I was told Willis' contract called for him to be able to fire any member of the crew who didn't perform to his liking, I almost gagged. Don't get me wrong: I really liked the man. Riding from the

Comes a Horseman *(1978)*

motel to the locations and back again took about four hours each day, and Alan, Hannah (the script supervisor), Gordon, and I got a pretty good fix on one another. I can only blame management for allowing Alan and Gordon the excessive time they took to shoot this movie. Had I been in charge, I probably would have been the guy being replaced!

From the moment I came on the job, I could see that Jimmy Caan wasn't his usual, light-hearted self. Something was bothering him. He wasn't very friendly with Pakula, Jane Fonda, or anybody except the stunt doubles. We had done two Hawks pictures together, but that was over 10 years before, when he wasn't a big star. Still, we got along just fine. The upsetting thing was he was chronically late on the set.

Jane Fonda must have inherited her discipline from her father, because she was always ready when called. Her then-husband, Tom Hayden (now an ex–state senator), together with her two little children, were with her on location much of the time. That must have brought her a certain amount of pleasure.

Beginning with the day she met me, I don't think she liked me, and I can't say I blame her. On the Sunday I arrived in Canyon City, I was in the transportation dispatcher's office talking to him (a man I'd worked with before) when a good looking girl came in to return some keys. She had borrowed a car to drive into Colorado Springs. After exchanging some small talk with her, the dispatcher introduced me.

"Oh, this is Paul, Jane. He's the new first assistant. He just arrived," he explained.

"Helmick. Paul Helmick. And yours?" I asked.

I blundered. I never had been told who was in the cast nor had I ever seen one of her movies. I honestly thought she was a girlfriend of the dispatcher and quite a pretty one, too.

She looked me square in the eye. "Fonda. Jane Fonda." And she was gone. And I was off to a hell of a start with the leading lady.

Behind the motel in which we stayed were several condominiums that were occupied by the actors, Pakula, and the staff and crew whose families accompanied them. James Caan and his brother, who was also screen-credited as the associate producer, also lived in one. One evening, after a day in which Caan was very late on the set, I decided to go over and talk to him, hoping to find out if there was something I could do to make him more cooperative. My trip was in vain because after some polite but brief conversation, I was shown out the door. Period.

Well, not quite. A day or two later, I was summoned to Fonda's dressing-room trailer, where she and Jason Robards accused me of conspiring with James Caan against the director, Alan Pakula. Somebody had told her that they saw me entering and leaving Caan's condo. How or why I kept my cool puzzles me to this day, but I did as I patiently explained the purpose of the visit. They would have done well to have first talked to Pakula because he and I had developed a wonderful working relationship. Now my interest in finishing this assignment became very real.

But, then, Miss Fonda had another reason to dislike me. When I came on the picture, one of the "picture cars" (a vehicle used in a movie) was an old 1928 or '29 Model A Ford truck driven by Miss Fonda and prominent in many scenes. When I asked, I was told by the transportation captain that not only had they no double for this rare vehicle, they had no spare parts—not even an extra wheel. I told him to start getting back-up parts from wherever he had to for things most likely to break down. When he told me that Miss Fonda liked to take her children for Sunday drives on those rough country roads, I could hardly believe it. Most politely, I told her we would get her another old car for the Sunday outings, as it was too risky to use the Ford except in the picture. Of course, I was well aware that she could quite easily have arranged for me to have supper at home in California that evening, but she didn't.

We came to a point one weekend where we had nothing to shoot Monday except a scene for which the location had yet to be found. What was required was a not-too-steep hillside overlooking a wide valley. We needed a fairly flat clearing where a rider (Richard Farnsworth) would be thrown by his horse. The horse would be spooked by some explosions which the camera must see down on the floor of the valley.

Not having anything to do Sunday afternoon, I got a four-wheel-drive vehicle and, together with the second assistant directors, set out to look for a place to work. Lacking any road, it was slow going through some hilly woods but we finally came upon a perfect spot. Logistically, the only practical way to use this location was to take the equipment up by pack mules with the staff and crew hiking up and the cast riding up on their horses. By the time we got back to the motel, it was too late in the day to take Pakula and Gordon Willis to see the place. I described it as best I could, not underplaying the difficulty of getting and working there. I answered all their questions but left it on a don't-do-me-any-favors basis. Pakula agreed we should go for it, and the second assistants and I set about organizing the trek. Monday morning, when

Pakula and Willis, two very game New Yorkers, got up to the spot for a look, one of them immediately named the place "Cardiac Hill." More than one crew member skipped going down in the valley for lunch, and I wasn't very popular with those who did. I got pulled up Cardiac Hill by holding onto a pack mule's tail after watching one of the wranglers do it.

Onwards and upwards!

Chilly Scenes of Winter (1982)

United Artists Studio was formed by two actors and one actress, all big stars, who were tired of being hired and who wanted to boss instead of being bossed. There was more to it than that, but let it suffice to move my story along. (Yes, I know that D. W. Griffith was also a partner.)

Two young New York actors and one actress, then, all of little or no renown, felt that motion picture producers had overlooked their acting talents all too long and decided to do something about it. They, somewhat like Douglas Fairbanks, Charlie Chaplin, and Mary Pickford, formed their own production company, calling it Triple Play Productions. They optioned a book by Ann Beattie called *Chilly Scenes of*

Chilly Scenes of Winter *(1982)*

Winter. Then they got a New York director, Joan Micklin Silver, to write the screenplay and direct the picture and easily persuaded a leading man, John Heard, to star. Then they came out to Hollywood and talked first with 20th Century–Fox and, when that fell apart, convinced United Artists to finance and release the picture. Oh, and they made sure there were acting parts in it for each of them. Then they had the good fortune to hire me as production manager.

The Triple players were Griffin Dunne (son of author Dominick Dunne, prominent in the O. J. Simpson trial), Mark Metcalf, and Amy Robinson. This was the first picture they produced. They had little or no experience and were smart enough to listen and learn. The director of photography, Bobby Byrne, and his crew worked with such ease and harmony that the meeting of East and West was a joy.

As was my job from beginning to end.

This could never be called a difficult picture for me or anyone else. Well, maybe it was for Mark Metcalf, one of the producers who also acted a rather brief but pivotal part. It seemed the director wasn't pleased to have him in the part and showed little patience with his scenes. Or at least I think Mark thought so.

I was very disappointed that United Artists didn't release the movie as these young people designed it. United Artists took over the editing, changed the ending, chose the music composer, and hence, the score, and even released it with the inane title *Head Over Heels*, which I thought might be more fitting for a 1935 Warner Bros. musical. At least they later had the good sense to recall the picture and re-release it with the original title, the original ending, and a good music score. It was moderately successful as an art house release, not including the video rentals which nowadays provide a significant part of the profits for almost any movie.

As things turned out, it was the last theatrical feature picture I was to have any part of, although I kept active in television production for a few more years until it was time to retire and pursue other interests. Such as, you ask?

Such as accounting for my life and finally recounting many of the times I had, some of the people I met, and a few of the things that happened while I plied my trade in a wonderful industry.

And Now a Word

One night on Olivera Street, a palm reader held my 18-year-old hand in hers and, looking me squarely in the eye, told me that I must make a big change in my life. However sweet it was at the time—what, with a promising future, a fairly nice car, clothes, money in my pockets—I must trust her, forsake everything, and go into the *air conditioning business*. I would be a tremendous early success if only I would obey the sign.

Certainly, there were air-cooled and heated vehicles and environments back in 1938, but air-conditioning as we know it had not come of age. So, you might say, the lady was perfectly safe in advising this occupation for almost any young man.

When I look at the great, tall buildings in every climate of the world, none of them with a window that can be opened, I go slack-jawed at the immensity of the problem of keeping people alive and comfortable inside.

Thus was I ill-equipped to face the rigors of surviving and maintaining a reputation in the movie business when there was always this little voice telling me to abandon ship and the make-believe world for, like Coca-Cola, the real thing. Especially when things went awry.

Here is a list of some of my favorite movies: *Music Man, One Flew Over the Cuckoo's Nest, Bridge On the River Kwai, My Darling Clementine, Lawrence of Arabia, Singin' in the Rain, Mrs. Miniver, Rose Marie, From Here to Eternity, Elmer Gantry,* and *Nobody's Fool.*

I had absolutely nothing to do with any of them except to enjoy watching them. But when I look over this amazing list and the list of the ones *I did* work on, I'm very proud and pleased to have spent my working life in this business and to have left the condition of the air to others.

The condition of man's spirit counts for something, too.

Annotated Filmography

The Pied Piper (20th Century–Fox, 1942) Director Irving Pichel. Monty Woolley, Anne Baxter, Otto Preminger, Roddy McDowall.
  I was impressed. Pichal was what a good director should be: bright, slow to anger. Good baptism for me. Second assistant director.

How Green Was My Valley (20th Century–Fox, 1942) Director John Ford. Walter Pidgeon, Maureen O'Hara, Donald Crisp.
  My second experience with the unforgettable John Ford. We were to remain friends for many years, although I never worked with him again. Second assistant director.

Ten Gentlemen from West Point (20th Century–Fox, 1942) Director Henry Hathaway. George Montgomery, Maureen O'Hara, Laird Cregar.

What a good director shouldn't be: miserable, easy to hate. I think Hathaway studied meanness under Preminger. Second assistant director.

Thunder Birds (20th Century–Fox, 1942) Director William Wellman. Gene Tierney, Preston Foster, John Sutton.

All about training pilots for the Army Air Corps. Little did I think I would soon become one. Second assistant director.

Rings on Her Fingers (20th Century–Fox, 1942) Director Rouben Mamoulian. Henry Fonda, Gene Tierney, John Carradine.

On December 7, we were shooting on Catalina Island when we were told to be on the 2:00 steamer with all our equipment. We were at war with the Japanese, who had just bombed Pearl Harbor. Second assistant director.

Dark Corner (20th Century–Fox, 1946) Director Henry Hathaway. Lucille Ball, Clifton Webb, William Bendix.

Lucy, playing a dramatic part, was much in love with Desi and showed it when he visited her on the set. Hathaway was miserable as ever but reasonably nice to me. Second assistant director.

Nightmare Alley (20th Century–Fox, 1947) Director Edmund Goulding. Tyrone Power, Joan Blondell, Coleen Grey.

Why doesn't somebody remake this story? Or have they? Having lunch with Goulding and Tom Dudley, the first assistant, was a frequent treat, with the meals prepared by Goulding's Hungarian cook. Being English, Goulding called everyone "Chum." He'd write songs on the set, some of which were actually published. Second assistant director.

Captain from Castile (20th Century–Fox, 1947) Director Henry King. Tyrone Power, Jean Peters, Cesar Romero.

A tough assignment but worth it for the many lasting friends I made. I loved Mexico, where much of the picture was shot. Second assistant director.

Roadhouse (20th Century–Fox, 1948) Director Jean Negulesco. Richard Widmark, Ida Lupino, Cornel Wilde.

Nothing for me to remember about this picture except that it paid the bills. 2nd assistant director.

Fury at Furnace Creek (20th Century–Fox, 1948) Director Bruce Humberstone. Victor Mature, Coleen Grey.

The Italian Stallion on horseback. Mature was deathly afraid of horses, but played a U.S. cavalry officer. Second assistant director.

The Fan (20th Century–Fox, 1949) Director Otto Preminger. Jeanne Crain, Madaline Carroll, George Sanders.

My first encounter with Obnoxious Otto but certainly not my last. Undoubtedly the most charming host of his end-of-picture party one could hope for. Mr. Jekyll and Hyde himself! Second assistant director.

Come to the Stable (20th Century–Fox, 1949) Director Henry Koster. Loretta Young, Celeste Holm, Elsa Lanchester, Regis Toomey.

We used Henry Fonda's farm-style Brentwood house, which I promised myself to buy after I "had arrived." It burned down in the Brentwood fire. A few Fonda children occasionally looked on, but I don't remember which ones. Second assistant director.

I Was a Mail War Bride (20th Century–Fox, 1949) Director Howard Hawks. Cary Grant, Ann Sheridan.

The beginning of a long, beautiful, and lucrative relationship. Hawks was the man who made things happen for me in the years to come. Second assistant director.

Broken Arrow (20th Century–Fox, 1950) Director Delmer Daves. Jeff Chandler, James Stewart, Debra Paget.

We must have shot in beautiful Sedona, Arizona, for at least a week before somebody at the studio discovered that Debra Paget's eyes were blue and Indian maidens' eyes are not. Contact lenses were the answer, uncomfortable as they were in those early days. Second assistant director.

A Ticket to Tomahawk (20th Century–Fox, 1950) Director Richard Sale. Dan Dailey, Anne Baxter, Rory Calhoun, Walter Brennan.

Oh, a newcomer named Marilyn Monroe played one of the prostitutes. Should have been a better picture than it was for all the hard work on everybody's part. Second assistant director.

Two Flags West (20th Century–Fox, 1950) Director Robert Wise. Joseph Cotton, Linda Darnell, Cornel Wilde.

Nothing much to remember about this movie except maybe the pleasure of working with Bob Wise, always the considerate gentleman. Second assistant director.

Love Nest (20th Century–Fox, 1951) Director Joseph M. Newman. June Haver, Bill Lundigan, Jack Paar, Marilyn Monroe.

An easy and pleasant assignment for a change, allowing me dinner at home with my family almost every night. I was quite surprised to see that Marilyn could actually act, sort of. Second assistant director.

Fixed Bayonets (20th Century–Fox, 1951) Director Sam Fuller. Richard Basehart, Gene Evans.

My first outing as an official first assistant director, and it's the Korean War in the winter as fought quite convincingly on Stage 8. First assistant director.

Kangaroo (20th Century–Fox, 1952) Director Lewis Milestone. Peter Lawford, Maureen O'Hara, Richard Boone.

If I had to go on a distant location again, I was glad it was Australia, where I had spent three months flying during the war. The first assistant director was a nice enough guy but seldom around, so I was doing his job as well. I came home tired and glad to have this one behind me. Second assistant director's pay for doing both jobs.

Monkey Business (20th Century–Fox, 1952) Director Howard Hawks. Cary Grant, Ginger Rogers, Marilyn Monroe, Charles Coburn.

Hawks to the rescue! Once I caught on to the way he works, it became a pleasure to go to work in the morning. First assistant director.

The Ransom of Red Chief (20th Century–Fox, 1952) Director Howard Hawks. Fred Allen, Oscar Levant, Lee Acker.

Hawks was a damned good writer, but this O. Henry classic wasn't his bag. Good for a few laughs on the set, but not so good in theatres. First assistant director.

Destination Gobi (20th Century–Fox, 1953) Director Robert Wise. Richard Widmark, Don Taylor.

The only consolation for being back in the position of second assistant director was getting to work with Bob Wise again. Shot somewhere in Nevada, as I recall. Second assistant director.

Gentlemen Prefer Blondes (20th Century–Fox, 1953) Director Howard Hawks. Marilyn Monroe, Jane Russell, Charles Coburn, Elliot Reid.

Hawks' first and only musical, and, loving music like he did, he had a good time for himself—that is, when he wasn't giving acting lessons to Marilyn. First assistant director.

River of No Return (20th Century–Fox, 1953) Director Otto Preminger. Marilyn Monroe, Robert Mitchum.

From the very beginning to the bitter end, this was quite the most incredible movie experience I have ever had. Best thing that ever happened to me, looking back on it now. First assistant director.

How to Marry a Millionaire (20th Century–Fox, 1953) Director Jean Negulesco. Betty Grable, Marilyn Monroe, Lauren Bacall.

This was to be my final stint at this studio for a few years. I felt a debt of gratitude for all the years they put up with me so I was well-trained to go out into the other world. Second assistant director.

Land of the Pharaohs (Warner Bros., 1942) Director-producer Howard Hawks. Jack Hawkins, Joan Collins, Sidney Chaplin.

For all the hard work on everybody's part, I only wish this one had enjoyed greater success. I got to know Hawks a lot better. First assistant director.

Desert Sands (Eagle-Lion Productions, 1942) Director Les Selander.

Nobody in the cast I ever heard of, before or after. War in the sand dunes of Yuma! Tired feet and legs at the end of a day on the dunes. First assistant director.

Marty (United Artists, 1955) Director Delbert Mann. Ernest Borgnine, Betsy Blair, Joe Mantell.

A most pleasant and successful piece of work. First assistant director.

The Helen Morgan Story (Warner Bros., 1957) Director Michael Curtiz. Paul Newman, Ann Blyth, Gene Evans, Cara Williams

My first picture with the top money-making director in the business, the Mad Hungarian with whom I managed to get along. One of Paul Newman's early pictures. First assistant director.

The Proud Rebel (United Artists, 1958) Director Michael Curtiz. Alan Ladd, Olivia de Havilland, Dean Jagger.

A darned good Western, well-cast and directed by another hard-to-get-along-with but well-intentioned director. First assistant director.

Defiant Ones (United Artists, 1958) Director Stanley Kramer. Tony Curtis, Sidney Poitier, Theodore Bikel.

A tough miserably cold and wet movie for cast and crew, but a good one, as were all of Kramer's. First assistant director.

Annotated Filmography

Teenage Thunder (Howco International, 1958) Director Paul A. Helmick. Bob Fuller, Chuck Courtney, Tyler McVey.

A well-deserved opportunity for me, I thought; I made the most of it in the six-day schedule I was given.

Rio Bravo (Warner Bros., 1959) Director-producer Howard Hawks. John Wayne, Dean Martin, Angie Dickenson.

Back in the saddle again on a real winner. Still a popular picture worldwide. First assistant director.

Porgy and Bess (Columbia, 1959) Director Otto Preminger. Sidney Poitier, Dorothy Dandridge, Sammy Davis, Jr., Pearl Bailey.

What a pity the great Gershwin legacy can't be carried on through the re-release of this picture. Children will be children, I suppose. First assistant director.

Thunder in Carolina (Howco International, 1960) Director Paul A. Helmick. Rory Calhoun, Connie Hines, Alan Hale, Jr., John Gentry.

Another break for me, this time with a considerably larger budget. Re-write by Paul Helmick, Howard Hawks and Leigh Brackett.

Hatari! (Paramount Pictures, 1962) Director-producer Howard Hawks. John Wayne, Elsa Martinelli, Bruce Cabot, Red Buttons, Gerard Blain.

A very happy time in my life, with so much to remember. Second unit director and associate producer.

Man's Favorite Sport (Universal Pictures, 1964) Director-producer Howard Hawks. Rock Hudson, Paula Prentiss, Maria Perschy.

A fun picture with fun people from top to bottom. Second unit director and associate producer.

The Great Race (Warner Bros., 1965) Director Blake Edwards. Tony Curtis, Natalie Wood, Jack Lemmon, Peter Falk.

I was hired as the second unit director, but about all I can take credit for was helping to find locations, plus a small amount of shooting before the second unit and I were banished. Second unit director.

Redline 7000 (Paramount Pictures, 1965) Director-producer Howard Hawks. James Caan, Laura Devon, Charlene Holt, Norman Alden.

Hawks, who in 1932 made the highly successful *The Crowd Roars* with big stars, tries another race-car picture with virtual unknowns and wished he hadn't! Associate producer.

A Guide for the Married Man (20th Century–Fox, 1967) Director Gene Kelly. Walter Matthau, Robert Morse, Inger Stevens.

Lean times, and back to first assistant director I went. Looking back on this and two more movies with Gene Kelly, I'm glad. First assistant director.

El Dorado (Paramount Pictures, 1967) Director-producer Howard Hawks. John Wayne, Robert Mitchum, James Caan.
   Back with my good and loyal friend, I think we made one of his usual good movies. Associate producer.

Funny Girl (Columbia Pictures, 1968) Director William Wyler. Barbra Streisand, Omar Sharif, Walter Pidgeon.
   My chance to work with one of Hollywood's masters, Willie Wyler. Unit production manager.

Hello, Dolly! (20th Century–Fox, 1969) Director Gene Kelly. Barbra Streisand, Walter Matthau, Michael Crawford.
   A difficult job made even more difficult because of personality clashes. First assistant director.

The Cheyenne Social Club (National General, 1970) Director Gene Kelly. James Stewart, Henry Fonda, Shirley Jones.
   From start to finish, a most enjoyable picture to be associated with. First assistant director and production manager.

Rio Lobo—(Cinema Center Films, 1970) Director-producer Howard Hawks. John Wayne, Jorge Rivero, Jennifer O'Neill.
   Hawks not up to his usual performance on this one, partly my fault. Associate producer.

The Culpepper Cattle Company (20th Century–Fox, 1971) Director Dick Richards. Gary Grimes, Billy "Green" Bush.
   This one could have put me on easy street, but I guess it just wasn't to be. Producer.

The Migrants (Lorimar, for CBS, 1974) Director Tom Gries. Cloris Leachman, Ron Howard, Sissy Spacek.
   A big challenge, but certainly the best TV-movie I ever had any part of. Associate producer and unit manager.

Comes a Horseman (Chartoff-Winkler Productions, 1978) Director Alan J. Pakula. James Caan, Jane Fonda, Jason Robards.
   Another unusual experience while making pictures and money. Thoroughly boring people. First assistant director.

Chilly Scenes of Winter (United Artists, 1982) Director Joan Micklin Silver. John Heard, Mary Beth Hurt, Peter Riegert.

An interesting picture with three young producers who did not pretend to be all-knowing and who were willing to listen. Production manager.

When I wasn't working on movies, I was kept fairly busy directing television commercials, which for the most part I thoroughly enjoyed doing.

Then there were numerous assignments in episodic television and movies-of-the-week. These include (in no particular order): Schlitz Playhouse of Stars, The Loretta Young Show, The Ozzie and Harriet Show, The Real McCoys, All the Kind Strangers, Skin Game, Khan, Spencer's Pilots, Three for the Road, Gemini, Skag, The Living Christ Series.

Index

Academy Awards 209, 210
Acker, Lee 36, 37
Agriculture, Department of 212
airboat 50, 51
air-conditioning 83, 222
Akins, Claude 120
The Alamo 146
Alaska 169
Alberta, Canada 47
Albright, Madelene 167
Allen, Fred 36, 37
Allen, Gene 198, 203
Anderson, Carl 146, 179
Army Air Corps 9, 17, 18, 101
Arusha 146, 147, 153-155
Aruza, Carloa 123

assistants 69, 70, 72, 77, 80
Australia 22-24
Austria 169

Baba, Ali 72
Bacall, Lauren 33, 60, 65, 119
Bailey, Pearl 126, 127, 129, 130
Bailey, Rex 135
Ball, Lucille 199
Ballard, Lucien 28-30
Bancroft, Ann 43
Banff Springs Hotel 53
Banks, Monte 32, 33
"The Barlows" 212
Barrett, James Lee 203
Bayless, Luster 210

233

Index

Beat the Devil 65
Beattie, Ann 220
Beauchamp, Clem 105, 108, 111, 168, 169
Bel-Air Hotel 95, 96
Belson, Louie 129
Ben-Hur 206
Bentley (car) 67, 68
Bernstein, Jimmy 90
Besche, Bob 207
Beverly Hills Hotel 95
Bidell, Sid 92, 93
bidet 64
The Big Sleep 68, 69
Blair, Betsy 100
Bloom, Jack 64
Blumenthal, Herman 195
Blythe, Ann 104
Bogart, Humphrey 33, 65
Bond, Ward 119, 121
Borgnine, Ernest 100, 101
Bow River 47, 50, 51
Bowen, Sid 53, 54
Bowers, Hoyt 208, 209
Brackett Leigh 74, 119, 121, 122, 133, 144, 146, 179
Brady, Joe 189–191, 198, 212
bravery 83, 84
Brennan, Walter 74, 119–122
Brice, Fanny 185
Bricktop's (Rome) 65
briefcase (Hawks') 74
Broken Arrow 43, 44
Brown, Russ 145
Brun, Joe 136, 139, 140, 149, 157
Bruno (the bear) 31, 32
Buick Riviera 167
bull charge (near Napoli) 84
bullfighters (Portugal) 84
Burger King 72
Burns, Cookie 115
Burrows, James 95
Butch Cassidy and the Sundance Kid 138
Byrne, Bobby 221
Byron, Melinda 115, 116

Caan, James 172, 181, 182, 216, 217
Cabot, Bruce 158
Cadillac driver 164
Calhoun, Rory 132

Callahan, Gene 187, 188, 193
camp drums 14, 15
Canutt, Joe 183
Canyon City, Colorado 215, 217
Capa, Bob 64
Caplan, Harry 176
Captain from Castile 19, 20
car magazines 85
Cardiac Hill 218, 219
Carlson, Bob 95, 96
Carney, Art 176
Carrere, Ferddie 169
Carroll, Diahann 126
Carter, John 179
Casablanca 102
Castles, Neil (Soapy) 139
Catfish Row 126
Cedar City, Utah 105
Century City 7, 176
Chaplin, Charlie 220
Chaplin, Sidney 86, 87
Charlotte, North Carolina 116
Chartoff-Winkler Prods. 215
The Cheyenne Social Club 202–205
Cheyevsky, Paddy 99, 100
Chicago 135
Chilly Scenes of Winter 220, 221
Cinema Center Films 206
Cinemacope 60, 86
Circle Blue Line Ferry 191, 192
Ciro's 144
Claridge Hotel (London) 66, 67
Clarke, Charles 24
Clive of India 174
Clothier, Bill 202, 208
Coburn, Charles 32, 33, 41
Coca-Cola 223
Cohn, Harry 7
Cole, Jack 39, 40
Collins, Joan 86, 87
Columbia Pictures 184, 186, 187, 200
Colvin, Bob 133–135
The Comancheros 110
Come and Get It! 119
Comes a Horseman 215, 219
Conners, Tom 95, 166
Coonan, John 182
Cooper, Gary 70
Courtney, Chuck 115, 117

Index

Crawford, Michael 196, 197
crop dusters 123
The Crowd Roars 133, 171, 172
Cukor, George 203
Curtis, Tony 112, 169
Curtiz, Michael 102–110, 196

dancing dolly 41
Dandridge, Dorothy 126, 130
Darby, Ken 126, 130
Darlington Southern 500 132, 139
Darnell, Linda 15, 16
Daves, Delmer 43, 44
Davis, Sammy, Jr. 126, 134
Day, Chico 196, 201
de Beer, Willy 150, 151, 154, 155, 157, 158, 160
DeCuir, John 195
Defiant Ones 111–113
deHavilland, Olivia 105, 107, 108
DeMaggio, Joe 57, 58
Denault, Edward 211
Desert Sands 91
Destination Gobi 38
DeTois, Jerry 150
Dickenson, Angie 119, 172
Directors Guild of America 61, 90, 126
Drums Along the Mohawk 13–16
Dunne, Griffin 221
Durkus, Andy 182, 183

Eagan, Betty 204
Eagle-Lion 90
earthquake 170
Eason, Bert 153
Eastman-Kodak 160, 192
Eaves, J. W. 203
Ebele, Ed 4, 8
Edens, Roger 196
Edwards, Blake 168–170
Eells, Col. Irving 69, 83
Egyptian army 75, 76
Eiffel Tower 169
El Dorado 179–183
elephants 161, 163
elephant hair bracelet 185
Elks Club, Florence 142
Erlichman, Marty 199
Evans, Gene 28
Excelsior Hotel 65

Fairbanks, Douglas 220
The Fan 45
Farnsworth, Richard 218
father 4, 5, 9
Faulkner, William 64–66
Fehr, Rudi 86
film editors 85, 86
Fixed Bayonets 26, 28
Fonda, Henry 203–205
Fonda, Jane 217, 218
food (Egypt) 71, 81, 82
forced-perspective 83
Ford, John 14–16, 74, 103, 121, 122, 124
Ford, Model A Truck 218
Ford Motor Company 40, 95
Formosa 90, 101
France 169
Frankovich, Mike 186
From Here to Eternity 198
Fuller, Bob 115–117
Fuller, Sam 28–30
Funny Girl 184–193, 194, 199, 200
Furthman, Jules 119
Fury at Furnace Creek 20

Gable, Clark 64
Game Department (Tanganyika) 146, 154, 160
Garmes, Lee 70
Garrison's Landing 198, 200, 201
Gearhart, Oregon 170
General Service Studio 95
Gentlemen Prefer Blondes 38–42
Geridon, Michelle 162, 163
Germany 169
Georges 66
Gershwin, George 125, 133
Gershwin, Ira 125, 128
Gershwin estate 126, 128
Gilmore, Stu 163
Girl Who Almost Got Away 164
Golden, Max 30
Goldsmith, Stanley 44
Goldwyn, Frances 129
Goldwyn, Sam, Jr. 105, 109, 125
Goldwyn, Sam, Sr. 125, 127, 128
Goldwyn Studio 100
Gone with the Wind 44
Gordean, Jack 144, 165

Index

Gordon, Billy 40
Gosnell, Ray 189
Goulding, Edmund 144
Grable, Betty 60
The Graduate 195
Granger, Stewart 123
Grant, Cary 31–34
Gray, Coleen 21
The Great Race 168

Gries, Tom 211–214
Griffith, D. W. 20
Guatemala 43
Guess Who's Coming to Dinner 111
A Guide for the Married Man 175, 178

Hale, Alan, Jr. 137
Hamilton, Ed 121
Hansen, Chuck 69, 71, 80
Harlan, Russ 70, 76, 77, 79, 80, 85, 123, 147, 148, 161, 168, 173
Hatari! 143–163
Hawkins, Jack 84, 86, 87
Hawks, Dee Hartford (3rd Wife) 64, 65, 84
Hawks, Gregg 152, 183
Hawks, Howard 31–42, 60–86, 92, 118–124, 133, 134, 143–164, 171–174, 179–203
Hawks, Slim (2nd Wife) 32
Hayden, Tom 217
Head, Edith 166, 167, 179
Head Over Heels 221
Heard, John 221
Hecht, Harold 99, 100
Hecht-Hill-Lancaster 98
Hehr, Addison 44, 45
Heimlich maneuver 173
Helen (wife) 10, 266, 27, 61, 81, 109, 129, 130, 186, 188, 204
Helen Morgan Story 102–105
Hello Dolly! 193–201
Hemingway, Ernest 64
Henderling, Jim 158
Henderson, Marcia 94
Hersh, Ben 185
Heston, Charlton 183
Hines, Connie 135
Hog Canyon Farm 39
Holiday Inn 213

Holt, Charlene 163, 173
Hopper, Hedda 29
"Horse Soldiers" 103
Houck, Joy 115, 116
Hough, Lefty 30, 60
Howard, Noel 70, 86, 87
Howard, Ron 214
Howard, Ruth 5
Howco-International 114, 115
Hud 182
Hudson, Rock 166
Huston, John 65

I Was a Male War Bride 31, 68
Indians (to Utah) 16, 17

Jacobson, Arthur 31
Jakarta 210
Jasper Lodge 49, 53, 54
Jeep 149, 151, 158
Jensen, Roy 51–53
Jersey Central Railroad 187, 189, 190
Jersey City 191
Joe Camel 176
Johnson, Nunally 60
Johnston, Johnny 59
Jones, Davey 189
Jones, Shirley 203
Judgment at Nuremberg 111
Jurow, Martin 169
Justice, James Robertson 88

Kaiser, Henry J. 96
Kaiser-Jeep Corp. 149
Kanab, Utah 13, 20, 21, 108, 206–210
Kangaroo 22
Karp, Jack 143 144
Kaye, Nora 192, 193
Kelly, Fred 198
Kelly, Gene 101, 175–178, 193, 195–205
Kern River 112
Kerr and Downey 145
Kessler, Bruce 172, 173
Khayyam, Omar 86
Kidd, Michael 196, 197
Kilimanjaro 154
King, Henry 19, 20
Klune, Ray 27, 30, 44, 45, 54, 98, 100
Knickerbocker Hotel 116, 131

Index

Koch, Howard 90, 173
Koenig, Doris (wife) 11, 12
Koenig, William 8, 9, 11, 12
Kohner, Paul 193, 203
Kramer, Stanley 111–113
Krick, Dr. Irving 47
Kruger, Hardy 188
Kurnitz, Harry 64, 65, 144

labor contractors 76
Ladd, Alan 53, 104, 108, 109
Ladd, David 105, 108, 109
Lake Manyara Hotel 156
L'Amour, Louis 203
Land Rover 152
Lansing, Sherry 209
La Shelle, Joe 47, 50, 100
Las Vegas 109
Lauter, Ed 214
Lavigne, Emil 86
Leachman, Cloris 213, 214
Legion of Honor 65, 66
Lehman, Ernest 195, 196
Lenhart, Isobel 193
Levant, Oscar 36, 37
Lewis, Jerry 119
Lewiston, Idaho 50, 51
Life magazine 79, 199
Lindy 90
Litez, Natasha 54–56
Lofton, Cary 137, 138, 149, 150, 158, 159
Lombard, Carol 119
Long Island Mansion 188, 189
Longido 150
Lorimar 211
Lowe, Mildred 3, 4, 5, 9, 11, 12, 27, 28
Luce, Claire Booth 167

The Mad Hungarian 102–110
Magnum photographers 64
Mamoulian, Rouben 126, 127
Mancini, Henry 163, 164
Mann, Delbert 98–100, 175, 210
Man's Favorite Sport 164–167
Marine Corp Band & Choir 140
Marquette, Jack 114–117
Marquette Productions 115, 117
Martin, Dean 119, 180
Martinelli, Elsa 161, 163

Marx, Enid 84
Marx, Groucho 84
Mary Jane 93
Matthau, Walter 175, 200, 201
Mature, Victor 21, 22
Mayer, Louis B. 7, 178
McCarthy, Frank 176, 177, 198
McClelland, Lois 197
McCord, Ted 104, 105
McDonald, Joe 60, 176
McDonald's 72
McEdwards, Jack 168, 169
McEwen, Scotty 24
McNeil, Alan 174
McNeil, Steve 165
McVey, Tyler 117
Melton, Ray 140
Mena House (Cairo Hotel) 71, 72, 82
Meredith, Bess 103, 104
Merman, Doc 126, 130, 195
Metcalf, Mark 221
Mexican National Railways 207
Meyer, Fred 8
MGM 178, 180
The Migrants 211–214
Milestone, Louis 24
mimeograph operator 4, 5
Mitchum, Robert 42, 49, 56, 57, 173, 180, 186
Momella 146
Mongoose (Squeaky) 161–163
Monkey Business 32–34
Monroe, Marilyn 32, 33, 39–42, 47, 54–58, 60, 172
Monty, Harry 52, 58
Moore, Ray 44
Morse, Eddie 172, 179
Morse, Robert 175
Mosely, Keith 152–154
Moshi 154
mother 3, 4, 9, 18, 132, 133, 135, 205
Movin' On 120
Murray, John Fenton 164, 165
museums (Egypt) 82
musical instruments (Egypts) 82
musicians (Egypt) 85

National Enquirer 172
National General Studio 203–205
Navy 198

Index

Negulesco, Jean 60
Nelson, Ralph 93
Nelson, Ricky 119, 121, 122, 124
New Jersey 187, 189, 198, 212, 213
New York 135, 186
New York Harbor 110
New York Streets (from *Hello Dolly*) 195, 197
Newman, Paul 104, 138
Ngorongoro Crater 155, 156, 160
Nipomo, California 95
Nogales, Mexico 123
Nyby, Chris 173

O'Fearna, Eddie 16
O'Hara, Maureen 22
Old Tucson Western Street 121–123, 179
Oldsmobile Tornado 192
Olin, Earl 179
Olivera Street 222
O'Neil, Carey 20
O'Neil, Jennifer 172
Ovitz, Michael 6
Ozzie and Harriet 119

Packard 105
Pakula, Alan 216–219
Palamino (horses) 181
Palm Springs 209
Pan American Clipper 64
Paramount Studio 90, 103, 143, 145–148, 163–165, 171–173, 181, 197, 209
Pareoli Apartment (Rome) 83
Paris 169
Parry Brothers 20, 21
Penicillino 207
Picitinny Arsenal 190
Pickford, Mary 220
Piper Cub 152
Planet of the Apes 120
Platt, Edward 94
playback 122, 126, 195
Playhouse Ninety 98
Poitier, Sidney 112, 126, 130
Pollack, Sidney 95
poodle dog 84
Porgy and Bess 47, 54, 125–130, 131, 134, 175

Port Augusta 24
Power, Tyrone 19, 20
Pratt, Jim 165, 167
Preminger, Otto 45, 47–49, 53–57, 126–132, 203
Prentiss, Paula 119, 166
Presley, Elvis 196
Previn, André 126, 130
process plates 50
production office 6, 7
The Proud Rebel 105–110

quarry (Egypt) 80

Rackin, Marty 103
Ramadan 76
Rancho Encantada 204
Rancho Golf Course 176, 177
Ransahoff, Marty 95
The Ransom of Red Chief 35–37
Redline 7000 171–174
Retig, Tommy 51, 57
rhino 154, 155, 157–159
Rings on Her Fingers 18
Rio Bravo 118–124, 179, 184
Rio Lobo 206–210
Ritchie, Con 149
River of No Return 43–58, 127, 203
Rivero, Jorge 208, 209
Robards, Jason 218
Robb, Don 15, 146
Roberson, Chuck 210
Robinson, Amy 221
Rocky Mountain Oyster Club 123
Roe Jack 189
Rogell, Sid 40
Rogers, Ginger 32
Rogers, Will 174
Rolls Royce showroom 67
Rome 65, 83
Ross, Herb 189, 190, 192, 193
Rossen, Hal 180–182
Roth, Harold 24
Rubin, Stanley 45
Rungren, Eric 145
Russell, Betty 8, 11, 12
Russell, Jane 39, 40
Russell, John 119
Russell, Roz 172

Index

Salamunovich, Mike 127, 129
San Diego Zoo 155
San Fernando Valley 116
San Moritz 64
Santa Fe Western Street 204
Saturday Evening Post 164
Saunders, Russ 148, 153
Savage Splendor 148
Sawyer, Joe 192
Schell, Hannah 217
Schenck, Aubrey 90
Schlitz Playhouse of Stars 92, 93
"Scrunt" 142
Sedona, Arizona 44
Selander, Les 91
Self, Bill 92, 93, 95
Selznick, David 44
"September Song" 41
Serengetti Hat 166
Shameroy, Leon 127, 130
Sharaff, Irene 126, 194
Sharif, Omar 186
Sheridan, Ann 119
Shiek's party 79
Silver, Joan Micklin 221
Simmons, Jean 123
Siteman, Art 69, 70, 75, 83
Smith, Jack Martin 195
Snody, Bob 24
solitaire 66, 67
Solomon, Jack 194
"Somethingorother," Clem 50, 51
Sound of Music 172
Spacek, Sissy 214
Stark, Frances 185, 186
Stark, Ray 184–187, 193, 200
Steinbeck, John 64
Stewart, Don 71
Stewart, James 181, 202, 204, 205
Stockton, California 126, 128
Stradling, Harry, Sr. 187, 194, 196, 200
Streisand Barbra 186, 187, 192–194, 197, 200 201
Swink, Bob 192, 193

Tanganyika (Tanzania) 145
Tarloff, Frank 176, 177
Technicolor cameras 107
Teenage Thunder 114–117, 131, 132

television 6, 21, 22, 60, 96, 97
Thatcher, Margaret 167
The Thing 173
Thunder in Carolina 131–142, 171
Thurston, Helen 51, 52
Tiomkin, Dimitri 82, 122
Tom Swift and His Airship 198, 199
Trauner, Alexander 70, 71, 83
Travilla, Billy 39, 60
Treasure of the Golden Condo 43
Trilling, Steve 122
Triple Play Productions 220
True Grit 210
Tucson 209
Turner, Lana 20
Twentieth Century Films 4, 5, 9, 174
Twentieth Century–Fox Film Corp. 5, 62, 89, 204, 175, 193, 200, 221
Tyler, Nelson 189

United Artists Studio 108, 220, 221
Universal Studio 165, 167

Van Horn, Buddy 205
Variety 90, 168, 203
Vashtar 88
Veitch, John 184
Verdon, Gwen 39
Vineland, N.J. 212, 213
Vista, California 80

Wallace, Hal 196
Wally 213, 214
Walsh, Raoul 53
Warner, Jack 7, 65, 86, 110, 169, 170, 174
Warner Bros. 60, 61, 62, 65, 69, 85, 102, 103, 105, 106, 122, 165, 169, 172, 173
Waugh, Joan 172
Wayne, John 67, 68, 74, 103, 110, 118–124, 144, 146, 149, 154, 160, 163, 171, 173, 179, 183, 186, 197, 206–210
West Point 200
Western Union 16
Wheeler, Lyle 60

White, J. Francis 115, 116, 131–133, 135, 138, 141, 142
White, Ted 149, 150, 158, 159

White Christmas 102
White Tower Restaurant (London) 68
Wichita, Kansas 198
The Wild Goose (chef) 179
Wilde, Cornel 43
Wilder, Billy 83
Will Penny 212
Williams, Bill 94
Williams, Cindy 214
Williams, Tennessee 212
Willis, Gordon 216–219
Wilson, Lanford 212
Winchelll, Walter 103
Winds of War 57
Winslow, George 41, 42

Wise, Robert 38, 68, 104
World War II 9, 17, 39, 44, 61, 93
Worthington, Cal 67
Wray, Faye 43
Wright, Joe 39
Wright, Tenny 64, 102
Wyler, William 184, 186–188, 192, 193
Wyler, Mrs. William 192

Yonkers, New York 187
Yuma, Arizona 91

Zanuck, Darryl 4, 5, 7, 30, 35, 36, 44, 45, 47, 55, 56, 144, 174
Zanuck, Richard 172